The Big Dance

The Big Dance

The Story of the
NCAA Basketball Tournament

Barry Wilner & Ken Rappoport

TAYLOR TRADE PUBLISHING

Lanham • New York • Boulder • Toronto • Plymouth, UK

Published by Taylor Trade Publishing
An imprint of The Rowman & Littlefield Publishing Group, Inc.
4501 Forbes Boulevard, Suite 200, Lanham, Maryland 20706
http://www.rowman.com

Estover Road, Plymouth PL6 7PY, United Kingdom

Distributed by National Book Network

British Library Cataloguing in Publication Information Available

Library of Congress Cataloging-in-Publication Data

Wilner, Barry.
   The big dance : the story of the NCAA basketball tournament / Barry Wilner & Ken
Rappoport.
      p. cm.
   ISBN 978-1-58979-621-8 (pbk. : alk. paper) — ISBN 978-1-58979-622-5
(electronic)
   1. NCAA Basketball Tournament--History. 2. Basketball—Tournaments—United
States—History. I. Rappoport, Ken. II. Title.
GV885.49.N37W47 2012
796.323'630973—dc23

2011033207

Printed in the United States of America

For Howard Hobson, the coach who started it all.—KR

To the ever-growing Wilner clan,
without whose inspiration and understanding
I would never get anything accomplished.—BW

Contents

Acknowledgments

The authors wish to thank Geno Auriemma, Matt Bourque, Bill Fitts, Harry Flournoy, David Lattin, Deborah Jennings, Patrick McKenna, Jim O'Connell, John Paquette, Pat Summitt, and Dick Vitale for their valuable contributions to this book.

Introduction

It's a national passion that happens as winter melts into spring.

No, not baseball.

Think bracket sheets.

And "Selection Sunday."

In March, it would be hard to find an office, bar, or backroom where someone wasn't filling out bracket sheets for the National Collegiate Athletic Association (NCAA) basketball tournament in what has become a unique sports ritual in America.

Another ritual: the team selection process that takes place on the Sunday before the start of the NCAA playoffs. No matter how often the NCAA expands the size of the field, there is almost always some kind of controversy surrounding teams that are picked or left out.

As of 2011, the NCAA had added three more teams to make it 68 for the field.

And to think, it all started so inauspiciously in 1939 with the University of Oregon winning the first championship in an eight-team field. Hard to believe by today's standards, but the tourney actually lost money—$2,531, in fact—and coaches wondered if having another one was such a good idea.

Good thing that Harold Olsen, the Ohio State basketball coach and a key figure in the National Association of Basketball Coaches (NABC), kept the faith. He originally proposed the idea after taking note of the success of the National Invitation Tournament (NIT) in New York and the National Association of Intercollegiate Athletics (NAIA) tournament in Kansas City. He kept pushing for a tournament that would be managed by the NABC acting as an affiliate of the NCAA.

The original eight-team format featured one representative from each of the NCAA's eight geographical districts. As a representative from the West, Oregon's "Tall Firs" whipped Olsen's Midwestern Buckeyes, 46–33, for the first national championship.

It didn't take long for the fledgling tourney to start making money, albeit a modest sum at first. In 1940, the winning Indiana team and runner-up Kansas each received $750 in addition to having expenses paid from the net receipts of $9,523.

Soon, a revolutionary change: for the first time, four teams advanced to the finals in New York's Madison Square Garden in 1946. The concept of the Final Four was beginning to evolve as Oklahoma A&M (now Oklahoma State) beat North Carolina to become the first team to win consecutive championships. The finals were shown on TV locally in New York, with an estimated viewing audience of 500,000.

The tourney grew by leaps and rebounds. When the championship game was televised in prime time for the first time in 1973, a record audience of 13.5 million homes watched. They saw a great UCLA team destroy Memphis State for its ninth national championship. Two years later, the Bruins won their 10th title in 12 years under John Wooden, who then surprised the nation by retiring after coaching the greatest dynasty in college basketball history.

The size of the national audience in the 1973 finals was a healthy sign in the marriage of the NCAA and TV. It was obvious college basketball was meant for the spotlight of prime-time television.

Interest in the NCAA playoffs reached a new level when Michigan State, led by Magic Johnson, and Indiana State, behind Larry Bird, met in the compelling 1979 final, won by the Spartans.

The game was a turning point in playoff popularity. March Madness would never be the same. And the stakes continued to skyrocket.

Forget about millions. Think billions: $10.8 billion, to be exact.

That's the staggering figure the NCAA collects in its most recent deal with CBS and Turner Broadcasting for the privilege of televising its tournament, every game live on four outlets.

Here, then, are stories of the movers, shakers, and shot-makers who have made the NCAA basketball tournament an American phenomenon.

1.

McGuire's Miracle

Something mystical was going on.

North Carolina's nerve-racking high-wire act during the 1956–57 basketball season convinced Frank McGuire of that.

"There was something eerie about winning 32 straight," the Tar Heels coach said. "We won several games we should have lost, we got breaks that were out of this world."

As the Tar Heels' winning streak continued to stretch during the season, fans offered McGuire good-luck charms and "lucky" coins to keep the team on course to the Final Four. By the time the Tar Heels entered the championship round at Kansas City, they had already won 30 straight and were ranked No. 1 in the country.

What happened next must have seemed even more "eerie" to McGuire: First, the Tar Heels beat Michigan State in triple over-time in the national semifinals. The very next night they went into triple overtime again to beat Kansas for the national title.

Two triple overtimes in two days for the national championship. Can you beat that? McGuire was still pinching himself a year later.

"What happened couldn't happen again, in a thousand years," McGuire said.

Believe it—no Final Four ever matched that one in excitement, thrills, and spills. And with their 32–0 record, the Tar Heels set the mark for most victories by an unbeaten champion—later matched by Indiana's 1975–76 team.

To say McGuire was the most popular man on campus was an understatement. Even before he led North Carolina to the national championship, he was presented with a sparkling 1957 Cadillac, courtesy of alumni, admirers, and even students, who were not allowed to chip in more than a dollar. Naturally, it was blue and white to reflect the school colors.

In a lighthearted editorial, the *Charlotte News* took this wry jab at McGuire:

"We certainly don't begrudge Mr. McGuire a single cylinder of his prize. We just wish that his less fortunate colleagues could enjoy similar rewards. We understand Dr. James L. Godfrey is having an unusually good year in history but not a whisper have we heard about outfitting him with a new car."

McGuire was in the driver's seat, no doubt. A transplanted New Yorker, he had brought his "City Game" to the South with speedy results.

"To play our kind of basketball, you've got to have discipline above everything else," McGuire said in explaining "New York basketball."

"It's the kind of game that concentrates on controlling the ball. We take only the good shots. If an opponent is slow, we'll tend to run and shoot a bit."

The starting players on the 1956–57 Carolina team were all from the New York area, McGuire's most fertile recruiting ground. Overall, the so-called "Underground Railroad" was responsible for nine of the 12 players on the 1956–57 squad.

McGuire's main contact for recruiting in the Big Apple was super scout Harry Gotkin, an old friend. There was a longtime personal history between them, going back to the time Gotkin's brother, Java, had played with McGuire at St. John's.

Harry Gotkin remembered how McGuire, who hated ethnic putdowns, would stick up for his brother.

"Sometimes a player on the other team would make a crack about Java's being Jewish," Gotkin said. "That's when Frank would step in. He'd say, 'You want to make cracks about him? Make them to me first, and then fight me first.'"

To put up his fists at the drop of a hat would not have been unusual for the quick-tempered McGuire. And he was a formidable figure—right out of Central Casting in Hollywood if you were looking for an old-fashioned Western hero.

"Husky, broad-shouldered, square-jawed, his reddish-brown hair thick and wavy, McGuire looked convincing (to play in a) Western," said *Sports Illustrated.*

The son of a New York policeman, McGuire grew up with 12 sisters and brothers in one of the city's toughest neighborhoods, which at that time was Greenwich Village.

"I grew up on the sidewalks of New York and you had to get along with all kinds of people," McGuire said. "You had to get along with them or fight them. We did considerable getting along and considerable fighting."

McGuire never used any more deadly weapons than his own two fists.

Speaking of fists, the neighborhood produced, among others, heavyweight champion Gene Tunney. Also Carmine DeSapio, who ran Tammany Hall with an iron fist.

McGuire put all of his energies into sports. He played basketball just about every day—in driving rain, the snows of New York winters, and the steaming heat of summer.

Selected all-city in basketball at St. Francis Xavier High School in Brooklyn, McGuire continued his exploits at St. John's University, where he captained both the basketball and baseball teams.

Following a successful coaching stint at St. Francis, McGuire was back again at St. John's—as a basketball coach.

In relatively little time, McGuire built St. John's into a national contender. In the 1952 NCAA tournament, the Redmen upset top-ranked Kentucky to advance to the finals.

They lost to Kansas.

Recalling that depressing loss to the Jayhawks, McGuire said, "After the gun went off, everybody mobbed the Kansas players and there we were—me and 12 basketball players. We were second in the United States. But we might as well have been 50th. It was a lesson."

McGuire coached the St. John's baseball team as well. In 1949 he led the Redmen to the College World Series, where they lost in the first round to Texas, the eventual champion. He became one of only three coaches to reach the Final Four of the NCAA tournament in basketball and also achieve a place in the College World Series.

But it was basketball that propelled McGuire to the forefront of coaching. He had turned out powerhouse teams at St. John's, winning 102 games in just five seasons.

The North Carolina Tar Heels came calling.

McGuire remembered Chapel Hill with affection from his days stationed at the university with the navy's V-5 training program during the Second World War. He still had friends there, and plenty of supporters.

He had a growing family, including young Frankie, who was stricken with cerebral palsy. He felt his family would be better off living in a college community, where the pace of life—unlike in New York—was unhurried.

McGuire seized the opportunity to coach the Tar Heels basketball team. He brought along Buck Freeman, his valuable aide from St. John's whom McGuire had called "my good right arm."

McGuire took over the Tar Heels in August 1952. It wasn't until the 1955–56 season that the team started to come into its own. By then, the key players were in place: Lennie Rosenbluth at forward along with Pete Brennan, Joe Quigg at center, Tommy Kearns and Bob Cunningham at the guard positions. Tony Radovich, Bob Young, and Danny Lotz were key players coming off the bench.

Rosenbluth, who had led the Tar Heels in scoring as a sophomore with a 25.5-point average, continued his prolific scoring as a junior. He averaged 26.7 points to lead North Carolina to an 18–5 record, prompting the Tar Heels' media guide to rave about Rosenbluth's "golden touch." Although the Tar Heels didn't gain a berth in the NCAA tournament, they managed to finish tied for first in the Atlantic Coast Conference (ACC).

Rosenbluth was not only the Tar Heels' leading scorer, but he also led the team in ailments, real or imagined. He hated out-of-town eating arrangements when the team was on the road. He was positive he would catch virulent germs. This laughable hypochondria at times reached ludicrous extremes.

One night McGuire was giving a pregame talk in the locker room when Rosenbluth lapsed into one of his world-class coughing fits. The coach stopped his talk and addressed his star player.

"Lennie, you're obviously dying," McGuire said wryly, putting his arm about Rosenbluth. "Now, I don't want you to die any place but Chapel Hill. Get dressed, Lennie, and we'll call off the game and drive you home."

With Rosenbluth's teammates all laughing, McGuire promised the player "the finest three-day Irish wake in the history of North Carolina."

At that point, Rosenbluth decided it would be best for him to play. He did, scoring 30 points as North Carolina beat Wake Forest, 69–64.

Rosenbluth was not always the object of laughter, but rather of jealousy. Some teammates resented the fact they played a subordinate role to the star forward.

"I was asking the other boys to sacrifice themselves for Rosenbluth for the good of the team," McGuire said. "Apparently I hadn't sold the idea."

Brennan and Quigg were two frontcourt players who had been stars in their own right wherever they had played.

"It looked as if cliques would form," McGuire observed.

McGuire threw the problem in Rosenbluth's lap, particularly because Rosenbluth was the team captain.

"After dinner hold a meeting with the boys," McGuire told Rosenbluth. "I don't want to know what this is all about. I just want this thing settled."

Rosenbluth did as he was told, then reported back to McGuire.

"Everything will be all right," Rosenbluth told the coach. "We had a meeting and it got it settled. A lot was my fault, some theirs. There'll be nothing to worry about from now on."

There wasn't anything to worry about on the court, at least, until a close-call overtime victory over South Carolina in the season's fourth game. The Tar Heels had another tough battle against Holy Cross, falling behind by 13 points before rallying to run their winning streak to eight.

The Tar Heels faced one of their biggest tests against nationally ranked Utah in the opening of the carnival-like Dixie Classic in Raleigh, North Carolina.

Jack Gardner, the Redmen's coach, didn't think his team would have trouble with the Tar Heels. "We'll beat North Carolina because they aren't quick enough to contend with our fast break," he boasted.

He was wrong.

The Tar Heels bolted to a 22–4 lead. They polished off Utah, 97–76, and swept past Duke and Wake Forest to win their first Dixie Classic.

The Tar Heels suddenly found themselves ranked No. 2 in the country, behind Kansas. And McGuire found life a little more hectic.

"The phone at home started ringing more," McGuire said.

Not as much as it would after the Tar Heels took over the top spot in mid-January, thanks to a Kansas loss and North Carolina's win over North Carolina State. It was the Tar Heels' 15th straight victory, and now North Carolina supporters were coming out of the woodwork.

One student kept his car parked in one spot, despite an accumulating pile of parking tickets, so as not to spoil the spell.

"People would stop me on the street and say, 'You're going all the way,'" McGuire recalled.

It made McGuire uncomfortable. He suddenly expressed a "fear of losing."

Two games later, it looked like McGuire's worst fear would come true. The Tar Heels trailed Maryland by four points with two minutes left. But they tied the game in regulation, then won it in double overtime.

"The boys told me, after that game, that they did not intend to be beaten," McGuire said. "That victory gave them a tremendous lift."

By the end of the regular season, the Tar Heels were flying high with a 24–0 record. But they still had a long way to go. First, the Atlantic Coast Conference playoffs.

Despite their great regular season, the Tar Heels needed to win the league playoffs in order to advance to the NCAAs.

The Tar Heels would have to be at their best—and no one was better then Rosenbluth, their heroic hypochondriac.

The unstoppable Rosenbluth scored 45 points against Clemson, 23 against Wake Forest, and 38 against South Carolina to lead the Tar Heels to the ACC title.

Rosenbluth personally knocked off a tough Wake Forest team in the semifinals. With 55 seconds left, the Tar Heels trailed, 59–58. But Rosenbluth scored on a three-point play to put the Tar Heels ahead to stay, 61–59.

"No game was tougher that season than the last Wake Forest game," McGuire said.

Rosenbluth's assault continued in the NCAAs: 29 points as Carolina beat Yale, 90–74; 39 in an 87–75 victory over Canisius; and 23 in a 67–58 win over Syracuse that vaulted the Tar Heels into the Final Four in Kansas City.

And what a Final Four it would be!

Awaiting the four finalists was the largest press-radio group in college basketball history at the time, featuring an 11-station TV network and live radio broadcasts by 73 stations in 11 states.

The Tar Heels faced a Michigan State team full of surprises. The Spartans were playing their best basketball of the year, having shocked No. 3-ranked Kentucky in the regional final. The Spartans didn't make it easy on themselves, rallying from a 12-point half-time deficit to win, 80–68.

The other regional final was also a nail-biter. San Francisco beat California, 50–46, in a game that featured nine lead changes and three ties in the last 19 minutes.

Could things get any more exciting?

Sure—particularly in the North Carolina–Michigan State game.

While Kansas and Wilt Chamberlain were crushing San Francisco, 80–56, to deny the Dons a chance to win a third straight national championship, the North Carolina–Michigan State game went down to the wire—and then some.

Take note: the teams were tied 18 times and were never more than six points apart from start to finish.

"The game had a dozen highlights and turning points as it see-sawed throughout," reported United Press International.

After one half, the teams were tied at 29. After regulation, it was 58–58, thanks to John Green's two free throws for Michigan State.

With three seconds left in the first overtime, Brennan hit a short jump shot for the Tar Heels to tie the game at 64.

The second extra period ended 66–66 as Green tipped in a basket with seven seconds left.

Third overtime.

No surprise, Rosenbluth took over. He scored twice on jump shots to complete a 31-point game. Kearns added two free throws to clinch it for the Tar Heels, 74–70.

No way the national finals could be equally as exciting, right?

The big stumbling block for North Carolina, with the emphasis on B-I-G, was Chamberlain. His stunning 7-foot size had intimidated and demoralized some very good teams. In his very first varsity game, "Wilt the Stilt" had scored 52 points and picked off 31 rebounds. He was the tall terror of college basketball.

Because of Chamberlain, the "smart" money was on Kansas, even though the Jayhawks were ranked No. 2 to Carolina's No. 1.

The Tar Heels didn't seem worried, particularly Kearns, the team's fiery backcourt man. Asked how the Tar Heels were going

The Greatest Game

The Shot Heard 'Round the World.

Any sports fan with a sense of history will remember Bobby Thomson's heroic home run that decided the 1951 National League playoffs.

Basketball has its own version.

Appropriately, it was a play called "Home Run."

Like Thomson's homer for the New York Giants against the Brooklyn Dodgers, the tense basketball moment had a lot riding on it.

And like Thomson's blast, it could arguably be called the most memorable contest in its sport's history.

The game: the 1992 NCAA East Regional final.

The teams: Duke and Kentucky.

The stakes: a berth in the Final Four.

It took no less than the final shot to decide the outcome, and a smooth one at that by Christian Laettner, the "Bobby Thomson" in basketball's version.

The Spectrum in Philadelphia was filled to capacity with a roaring, emotional crowd there to see two of college basketball's giants. Like two great heavyweight fighters, the Blue Devils and Wildcats slugged it out on the court with brilliant back-and-forth play.

At the half, Duke led the high-scoring contest, 50–45.

The best was yet to come.

With 11:08 to go, Duke went ahead by 12 points, 67–55. The Wildcats, using a man-to-man defense called the "mother-in-law" because of its "constant pressure and harassment," forced turnover after turnover. The pressure defense knocked the Blue Devils off their game and knocked their lead down to four points.

The crowd was stunned by what happened next. Driving to the basket, Laettner collided with Kentucky's Aminu Timberlake and both spilled to the floor. With the Kentucky player still on his back, Laettner purposely hopped up and planted a foot on the prone player's chest.

"That was unbelievably dumb," Duke coach Mike Krzyzewski shouted at his player from the sideline.

Like many others in the Spectrum, Krzyzewski might have surmised that Laettner would be thrown out of the game for unsportsmanlike conduct. Fortunately for Duke, he was not. He was called for a technical foul and allowed to continue.

Neither team was able to pull away as the game headed toward its ultimate dramatic conclusion.

At the end of regulation, it was 93–93.

In overtime, the teams were never more than three points apart. Laettner was in the middle of everything. After Kentucky went up, 101–100, with 19 seconds left in the overtime period, Laettner went to the foul line for two free throws. He hadn't missed a shot all day.

"The sucker's never going to miss," complained Kentucky coach Rick Pitino.

He didn't. Duke went ahead, 102–101, with 7.8 seconds to go.

Kentucky ball. Still plenty of time left for the Wildcats.

If Kentucky scores, Duke's Bobby Hurley reminded his teammates, remember to call a timeout. It was a crucial reminder.

Sean Woods banked a shot off the glass to give Kentucky a 103–102 lead.

Timeout Duke. Time left: 2.1 seconds.

Coach K diagrammed the play for one last shot. It was a play the Blue Devils had practiced, a heave from the end line, 94 feet away. Grant Hill would inbound the ball, hopefully into the waiting hands of Laettner, stationed about 17 feet from the basket. Laettner had to catch the ball, dribble, turn, and shoot, all in one motion.

"At the time I was thinking that there were two seconds left, which meant I had time to make a fake if I wanted to," Laettner told the *Sporting News* in a 2009 interview. "It was not a desperate heave. I had time to stay calm and be relaxed and take a nice, easy shot at the bucket. The last thing I remember thinking is that I had to catch the ball."

The Blue Devils had tried the same play in a game against Wake Forest earlier in the season, but Laettner was unable to handle Hill's pass.

"Grant's pass was like a curveball," Laettner said. "It took me out of bounds, and I wasn't able to shoot it."

Not this time. Hill's pass was right on the money.

"I just made a post move," Laettner said.

Laettner faked and shot a turnaround jumper. The ball settled into the net, giving the Blue Devils a nearly miraculous victory, 104–103. On to the Final Four for Duke. On to a second straight national championship.

"The rest is history," Laettner said.

Just like Thomson's home run.

to handle such a huge challenge, he replied, "We'll think of something. Chamberlain is not going to give us the jitters like he did to San Francisco and those other clubs."

Kearns, himself, was part of a master plan to contain the Kansas center, only one of the greatest forces in college basketball. When the players took the court for the opening tip-off, McGuire sent out Kearns, his shortest player at 5-foot-11, to jump against the 7-foot Chamberlain.

It was a bit of psychology McGuire hoped would disorient the Jayhawks star.

"Wilt looked 10 feet tall towering over Tommy, but they made such a ridiculous picture together that Chamberlain must have felt no bigger than his thumb," McGuire said. "At least that's the state of mind we wanted to get him into. What I wanted was for Chamberlain to get a good shock."

It was nothing like the shock Chamberlain later received facing a rugged Carolina defense. McGuire's game plan was to focus on Chamberlain and hope none of the other Kansas players suddenly developed a hot hand.

"We knew nobody could outrebound him, so we had to block him," McGuire said of Chamberlain.

With Carolina using a sagging zone, Chamberlain found Tar Heels players in front of him and behind him. As Chamberlain would say later, "I didn't get many shots off against that kind of defense."

His teammates, meanwhile, "couldn't put a pea in the ocean," Chamberlain said.

The Tar Heels were having better luck. They connected on 64.7 percent of their shots compared to 27.3 percent for the Jayhawks in the first half. Rosenbluth, as usual, led the way with 14 points as Carolina took a 29–22 halftime lead.

McGuire's game plan: so far, so good.

"When you have the ball, the other team can't score," McGuire said. "That was our object—to keep the ball away from the 'Stilt' by slowing up our game and always keeping an eye on him."

The second half was a different story.

The Tar Heels' shooting percentage dropped off, and the Jayhawks started to find the basket and moved in front, 40–37, with 10:20 left.

The Tar Heels, having survived the Michigan State marathon, were playing with tired legs. They got some help from an unexpected source: Kansas coach Dick Harp, who suddenly ordered his team to go into a stall.

"It was exactly what we needed," Rosenbluth said. "It let us catch our breath."

McGuire raised his hand and signaled to his team by spreading five fingers. His instructions: "Let them kill the ball until there are five minutes to play."

With five minutes left, McGuire signaled again, this time to speed up the game.

"They'd given us time to get our second wind and provided us a safety margin in the foul column," McGuire said.

For everyone but Rosenbluth, that is. Carolina's star player fouled out with 1:45 to go.

Kansas was leading, 46–43, at that point and Chamberlain recalled, "It looked like we had the championship in the bag."

Not so fast, Jayhawks.

Gene Elstsun, one of the Jayhawks' best free-throw shooters, missed a foul shot, and the Tar Heels eventually caught up, tying the game at 46 at the end of regulation.

Now Rosenbluth, who had averaged 28.2 points in Carolina's previous 30 games, could only watch helplessly from the bench as the Tar Heels battled the Jayhawks in three frantic overtimes.

Battle, they did. Literally.

Following a relatively quiet overtime period that ended 48–48, the second OT was wild by comparison—even though no points were scored. The lowlight of the period featured a wrestling match for the ball between Chamberlain and Brennan.

"They had to be pulled apart to keep from clashing," the Associated Press reported.

Harp rushed onto the court.

"I wanted to try to prevent a fight," the Kansas coach said.

McGuire, never one to shy away from a battle, joined the fray.

"Hot words were exchanged," the Associated Press reported. "Kansans said McGuire called them an ugly name. . . . And then, the North Carolina coach said a 'big guy' on the Kansas bench hit him in the stomach."

Kearns delivered his own retaliatory blow, driving for a field goal and hitting two foul shots for a 52–48 Carolina lead.

Back came the Jayhawks. Chamberlain scored three points, and Maurice King and Elstun each hit a free throw for a 53–52 Kansas lead with 20 seconds left in the third overtime.

The Tar Heels had made a habit of comebacks all season long. They needed another one.

So back they came.

Quigg was fouled by Chamberlain with six seconds remaining. He was awarded two free throws.

"I was nervous," Quigg said. "All I could think about during the timeout period was making those two shots. I got to thinking about the season we had . . . and I thought to myself that I couldn't let the team down now. I thought about this being the chance of a lifetime—a chance to win the NCAA championship."

Assistant coach Buck Freeman pulled Quigg aside and gave him some quick advice: "Don't forget to follow through and end up on your toes."

The North Carolina center let go with his first foul shot.

Score! Game tied.

"I knew it was in the moment it left my hand," Quigg recalled later. "You can just 'feel' whether a shot is good or not."

Quigg took a deep breath and then fired another shot.

"The second one wasn't as hard to make. I had the range—and I knew I could make that one, after sinking the first one."

Quigg then had his hand in a key defensive play, blocking a pass intended for Chamberlain to prevent a Kansas score. Kearns picked up the loose ball and tossed it toward the rafters of the Kansas City Municipal Auditorium as time ran out.

Final: North Carolina 54, Kansas 53.

Just another tight one for the Tar Heels in a season of close calls.

Call it a miracle or a team of destiny, if you wish. McGuire would not dispute that.

2.

The Dynasty Boys

John Wooden's UCLA Bruins had just beaten Louisville in the national semifinals at the 1975 Final Four. Why was he feeling so fearful?

As he walked off the court, he feared facing his players in the locker room, and then the media at the postgame press conference.

Even though he had coached the Bruins into their 10th championship game in 12 years and was still at the top of his profession, he had made up his mind to retire. It was going to be an emotional moment, for sure, for the coach they called the "Wizard of Westwood." He had given locker room talks before—plenty good ones—but this one would be the toughest of his career. Also one of the shortest.

The UCLA players sensed something was up when a grim-faced Wooden walked into the locker room. The game with Louisville had been one of the most thrilling of his career, but Wooden hardly looked uplifted.

There had been rumors floating around about his impending retirement. Wooden might have tipped his hand after the last game of the season at Pauley Pavilion when he acknowledged it would be the last home game "for a few people in this room."

Then, at the Final Four in San Diego, he made a brief announcement in the locker room following the nail-biting 75–74 victory over the Cardinals.

"I'm bowing out," he said. "I don't want to. I have to."

Remembering that emotional moment in later years, Wooden explained why he decided to retire at that particular time.

"It seemed the fact that we had been winning as much as we had, that it was getting to the point where people were critical and suspicious," Wooden said, "and I thought maybe it was the best just to get out of it. I was letting little things bother me. A succession of these things led up to my retirement."

The final straw: Wooden was hurt by accusations from the NCAA rules committee that he had always been a "problem." The committee lashed out when Wooden followed his common practice of closing the locker room door to the media.

Not a darling of the NCAA. Nor a darling of the press, that Wooden.

But simply the most successful coach March Madness has seen.

"I had been a part of this great basketball game," Wooden said, referring to the Louisville game. "But what made me feel different was that I found myself going off the floor almost dreading to go in before the wrath of the media.

"I had never let it bother me, and yet here I found myself almost dreading to do it. And I decided, I believe I'll just announce my retirement now."

Wooden's wife, Nell, couldn't have been happier. She had been trying to get him to retire for some time. But each year, something came up—like a championship.

Few coaches ever retired in such grand style. Going into the championship game against Kentucky two nights later, Wooden had led the Bruins to nine national titles in 11 years.

Starting in 1964, when the Bruins won their first title, they became just a four-letter word to their opponents. Cussed and discussed, UCLA ruled the sport under Wooden as no other college basketball team in history.

Evolution

At first, Walt Hazzard was almost as much trouble to John Wooden as he was to opposing teams.

"Hazzard was a tremendous passer and an outstanding ballhandler," Wooden recalled of his star guard. "But early in the year, I had some problems with him. I benched him. He was getting a little too fancy with the ball and I just wouldn't permit that. We lost a couple of games because I benched him."

It was the 1961–62 season, and Hazzard was playing in his first year as a sophomore with the Bruins.

"I had players who probably could pass as well as Walt," Wooden said. "But they didn't see the court the way he could. They didn't anticipate like Walt."

Hazzard was so far ahead of his teammates that he sometimes surprised them with his passes.

"He had the ability to anticipate the man getting open where the man himself couldn't anticipate it," Wooden said. "The ball would be there and they wouldn't handle it too well. He could handle the ball as well as any player I have coached."

Hazzard, a product of Philadelphia, was discovered by Willie Naulls, the player he would eventually supplant as UCLA's all-time leading scorer. After watching Hazzard in one high school game, Naulls felt he would be perfect for the Bruins' speed-oriented game.

Hazzard was, but it took some time for the Bruins to get used to him.

"The boys had never seen anything quite like him," Wooden said.

Nor had anyone else on the West Coast.

"He shoots passes through holes where you couldn't throw a golf ball," said *Sports Illustrated* in its March 19, 1962, issue.

Hazzard was as quick with his wits as with his hands. When a teammate announced one night at a training table meal that he was studying Africa so he could learn about Hazzard's background, the brilliant UCLA guard called out, "Coach, I think we've got a candidate for Little Rock here."

The Arkansas city, of course, was one of the early flashpoints for the civil rights movement.

Early in Hazzard's career, Wooden told him to stop worrying about his scoring and just play his floor game. If he did, the coach told Hazzard, he would eventually leave as UCLA's all-time leading scorer.

That turned out to be true.

Noted Wooden: "I mentioned this to him at the time he graduated, and he said, 'Yes, it will last one year.'"

Hazzard was referring to Gail Goodrich, who joined him a year later and eventually helped the Bruins win two national championships, in 1964 and 1965.

"They complemented each other very well," Wooden said of Hazzard and Goodrich. "Hazzard was a great ballhandler and Goodrich definitely was the better shooter."

Personality-wise, the two were dramatically different.

"Gail was a sensitive person," Wooden said. "You had to be careful at times taking him out of a game. He was one that you could never yell at. It would hurt his spirit. You'd have to pat him on the back more. Hazzard, for instance, would just get mad (and play better)."

Goodrich not only was a scoring machine, but also a key player in the Bruins' pressing defense. Only about 6-foot, he played "taller" than his height, according to Wooden.

"Kenny Washington was 6-3, or slightly over that, yet when the two were standing against the wall to measure their reach, Goodrich's fingers would be perhaps two inches higher up on the wall than Washington's," Wooden said. "Goodrich was closer to six feet, yet with his reach, he was more like a 6-4 man. So I considered him much bigger than he actually appeared to be."

Before Goodrich and Hazzard became a high-powered duo, the Bruins showed some signs of life with a good run in the 1962 NCAA tournament. They fell two points short against the eventual national champion Cincinnati Bearcats in the national semifinals. Played in Louisville, the game marked the first time local television carried the NCAA basketball tournament.

Between seasons, Wooden went back to the drawing board. Every year when basketball season ended, Wooden gave himself a project: How to make the Bruins a better team?

"I'd read anything I could find that had been written about basketball," Wooden said. "Periodicals like *Scholastic Coach* and *Athletic Journal*. Maybe one year I would be researching the fast break, the other it would be rebounding. Maybe the next year would be the jump shot."

This time, it was defense. Going into the 1962–63 season, Wooden thought about giving a pressing defense a try.

"I had used the pressing defense with great success in high school and at Indiana State. At UCLA, I had tried it for a while and disbanded it. Every year. Almost without exception, I would try it out and give it up too soon. In retrospect, I realized I was wrong."

It eventually became the hallmark of UCLA's championship teams.

"It didn't work well early in the year, but by the end of the year the pressing defense was good," Wooden said. "And it was the same pressing defense that took us through the next year undefeated."

Wooden credited Keith Erickson for his contribution to the Bruins' defensive strategy:

"He was certainly one of the key reasons for our championships in '64 and '65."

Wooden had scouted Erickson in junior college but wasn't impressed at first. Later, he got a better look and liked what he saw. The UCLA baseball coach wanted Erickson to play for him as well, but didn't have a scholarship to offer. He made a deal with Wooden to give Erickson a scholarship, allowing him to play both sports.

National Champions!

Goodrich and Hazzard in the backcourt, Fred Slaughter at center, and Jack Hirsch and Erickson at forward.

Wooden came into training camp in the fall of 1963 confident he had a championship-caliber starting lineup. He didn't realize at the time it would eventually be the deepest team the Bruins had put together since he took over the basketball program.

Would this be the year Wooden finally won his first national championship? The possibility existed, Wooden was sure.

Along with the starters, Wooden had two other players who would play key roles: forward Doug McIntosh and Washington, a guard-forward.

"I had what I liked to have—seven players that I considered starters," Wooden said.

Everyone knew the major names: Hazzard, Goodrich, Slaughter, etc. In the 1963–64 season, McIntosh and Washington were sophomores just trying to fit in. At the time, freshmen weren't eligible to play varsity ball.

"They came along and improved all year and added tremendous strength to this team," Wooden said of McIntosh and Washington.

The Bruins finished the regular season unbeaten (26–0) for the first time in their history. Even so, Wooden was very concerned about Seattle, UCLA's first-round opponent in the NCAA playoffs.

"They matched us as far as quickness was concerned," Wooden recalled, "and they were definitely bigger."

When Seattle went ahead in the second half, Wooden later told reporters he was more concerned about losing than at any other time during the season.

He needn't have worried—UCLA survived the West Regional opener, 95–90.

Next up: the University of San Francisco.

"I was more concerned with Seattle than I was with USF," Wooden recalled. "I really thought that we'd be quicker than USF."

Wooden might have had second thoughts when his team fell behind, 20–7.

"It was a very bad start," Wooden said. "No one actually got off to a good start, Hazzard and Goodrich in particular."

Early in the second half, Slaughter picked up his fourth foul and had to sit down. "Fred wasn't having one of his better ball games," Wooden said.

That's when UCLA's deep bench paid off. In came McIntosh to replace Slaughter.

"As the season wore on, I felt more confident in Doug and felt I could bring him in to the game in certain situations," Wooden said. "I had no hesitation in doing that in this particular game."

McIntosh contributed key points as UCLA chipped away at San Francisco's lead. Goodrich was suddenly back on his game, as was Hazzard. And Erickson joined the fun. With 1:24 left, the Bruins led, 75–72. Time for the delay game.

"We felt compelled (to go into the stall)," Wooden said. "It's only natural, with two minutes left in the ball game if you have a three-point lead. My feeling almost always was that if it was an odd-point lead, we would go into our deep protection game than if it was an even-point lead." (There were no three-point shots in those days.)

The strategy worked. The Bruins were on their way to the national semifinals to play Kansas State, a team they had beaten earlier in the year in a tough game at the Sunflower Classic in Kansas.

Wooden expected another bitterly fought contest in this second meeting with the Wildcats. The game matched his expectations.

UCLA fell behind late in the second half. A sportswriter joked that the Bruins were playing at a disadvantage—their cheerleaders and song girls had yet to show up for the game. Their flight had been delayed.

Finally, with six minutes left and the game tied at 75, they came bouncing onto the court "with a proper Hollywood entrance," according to one observer.

At this point, Slaughter was sitting on the bench in foul trouble. He had all he could handle in 7-foot Roger Suttner, who was easily a half-foot taller.

"So I brought in McIntosh," Wooden said. "McIntosh had improved during the year, and I had confidence in him."

UCLA went on to a 90–84 victory to advance to the championship game against Duke. Erickson scored 28 points.

"Somebody wrote it was our cheerleaders and song girls who gave us a shot in the arm," Wooden said. "I think that makes a good story, but what really made the difference was that our pressing defense began to take effect."

The day of the championship game, Wooden was standing in a hotel lobby with other coaches. The consensus seemed to be that UCLA was a great little team, but it was amazing that it had won 29 straight games. The general feeling: Duke should be a heavy favorite.

The exception to that sentiment came from one particular coach from Europe. He had visited several college campuses to pick up basketball techniques, including UCLA.

When the other coaches asked him how he thought UCLA would do in the championship game, he put up a hand and spread his five fingers.

"UCLA is team," he said in broken English. "UCLA will win."

"I thought that was a nice compliment," Wooden said, "because it's exactly what you want. You want your players playing as a team—you don't want a bunch of individuals out there."

For a while against Duke, the Bruins' pressing defense had little effect. The Bruins then reeled off 16 straight points to take a 42–30 lead at the half.

"By this time," Wooden said, "I had complete confidence in the press. I definitely felt at the half that we had this game absolutely won."

They did.

Final: UCLA 98, Duke 83.

The Bruins' first national championship, and first undefeated season at 30–0, was in the books.

Wooden said this team came as close as any of his squads to reaching its maximum potential.

"There was something in this season about the number 30," Wooden remembered. "I mentioned on national TV that it was our 30th victory and our daughter's 30th birthday on that particular day. She preferred that I hadn't mentioned it."

Repeating

At the start of the 1964–65 season, Goodrich, UCLA's star guard, was happy. Wooden had made him the Bruins' main ballhandler in his senior year.

"Of course he liked that," Wooden said. "He had always wanted to do that."

With Hazzard gone, Goodrich was the likely successor. Would he work as a point guard as well as a guard who could put up points?

Goodrich could score. That was obvious. But now he was being asked to fill the shoes of Hazzard, the national college player of the year in 1963–64. Wooden was asking Goodrich to be a playmaker as well as a scorer.

Goodrich was up to the challenge. He not only directed the offense, handing out timely assists, but he also was the Bruins' leading scorer in 1964–65 with an average of 24.6 points. But that was only part of his multifaceted game.

"Despite his limited height, Goodrich has a real instinct for the rebound," wrote *Sports Illustrated* on March 15, 1965. "He seems to anticipate the fluke bounces and be in the right spot to scoop up balls and toss them in for those 'garbage' baskets."

Who would have figured Goodrich to help lead UCLA to two consecutive national championships? When he was a senior in high school at Los Angeles Poly, few colleges were breaking down his doors—even though he led the school to the city championship. No doubt that had to do with his less-than-imposing 5-foot-9 height while in high school.

In fact, the only school seriously interested in him was UCLA. Gail Goodrich Sr. had starred at Southern Cal and was hoping his son would play there. But, like other schools that were wary of Goodrich's relatively short height, the Trojans failed to make a big pitch for him. The Trojans lived to regret that decision, as Goodrich grew to 6-foot or so and turned into a brilliant college player who later went on to professional glory with the Los Angeles Lakers.

Hazzard wasn't the only one gone from the 1963-64 national championship team. Slaughter and Hirsch also had played their last season at UCLA, leaving three starting positions to be filled.

Welcome, Edgar Lacey and McIntosh in the frontcourt and Fred Goss at guard. And welcome, full-court press, full-time.

With new personnel in the starting lineup, Wooden made some adjustments to his pressing defense at the start of the 1964–65 season.

"We were in with three new starters and a new type of pressing defense and it did take us longer to get going," Wooden admitted.

The Bruins lost to Illinois in the opening game of that season, a defeat Wooden called "one of the worst beatings we took." They managed to rebound and finish with a 14–0 record in their conference, then opened the NCAA playoffs against Brigham Young—in BYU's own gym.

"I was frankly concerned," Wooden said. "I had taken teams to BYU through the years and played there, and BYU gets tremendous support. They have great fans and really get behind their team. Deep down, I was concerned about how we would respond to that home crowd."

Especially in a tournament game.

"I think there should be alternate sites and a home team should never be playing in a tournament on their home floor when it comes to the NCAA (playoffs)," he said, with good reason.

Once the Bruins got their press going, it didn't seem to matter. UCLA rolled, 100–76, as Goodrich scored 40 points to break UCLA's single-game scoring record. Wooden was more impressed by Erickson's 28.

"Erickson is going to play a good ball game, but usually wasn't going to score a lot of points."

Next up was San Francisco, an old nemesis from the Bill Russell years in the 1950s and a difficult opponent only one year before. Wooden was again concerned, simply because "USF was a better basketball team."

Never mind. It was another scorefest for UCLA, which won, 101–93.

The Bruins added Wichita State to their list of victims with a 109–89 thrashing of the Shockers. That set up a championship game with Michigan, which was ranked No. 1 in the country almost all season and pretty much the choice to unseat UCLA as national champion.

"They had a big, powerful-looking team," Wooden recalled of the Wolverines. "They almost looked like football linemen."

These "linemen" included Cazzie Russell, Oliver Darden, and Larry Tregoning.

In many ways, the 1965 national championship game was much like the one in 1964. Both times, UCLA's opponent got off to a good start. And both times, the Bruins turned things around with their press.

"Our press really took a big toll on them," Wooden said after watching his team take a 47–34 lead over Michigan at the half. "We had the game essentially won at the half. It was more than just the score. You could just tell by the general appearance of the teams that I felt (that the game was over). I think the running had really gotten to them.

"I remember it was (Bill) Buntin shooting free throws just before the half. He took a deep breath, he was so tired. He threw the free throw up there and it was way short. It was just air."

Goodrich, meanwhile, had no trouble finding the basket, from the foul line or the floor. He scored 42 points, a championship-game record, and finished one point away from Clyde Lovellette's tournament record of 141 points for Kansas. And UCLA nailed down its second straight title, 91–80.

The Alcindor Era

When UCLA started classes in the fall of 1965, one student in particular stood out.

He was hard to miss. For one thing, Lew Alcindor was over seven feet tall. For another, his basketball skills had inspired Wooden to praise him as "awesome."

High praise indeed, considering the Bruins basketball coach was historically sparing in such endorsements.

"I felt that the team that has Alcindor has their foot in the door," Wooden said.

Wooden, of course, was speaking about winning a national championship.

"I hoped to be the first team to win three in succession," Wooden said.

Alcindor, who later changed his name to Kareem Abdul-Jabbar, was the most heralded freshman to ever play at UCLA—maybe anywhere in the history of college basketball. In an era when freshmen couldn't play for the varsity, Alcindor was clearly the most notable sports name on campus even before he played in his first basketball game.

In a tune-up against the varsity for the 1965–66 season, Alcindor scored 31 points to lead the freshmen to a 75–60 victory. That was versus a UCLA varsity that, incidentally, was shooting for its third straight national title.

"UCLA is No. 1 in the country, and No. 2 on its own campus," quipped one observer.

Ever since starring at Power Memorial in New York, and even before that, Alcindor usually guaranteed success for his teams. In high school, he led Power to 71 straight victories and two championships. He set New York City records for career points and career rebounds.

When it came time to announce his choice of a college, Alcindor's press conference on May 4, 1965, was a mega-event in New York and created lots of interest around the country.

Imagine how many coaches held their breath as Alcindor prepared to announce his choice. UCLA was where the celebrations began.

It took him a while to get used to UCLA.

He was 3,000 miles from home, living in a West Coast culture as different from the East as night from day. At first he was so homesick that he didn't unpack his bags for a week.

Wooden did everything he could to make UCLA a safe haven for his young star. The UCLA coach threw a protective wall around

Alcindor, just as Alcindor's former coach Jack Donohue had done at Power, keeping the media and other outside influences at bay.

Alcindor was unusually coordinated for a big man, a superb athlete who could adapt his game to any situation. His major weapon was no secret: the dunk. Sailing high over the basket, he jammed the ball through the hoop with ferocity, scoring many of his points with ease.

Alcindor did not have exclusive ownership of this crowd-pleasing shot, of course. The Houston Cougars, for one, featured a slam-dunking group led by the great Elvin Hayes.

They would not have use of this weapon for very long. The NCAA rules committee eliminated the shot from college basketball after the 1967 season. It was not allowed again until 1976, long after Alcindor and Hayes were gone from the college scene.

What did Alcindor do without the dunk shot in college? He simply developed a devastating outside hook shot that was impossible to stop. This was his trademark "skyhook" that he continued to refine in the pros, where he was a one-man wrecking crew as Kareem Abdul-Jabbar.

"Lewis felt the rules committee put in the 'no-dunk' rule because of him," Wooden said of Alcindor. "I don't think it was aimed at him. He might have had some influence on it, but all of the Houston team was in there dunking and bending the basket in the back before you could start a game. I think that's what influenced the rules committee."

No matter. It became widely known as the "Alcindor Rule."

While the UCLA varsity slumped to an 18–8 mark in 1966 and failed to make the NCAA playoffs, the "Baby Bruins" were on a roll. With Alcindor leading the way, UCLA's freshman team won 21 straight games. Waiting impatiently to join the varsity, he smashed the freshman scoring record by 150 points.

Alcindor was one of four sophomores in UCLA's starting lineup when the 1966–67 season opened. The other starters: forwards Kenny Heitz and Lynn Shackleford and guards Lucius Allen and Mike Warren, the only upperclassman in the bunch.

"Warren was as intelligent a player as I've ever coached," Wooden said of the junior guard.

Alcindor was the biggest name, though—the first true big man Wooden had coached. So much was expected of Alcindor as he nervously awaited the start of the season.

"I just want to go out there and be able to do my thing and see if it is good enough," he said.

He needn't have worried. In his first game, against Southern Cal, Alcindor scored 56 points as the Bruins routed the Trojans, 105–90.

As UCLA built a winning streak, Alcindor received more than his share of publicity.

"You read some of the things they say about you and get scared of yourself," Alcindor said. "I read all these things and I say, 'Is that me they're talking about?'"

Alcindor, good as advertised. The Bruins finished the season undefeated and cruised past Wyoming in their first NCAA tournament test. Wyoming coach Bill Strannigan said he thought the Bruins were the best college basketball team he had ever seen.

"If I were the opposing coach and were down 55–18 at the half, I would feel that way, too," Wooden said. "They were awestruck at seeing Alcindor and gave us no trouble at all."

Neither did the University of Pacific in the regional finals. UCLA waltzed, 80–64, as Alcindor scored 38 points and grabbed 14 rebounds, outplaying Pacific center Keith Swaggerty by a wide margin.

With Hayes, Houston seemed more of a worthy opponent for the Bruins. Just like Alcindor, Hayes was a frontcourt force. As the national semifinals in Louisville, Kentucky, approached, many newspaper stories focused on the battle of the big men.

"What I'm really looking forward to is a head-to-head situation with Alcindor," the boastful Hayes said. "I don't think Lew can stay with me when he's on defense. I think I have some real fine moves."

Hayes won the statistical battle, scoring 25 points to Alcindor's 19. UCLA won the game, 73–58.

"They left Shackleford open," Wooden said. "Apparently they were going to make him prove he could shoot from the outside."

He did, scoring 22 points as UCLA romped. It was one of the few times someone other than Alcindor was the Bruins' leading scorer.

To no one's surprise, the Bruins whipped Dayton by 15 points in the finals to cap a 30–0 season. Alcindor's line: 20 points, 18 rebounds, and four blocked shots—all early in the game.

"I felt the team had come along extremely well that year," said Wooden, who became the first coach in the NCAA's Division I to have two perfect seasons—and, not too long after, three straight national championships.

Wooden liked to point out that his Bruins became the youngest team ever to win the NCAA championship in men's basketball.

"At that time, we had already won with the comparatively smallest team ever to win the NCAA championship (1964). Now we won with the youngest."

Wooden was very optimistic about the coming year. And why not, considering the powerhouse he was coaching?

Alcindor, Part 2

It was a game made in basketball heaven.

The "Big A" vs. the "Big E," a Clash of the Titans, the Game of the Century. At the eighth wonder of the world!

If the hyperbole was coming in loud and clear, no wonder. The stage was set for a battle between UCLA and Houston, the two best college basketball teams in America in the 1967–68 season. Both were undefeated—UCLA was ranked No. 1 and Houston No. 2.

Even the setting was bigger than life: the famed Houston Astrodome, which had been sold out for months.

"We've had calls from Mexico City, Chicago, and San Francisco," said the ticket manager for the Dome. "If we hadn't run out, we would have sold 75,000 tickets, no doubt about it."

As it was, a record crowd for a college basketball game would attend, 52,693. In addition, the game on a January night in 1968 would have the largest television audience in the history of college basketball, shown by more than 150 stations in 49 states.

With Alcindor leading the way, UCLA had chalked up 47 straight victories. Led by Hayes, Houston was also unbeaten and had won 17 straight since losing to the Bruins in a sobering defeat in the previous season's national semifinals. The Cougars were particularly tough to beat at home, having won 48 straight.

Since losing to UCLA the year before, the slam-dunk-happy Cougars were aching for revenge—especially Hayes, who resented the fact Alcindor had received so much favorable publicity. Hayes believed that he, not Alcindor, should be recognized as the best college basketball player in the country.

Alcindor refused to get into any personal dialogue with Hayes about who was better. He was more concerned with winning, he said, than any personal accomplishments. But clearly he was not at his best after suffering an eye injury in a game against Cal. For the better part of a week leading up to the Houston game, Alcindor wore an eye patch and stayed in bed as the team knocked off Stanford and Portland.

The injury was a deciding factor against the Cougars, too.

Against Houston, Alcindor had the worst game of his career, making only four of 18 shots as the Cougars beat the Bruins, 71–69, and took over top ranking in the land.

By contrast, Hayes was at his best with 39 points and 15 rebounds. His two free throws clinched the game for Houston.

"Elvin Hayes had one of the greatest individual games I've ever seen a player have," Wooden said. "He just did everything extremely well in that ball game."

Hayes added insult to injury, downgrading Alcindor's talents with his usual run of trash talk.

"They had a lot to say about us and I don't think they were correct," Alcindor said. "They were annoying and insulting. We want to teach these people some manners."

All of a sudden, a personal feud was brewing between Alcindor and Hayes—and, in fact, between all of the players on both teams.

"I hope they come to L.A. undefeated," Allen said, referring to a possible rematch in March Madness. "That would be nice."

And, yes, UCLA got its chance for revenge when the teams met in the national semifinals in Los Angeles. Neither team had lost since their meeting in January, the Cougars riding a 31-game winning streak.

"It made for tremendous interest throughout the nation," Wooden remembered. "I never had a team more eager to play in the tournament than we were to play Houston."

Wooden usually used man-to-man defense but this time went to a "Diamond and One" zone to keep a tighter check on Hayes: play him tight on the outside and if he slipped through, Alcindor would be waiting underneath the basket. The strategy worked beautifully as the Bruins held Hayes to merely 10 points.

"I think the defense momentarily confused them," Wooden said, "and we got a great start."

A great finish, too. The Bruins buried the nation's No. 1 team, 101–69. In their personal statistical battle, Alcindor outscored Hayes, 19–10, and outrebounded him, 18–5.

"They wanted to prove that their win in the Astrodome was no fluke," Wooden said. "On the contrary, it showed it was a fluke. I know a lot of our players were thinking about that. I had no concerns. I could just tell by their general attitude that we were certainly going to be ready to play."

The 78–55 victory over North Carolina in the finals was almost anticlimactic.

"The game against North Carolina counted a lot," Alcindor said, "but the win over Houston was our most satisfying. Getting to play them again is something that we all prayed for. I guess you could say I definitely wanted to win that one more than any game I've played since I've been at UCLA."

Alcindor, Part 3

When the Bruins opened the defense of their national championship in the 1968–69 season, Wooden was understandably concerned. Sure, UCLA still had Alcindor at center and what Wooden called "the strongest front line in the history of college basketball." These players included returnees Shackleford and Jim Neilsen plus three highly touted sophomores: Curtis Rowe, Sidney Wicks, and Steve Patterson, who would form the nucleus of more championship teams down the road.

However, the backcourt was questionable following the graduation of the playmaking Warren and the absence of Allen, declared ineligible for academic reasons.

Going into training camp, Wooden wondered who was going to step up to replace Warren and Allen. "Whoever they are, they'll be the most inexperienced set of guards I've ever had at UCLA," he said.

Welcome, John Vallely. Vallely played center in high school and forward in junior college. With the frontcourt-heavy Bruins, Vallely made the transition to guard and opened eyes around UCLA with his shooting ability.

"By the middle of the year, the players were calling Vallely our money man," Wooden said. "He was the one they wanted to get the jump shot when you had to have the basket."

The other backcourt position was filled by Heitz, who moved over from forward and clicked with Vallely.

Meanwhile, it was business as usual for Alcindor, who won his third straight national player of the year trophy while leading the Bruins into another playoff appearance.

The Bruins were heavily favored to win their third straight NCAA championship without much opposition. Apparently Drake never got the memo.

Not much was known of the Bulldogs, who had not been nationally ranked until the final week of the season. Wooden knew about them, though, as he prepared his UCLA team for the Missouri Valley Conference champions in the national semifinals in Louisville.

"They weren't a big team, but they were a quick team," Wooden said. "I dread the quick teams."

From start to finish, the Bruins had their toughest test of the 1969 NCAA tournament.

"We never could pull away," Wooden said. "It seemed like we'd be getting ahead and then they'd close in. They were very quick, played us tight and rugged.

"Obviously with us being the opposite of the underdogs, they were the crowd favorite. Of the 18,500 people that were there, perhaps 15,000 were pulling for Drake."

With Vallely making a number of clutch shots as part of his team-leading 29 points, the Bruins took an 83–74 lead with a little more than a minute to play. It was hardly over.

The Bulldogs scored eight straight points to pull within one. That's as close as they got, as Shackleford made a pair of free throws to clinch an 85–82 UCLA win.

Two nights later, UCLA wore the champion's crown again with a 92–72 victory over Purdue, Wooden's alma mater, featuring the great Rick Mount.

The Alcindor Era at UCLA was at an end. With 37 points and 20 rebounds, he finished it in grand style as the Bruins became the first team in NCAA basketball history to win three straight championships. For Wooden, it was a great relief.

"In many ways, I was glad it had come to a close," Wooden said. "With Alcindor, I put great pressure on myself. I felt we should (win three national championships). Sometimes it becomes harder to do the things you should do than it is when you're not expected to do something."

A New Challenge

Wooden had a special name for his 1969–70 squad: "The Team Without."

"Of course it was the team without Alcindor," Wooden said. "Lots of coaches and people said now without the big man I would get my comeuppance."

But UCLA's opponents hadn't counted on the Bruins' ferocious pride.

"They wanted to prove to themselves that they had something in their own right," Wooden said.

It was Wicks' time to shine. As a sophomore the season before, he had played sparingly. But now he was front and center, as far as Wooden was concerned.

Wooden considered Wicks one of the greatest competitors he ever coached: never afraid to take a shot in the clutch or make a big defensive play. He was also good at bringing the ball up court against pressure.

Wicks was a lithe, 6-foot-8 forward who had come storming out of Los Angeles' black ghetto.

"He had a tendency to give you that hard stare," Wooden said. "But he was anything but tough. He'd do that to me a time or two when we disagreed and I'd say to him, 'Now, Sidney, you can scare other people, but I know you, you're all chicken inside.' Invariably, he would smile."

Wicks was paired at forward with the 6-foot-6 Rowe, another L.A. ghetto product. The formidable starting five also featured Patterson at center and Vallely and Henry Bibby in the backcourt. Without Alcindor, Wooden went to a high-post offense with Patterson in the middle, playing away from the basket.

"I feel more comfortable with this style," Wooden said. "We used the low-post offense solely because of Alcindor and the personnel we had with him."

Before the conference season opened, Wooden sat down with pencil and paper and played his annual guessing game. It was a habit of his to try to predict his team's record in the conference, something he had done ever since he had started coaching at UCLA. This year, he went through the schedule game by game and came up with an 11–3 mark. He sealed the paper in an envelope and gave it to his secretary.

Wooden was off by one—the Bruins finished 12–2 in conference play.

"I think we were a much better ball club after losing a couple," Wooden said. "You can learn as many lessons from a loss as you can from a victory. I went into (postseason play) actually with as much confidence and expectations as I had with Alcindor."

That confidence was justified as UCLA whipped Long Beach State, Utah State, and New Mexico State by sizable margins and rolled into the NCAA finals against Jacksonville.

The teams were a study in contrast: UCLA's tightly disciplined style under Wooden vs. Jacksonville's wide-open approach under the flamboyant, colorful Joe Williams.

"He was the wildest dresser I had ever seen," Wooden said of Williams.

In other words, the complete opposite of Wooden, who usually wore conservative, dark suits. One writer pointed out that by comparison, Wooden dressed with all the sartorial splendor of an undertaker.

Wooden's wife was upset when she saw the remark in the paper.

"She got me some blue shirts and yellow shirts and I started wearing some sports coats."

One thing Wooden did not change: his controlled practices. They were so different from the undisciplined, fun-loving workouts of Jacksonville, whose coach said of his team, "They do what they want to do."

In pregame warmups, the Jacksonville players entertained the crowd by whipping the ball around to the strains of "Sweet Georgia Brown," à la the Harlem Globetrotters.

"I felt watching his team practice to music, they didn't seem to have any discipline," Wooden said. "I didn't like that at all."

As was his practice, Wooden kept his players sheltered from the press. By the same token, the Dolphins were crying out for media attention.

As Wooden was imposing his media ban, Jacksonville's Artis Gilmore called out from the other end of the court, "Hey, man, we'll talk to you."

One other difference: this time, it was UCLA's opponent that featured the big man, the 7-foot-2 Gilmore. And he was giving the Bruins a lot of problems early in the game as Jacksonville took a 14–6 lead. At this point, Wooden called a timeout and made some adjustments. It was Wicks' idea to play behind the big man in the low post.

"I knew it wasn't going to be any worse," Wooden said, "so I switched Sidney behind him."

The tactic worked, as Wicks blocked five of Gilmore's shots.

"The dunk rule really helped me," Wicks said, referring to the ruling that outlawed the dunk shot in college ball. "If Gilmore could have dunked, he would have killed me."

And with an 80–69 victory over Jacksonville, the Bruins had sewn up their fourth straight national championship.

Going After More

For most of the 1970–71 season, Patterson was overshadowed by Wicks and Rowe in the frontcourt. With those two carrying much of the offensive load along with Bibby in the backcourt, Patterson usually was an afterthought when observers went over the game's box score.

"Rowe and Wicks received more acclaim and were more in the public eye," Wooden said. "And Bibby was somewhat spectacular at times shooting from the outside."

Not that the 6-foot-9 Patterson wasn't fulfilling a very valuable role at center.

"I felt at this time he played about as well in my high-post offense as any center I've ever had," Wooden said.

That went way back to the days of Naulls, one of the great high-post centers in UCLA basketball history.

Not that Patterson was always perfect. He had gone through a streaky, erratic year and had been benched at times for lethargic play. In UCLA's 68–60 victory over Kansas' Big Eight champions in the national semifinals at the Houston Astrodome, he managed only six points.

Against Villanova in the finals, he suddenly turned into Mr. Automatic. Scoring inside and out, Patterson piled up 20 points as UCLA charged to a 45–37 lead at the half.

Patterson finished with a career-high 29 points as UCLA survived its closest test in seven years in the finals, 68–62. The Wildcats had done a good job holding Wicks and Rowe to a combined total of 15 points. They had forgotten that Patterson was on the court, too.

Patterson was a redshirt with the Bruins when they had played in the Astrodome three years earlier. This time, he was the star of the game, as Wooden took advantage of Villanova's zone defense.

"We used a certain play against that zone defense where we'd roll him down deep suddenly, and he picked up some easy baskets," Wooden said.

Patterson's play wasn't the only unexpected occurrence in the game. At the start of the second half, Wooden went to a ball-control tactic—something he rarely did. But he wanted to make a point.

For years he had been pressing to install a 30-second clock. He felt that "non-action games" featuring ball control were hurting college basketball.

"From a technical point of view, it might have been wrong," Wooden said of the slowdown tactics against Villanova at that particular time. "I was doing this for the rules committee."

Wooden wouldn't have done it, of course, if it might have cost him the game.

"It was one of those games I just felt that we weren't going to lose."

Not even when Villanova pulled within 61–58 on a baseline jumper by Howard Porter. Bibby took over late in the game. The sharp-shooting guard scored eight of UCLA's last 10 points. Patterson had the other two points.

The game was memorable to Wooden for other reasons.

"Two things happened at the end of this game which made me feel as good as anything I've ever had in my coaching career and they happened in regard to Sidney Wicks and Curtis Rowe," Wooden said.

In one instance, Wooden had just returned to the dressing room after meeting with the media. As he walked in, he heard a reporter ask Rowe about rumors of racial problems on the Bruins.

"We don't have any racial problems on this team," Rowe quickly responded. "Coach Wooden doesn't see color, he just sees basketball players."

This, of course, pleased Wooden very much.

"I'd like to feel that I had no prejudice in that way," Wooden said. "That left a good feeling."

The other instance occurred near the end of the game. Bibby was at the foul line, and a timeout was called. Wicks came over to Wooden and said, "Congratulations on another championship, Coach." Wicks turned and walked back to his position on the court, but quickly returned.

He leaned down and put out his hand again, smiling as he did so.

"Coach, you're really something," Wicks said.

That pleased Wooden to no end.

"That meant a lot to me in that I had to discipline him a little just before then. We had a disagreement, but that was forgotten. Sidney would get awfully upset, but then things would get over and they're gone, past, and forgotten."

The Walton Gang

Bill Walton arrived on the UCLA campus with almost as much fanfare as Alcindor. It was well-deserved, according to Wooden.

"Alcindor was the most valuable player I've ever coached," Wooden said. "Bill Walton is the second most valuable player, and you can put up a pretty good argument that he was as valuable as Alcindor."

Both were excellent team players. And both had great maneuverability for big men. Over the course of his college and professional career, Alcindor reached a height of 7-foot-2. Walton was 6-foot-11.

Their playing personalities were distinctly different, Alcindor going about his business with grim determination, Walton playing with childlike enthusiasm.

"Bill was an animated player, whereas Lew was not too animated," Wooden said. "He would give you the sense of being an introvert. Bill would give you the feeling he was an extrovert, a rebel in many ways."

Walton was always ready to express an opinion about world affairs, whether it was politics, drugs, or the environment. His outspoken behavior occasionally got him into trouble with the law. He was arrested for taking part in an antiwar demonstration near the UCLA campus.

He answered reporters' questions with a startling frankness. Not that he enjoyed talking to the media at all. That was another trait he shared with Alcindor, who did interviews grudgingly and sparingly.

"My basketball life is open to everyone," Walton said, "but what I do off the court for my own recreation and entertainment is my own business. I do what I want to do and people don't have to know. Even Coach Wooden doesn't know what I do."

Wooden allowed Walton to be as free-spirited as he wished, so long as he kept up his grades and worked hard at basketball. In both cases, Wooden gave Walton a high passing mark.

Walton played with inflamed knees that needed constant medical attention. It didn't seem to affect the quality of his play.

No college basketball player in America had Walton's unique ability to pick off a rebound and trigger a fast break.

"On defense, I make a point of knowing where all my guys are, all of the time," Walton said, "so when I get the ball, even while facing the basket, I am thinking about the fast break."

Even though he was only a sophomore in the 1971–72 season, Walton was expected to make a giant contribution. "Naturally, the style of play is going to revolve around Bill Walton," Wooden said.

Wooden had no choice but to rely on Walton for a major role. He had to replace four starters from his '71 championship team. The only remaining starter: Bibby, the veteran sparkplug guard who was starting his third straight year. With all the inexperienced players on the team, Wooden was counting on Bibby to take the leadership role.

If there was a shortage of experience, there was no shortage of talent as UCLA launched the 1971–72 season. Keith Wilkes and Larry Farmer joined Walton in the frontcourt. Along with Bibby, the other guard position was shared by Greg Lee and Tommy Curtis.

Swen Nater and Larry Hollyfield were the first two players off the bench. Although the 6-foot-11 Nater never started a game at UCLA, he proved to be invaluable as a practice opponent for Walton.

"He was a big, strong player," Wooden said of Nater, who went on to a solid professional career. "Bill Walton made the remark that Swen Nater was as tough as anyone he played against at any time. Swen didn't get the credit very much."

The Bruins opened the season with a 105–49 blowout of The Citadel—a score not uncommon as the season progressed.

"The surprising thing about this team, we hardly were pressed in any game all year," Wooden said. "We won by a pretty good margin consistently game after game. Teams tried different styles against us."

After losing 114–56 to UCLA early in the season, Notre Dame went into a slowdown game the next time they met, to no avail. The Bruins beat the Irish by a mere 25 points, 57–32.

Not until UCLA faced Florida State in the NCAA tournament finals did the Bruins play in a truly competitive game. The Seminoles, coming off three years of probation for recruiting violations, featured two powerful frontcourt players in Reggie Royals and Larry McCray, and a sharp-shooting guard in Ron King.

None of them added up to Walton, who had 24 points and 20 rebounds as UCLA held off Florida State, 81–76, to complete Wooden's third perfect season. Championship number eight was in the books for the Bruins.

Walton was a terror in the Final Four that year, scoring 33 points and grabbing 21 rebounds in a 96–77 win over Louisville in the semifinals before his stellar performance in the championship game.

"He was really animated and particularly really up for (the championship game)," Wooden said.

It was a mere appetizer for what Walton would cook up the next year.

Nobody's Perfect—Except UCLA

How do you improve on perfection? In the 1971–72 season, UCLA had beaten its opponents by an average of 32 points en route to a 30–0 record.

With his top players all juniors and more experienced, Wooden expected better years from them in 1972–73.

"I think I picked us to win them all this year," said Wooden, referring to his annual preseason tradition of predicting his team's record.

Sitting at his desk, Wooden jotted down "30–0." He put the paper into an envelope, to be sealed away like the Academy Awards until after the conclusion of the season.

Another perfect season was in order, then, for the UCLA team. Who would doubt it, with the likes of Walton, Wilkes, and Curtis returning?

And through the regular season, it was so far, so good.

By the time the 1973 playoffs began, the Bruins were riding a 71-game winning streak built over two seasons. Along the way, they had broken San Francisco's record of 60 set in the 1950s.

In the NCAA playoffs, more of the same. The Bruins added to their monster streak with victories over Arizona State, San Francisco, and Indiana before meeting Memphis State in the finals.

Even though the Bruins had won the championship in 1972, Walton was dissatisfied with the way the team had played. "We didn't dominate the way I know we can," a dour Walton said at that postgame press conference.

In the '73 finals, things were no different—at least for the first half.

Behind Larry Kenon and Larry Finch, the Tigers gave the Bruins all they could handle. The game was tied, 39–39, at halftime, and UCLA even fell behind at the start of the second half.

Walton had seen enough. He broke out, continually scoring on easy shots near the basket after taking passes down low from Lee.

"Our eyes meet and I whale it up there," said Lee, explaining the ease with which he connected with Walton.

The UCLA center missed only one shot all night, scoring on 21 of 22 tries in one of the greatest statistical performances in NCAA playoff history. And one of the most dominant.

He finished with 44 points as UCLA whipped Memphis State, 87–66.

The 21-point victory was more to Walton's liking than the mere five-point win over Florida State in the 1972 championship game. But as far as Walton's spectacular, near-perfect show in 1973, Wooden didn't necessarily think it was the center's greatest performance.

"The way they were playing," Wooden said, "most of those baskets were right underneath, or those short bank shots from just off the key area, maybe seven or eight feet.

"Actually, I felt that Bill had many better games for us than this particular game. He didn't have to work that hard in this ball game because so many of those shots were easy. I've seen him hit 25 or 30 in a row of that type of shot."

Walton also was strong on the boards with 13 rebounds, the only player on the court with double-digit rebounds. He accomplished a lot of this in foul trouble, finishing with four.

"He did so many things so well that we just couldn't stop him," said Memphis State coach Gene Bartow, who would later succeed Wooden as coach at UCLA. "He's the best collegiate player I've ever seen."

Walton could have left college at that point. It was rumored he had received a pro offer that would make him a millionaire. But he was having too much fun at UCLA, he said, to leave school early for the NBA. Besides, money had never been a driving force in his life.

UCLA's winning streak was eventually bound to end, and it did on a January night at South Bend, Indiana, in the 1973–74 season. It was there that the Bruins lost by one point to Notre Dame, 71–70, to end their record winning streak at 88 games.

"This was great for college basketball," Notre Dame coach Digger Phelps said. "I'm sure everyone was rooting for us the way they used to root against the New York Yankees."

The Bruins had dominated from the start, twice leading by 17 points in the first half. Then, with 3:30 to go, they blew an 11-point lead. Dwight Clay's jump shot from the right corner with 29 seconds remaining clinched the victory for the Fighting Irish.

"It was one of the greatest feelings I've ever had," Clay said of his winning shot. "I looked out at Gary (Brokaw) with the ball when he was trying to get it into (John Shumate). Then I saw the defense shift in to Gary and I was alone, so I called to him for the ball."

Then it was March Madness in January.

"The crowd of 11,343 fans in Notre Dame's Athletic and Convocation Center was almost stunned," the *New York Times* reported. "It was a few seconds before belief registered, apparently, and then the fans swarmed on the court, smothering the Irish players and coach Digger Phelps with wild undergraduate enthusiasm."

The Bruins quickly redeemed themselves one week later by whipping the Irish in a return game in Los Angeles, 94–75.

Another surprise happened to the Bruins on the way to an eighth straight national title.

In an epic back-and-forth struggle, UCLA and North Carolina State played a game for the ages in the 1974 national semifinals.

The teams took the thrilling contest into one overtime, then another.

In the second overtime, the Bruins bolted to a seven-point lead and seemingly had the game wrapped up. At least, that's what most everyone thought.

But North Carolina State held its composure.

David Thompson, Tommy Burleson, and Monte Towe led a late rally for the Wolfpack. "Trailing by 7 points with 3 minutes 27 seconds to go in the second five-minute overtime period, N.C. State showed no signs of panic," reported the *New York Times*.

For the first time in 39 playoff games, the Bruins wound up on the short end of the final score, 80–77, in double overtime.

Not only did the stunning loss stop a record playoff winning streak at 38 for the Bruins, but also a national championship streak at seven—a number unlikely to be approached again.

"It was inconceivable that in the second overtime we could dissipate a seven-point lead," Wooden said. "But it was an outstanding basketball game, and certainly I couldn't fault my team too much."

Back on Top

When practice opened for the 1974–75 season, Wooden had a major reconstruction job on his hands. It was nothing new for Wooden, who had seen great players come and go through the years. This time, though, he had to find a replacement for Walton and Wilkes, two of UCLA's all-time greats.

As the only returning starter, forward Dave Meyers was being counted on by Wooden to be one of his key players.

Marques Johnson, Richard Washington, and Ralph Drollinger were three others who primarily played in the frontcourt. The starting guards, for the most part: Pete Trgovich and Andre McCarter.

A good group of players, yes, but one that paled by comparison with the teams that had featured Walton and Wilkes. Or Alcindor and Allen. Or Wicks and Rowe.

"People thought we'd have a pretty good team," Wooden said, "but nobody felt we'd be in contention for the national championship."

From the start of the season, the Bruins had to overcome health problems to key players. Johnson, for one, had come back from hepatitis.

"I was under restrictions not to get him too tired," Wooden said.

Meyers, meanwhile, wasn't the same player in the second half of the season following a groin injury.

"It hurt our team quite a bit because he played our number one pressing defensive position and he was not able to function," Wooden said. "I had to quit using our press, and our press was one of our strengths."

No perfect record this time, but at least a spot in the NCAA playoffs.

Welcome again to the "UCLA Invitational," as one writer had dubbed the NCAA playoffs in the midst of the Bruins' amazing run.

Except for a 14-point win over Arizona State, not too many things came easily for UCLA in the 1975 tournament. The Bruins nearly were beaten by Michigan before pulling out an overtime win. They managed to hold off Montana by three points and later nipped Louisville by one in overtime in the national semifinals.

Then, more drama as Wooden made his announcement he would be retiring following the national championship game.

And the finale, a 92–85 victory over Kentucky for Wooden's 10th title in 12 years.

Hollywood couldn't have scripted a better ending.

3.

The First

They were called the "Tall Firs."

Howard Hobson's Oregon Ducks, the first NCAA champion in 1939, had it all: size, speed, and a superlative coach.

The front line was among the tallest in the country. Urgel "Slim" Wintermute was the biggest of the bunch at 6-foot-8. John Dick and Laddie Gale were each close to 6-foot-5. By 1939 standards, the Ducks' front line was huge, something to behold.

"A player the size of Wintermute was a novelty in the East," Hobson said.

"Tall Firs," indeed. But unlike the majestic state tree of Oregon, the Ducks didn't stay planted very long.

While the rest of the West Coast was mainly playing a conservative game, the Oregon basketball team was rolling right along with a devastating fast break. No sitting ducks, for sure.

The architect of this racehorse style was Hobson, a legendary coach responsible for a basketful of key innovations in the sport.

No, he didn't invent the fast break, but he certainly polished it to a high degree. It was something rarely seen before on the West Coast, especially the way the Ducks did it.

"Our fast break was a little unusual in that we looked for it on every possession," Hobson said in a 1979 interview. "It was a break that we always attempted after we gained possession, with the two guards handling the ball most of the time, the two forwards down ahead, and the center trailing and coming in on the rebound."

The result usually created an imbalance on the court, leaving an Oregon player open to shoot. More often than not, that player was 6-foot-4 forward Laddie Gale, who led the Pacific Coast Conference (PCC) in scoring.

Gale was known for his gigantic hands that allowed him to fake out opponents under the basket. Gale could switch the basketball with ease between his huge hands while driving for a score. It made it tough for an opponent to block his shot.

"He'd come under the basket and, instead of turning and shooting, he'd flip the ball back over his head with one hand from the other side of the basket," said reserve guard Ford Mullen.

Mullen said he would never forget the first time he shook hands with Gale. "My hands were lost in his."

Hobson's speed-oriented philosophy was not only a weapon on offense, but also on defense.

"We had assignments for spots that we had to run back to on defense," recalled Dick, the other starting forward on the Oregon team. "We were constantly fast-breaking going back as well as going down the court."

The constant running created a dizzying turmoil for Oregon's opponents.

"We ran on everything," Dick said. "We wanted to keep the pressure on them mentally—more so than physically. Never give them a moment's rest."

Height and speed weren't the only hallmarks of this team. There was also Bobby Arnet, a 5-foot-8 sparkplug. As team captain, Arnet had more responsibilities than the players do today.

In the 1930s, coaches were not permitted to start a conversation with officials. Only the captain could talk to a referee or call timeout. Arnet was superb in this role.

Arnet commanded the backcourt, playing alongside Wally Johansen. They had played together since junior high school in Oregon and had won state high school championships together. They were both directed to Oregon, along with other players, by Astoria High School coach John Warren, who eventually became the freshman basketball coach at Oregon.

"Bobby was the best dribbler I have ever seen," Dick said of Arnet in an interview with the *Oregonian*. "He had short legs and a long trunk and long arms, so he could run erect and dribble like nothing I had ever seen."

Arnet actually preferred to pass rather than shoot. He left the shooting up to his fellow guard. Johansen was a skilled outside marksman, particularly devastating with his two-handed set shot.

The Ducks' 1938–39 team featured more than just the sterling top five, of course.

"Through the season, I'd say we used nine players a lot," Dick said. "We used four guys off the bench a great deal."

They included Ward Mullen and Matt Pavalunas in the back-court and Ted Sarpola and Bob Hardy at the forward positions.

"We didn't have another center as such," Dick said. "Laddie could play center and I could play center if we wanted to spell Slim. I just moved over and took over his center spot and we would just put in another forward. Hobbie always used his substitutions. He'd spell people normally in the middle of each half."

In the middle of everything, there was Hobson directing this unusual team like a supreme puppet master.

In his first year at Oregon, 1936–37, Hobson barely won more games than he lost, with a 13–11 record. The following year was better at 17–9, but the Ducks finished the year with a loss to Stanford. The team decided to do something about it and had a closed-door meeting, closed even to Hobson.

The result?

"They told me they had met and decided that next year, they would go all the way to the Pacific Coast championship," Hobson said.

The innovative Hobson would be the one to lead the way. He knew just what to do; he had learned his lessons well. The Ducks were going to become road warriors through a unique plan.

"He was a very astute basketball coach," Dick said, "and he was great to play for. The thing I remember most about Hobby was his meticulous attention to detail. He kept the most voluminous records you could imagine of everything that happened, in practices as well as games."

Hobson charted not only the number of shots taken by each player but where they were taken from on the floor. He did the same for rebounds and turnovers.

Hobson was not only a coach, but a coaching pioneer. His 13-year analysis of basketball for a doctoral thesis would eventually lead to several important rules changes. They included, among others, proposals for a three-point field goal, a shot clock, and wider free throw lanes.

So how did this creative basketball genius get started?

Growing up in Portland, basketball didn't enter Hobson's life until he was 12, when he played in his first organized basketball game, held in an old grammar school gymnasium. Hobson was about to learn his first real lesson in basketball.

One of the opposing players was scoring at will against Hobson's team. Hobson's assignment: stop him.

"This I tried to do without having the slightest idea of what methods to employ," Hobson recalled.

Hobson dived at the player. That stopped him, all right, but also stopped Hobson. He lost two front teeth.

"I was severely reprimanded when I got home," Hobson recalled in his book about Oregon basketball, *Shooting Ducks.*

"But I learned something about basketball. I realized, even then, that attention needs to be paid to the proper methods of play."

He became meticulous about attention to detail.

Hobson had played at Portland's Franklin High School before captaining the University of Oregon basketball squad. After college, he coached on the high school level before winning three straight league championships at Southern Oregon Normal (eventually Southern Oregon State College). Then the offer came in 1936 to coach the Ducks.

At Oregon, Hobson put together a well-oiled machine with tough practice sessions. Remembered Dick:

"We scrimmaged for two hours or more every day, and that didn't count all the preliminary stuff that led up to the scrimmage. The emphasis was on running, so it seemed when you got into a ball game, it was a piece of cake. We were always the best-conditioned team out there."

Hobson was approachable, but strict with his players. His locker room manner was cut and dried, but efficient.

"He'd have his outline on the backboard and would quietly tell us what he thought we were doing right or wrong, and what we should do," Gale remembered. "There were no inspirational speeches."

To prepare the team for the rugged Pacific Coast Conference race, Hobson had a plan. His team was going on a barnstorming train trip across America. It was the first time a college basketball team from the Northwest had made such a challenging intersectional trip.

Before the Ducks hit the road, Hobson had everything carefully planned out.

"Before we'd leave on that trip, Hobby would give us an itinerary and we knew every minute from the time we left where we were going to be, right down to the hotels we were staying in, the trains we were riding in, the car numbers, the berth numbers, what we were going to eat," Dick said.

The Ducks, called the "Wandering Webfoots" by the student newspaper, made stops in many major cities in December 1938: New York, Philadelphia, Cleveland, Buffalo, Detroit, Chicago, and San Francisco, playing a total of 10 games in 22 days.

One thing that Hobson couldn't plan for: sleeping conditions on the train.

Wintermute's knees touched the top of the Pullman berth on the train. His long arms hit something every time he turned in his sleep. He was extremely uncomfortable and didn't get much sleep. His play the next day showed it. Hobson, to encourage him, told him he would do better the next game. He didn't.

Hobson finally said, "If I were a 6-foot-8 center, I'd expect to play better ball than you've been playing."

Slim answered, "If you were a 6-foot-8 center and had to sleep doubled up in knots for two nights, you wouldn't play any better, either."

Hobson's solution? Three upper berths split into two.

"We would take a slat out and we would be sleeping in one berth, but our feet would be sticking into the middle of another," Gale said. "We would have three berths, two men, and our heads would be opposite one another and our feet would be next to one another."

The occasional discomfort extended to the arenas the Ducks visited but brought them closer as a team, as Hobson remembered.

"We became a family," Hobson told the Associated Press. "It was a great morale booster because we had a very close relationship. When we got back, we were a force because the boys were used to playing on all kinds of courts with all kinds of officiating."

And against all kinds of roughhouse play.

"We learned a whole lot about body checking and things back there that we hadn't run into," Gale said.

The 1938–39 season presented a special incentive for the Ducks: a new national tournament to challenge the NIT. The tournament was put together by the National Association of Basketball Coaches

(NABC) under the auspices of the NCAA and included teams from across the nation from each of the NCAA's eight regional districts. The NCAA had given its approval on October 3, 1938, on the condition that the coaches themselves handle the tournament.

"We knew in our junior year that we could look forward as seniors to hopefully play in a national playoff," Gale said. "I thought it was very important to have that incentive."

The first challenge for Oregon's Ducks, of course, was to win the Pacific Coast Conference. The Ducks were ready for anything after facing some of the country's top teams on their celebrated road trip.

First up, the Northern Division playoffs. The Ducks took on a rugged, fast-breaking Washington team similar to Oregon's speedsters.

"I remember in the Washington series, both teams used a fast break that was dazzling," Gale recalled.

It was a contest of conditioning between Oregon and Washington—which one was in better shape? First one to call a timeout loses.

"It seemed to me that we were told to run them into the ground and their coach (Hec Edmundson) had told their players to run us into the ground," Gale said.

No timeouts, just running up and down the court.

"We finally won it—we made Washington take a timeout," Gale said.

The Ducks won the first two games of the series to clinch the Northern Division title.

Up next, the California Golden Bears, the Southern Division champions.

"They were one of the few teams we played that was as big as we were . . . in fact, a little bigger," Dick said of Cal.

Nevertheless, the Ducks whipped the Bears two straight times to win the PCC title.

Next assignment: the Western Regional of the new NCAA tournament set up by the coaches. Oregon was part of a group that included Utah State, Oklahoma, and Texas. The western stage of the tournament was held in the Sports Coliseum at Treasure Island, an exhibition area smack in the middle of the San Francisco Bay.

The Eastern Regional included Ohio State, Villanova, Brown, and Wake Forest—all teams selected by a coaches committee.

All of the teams in the field except Oklahoma were chosen on the basis of their outstanding records. After Missouri pulled out, the Sooners survived a playoff in their region to gain the final tournament spot.

The Ducks didn't know much about Texas, their first-round opponent. It didn't matter. Oregon opened with a 15-point blowout of the Longhorns, 56–41.

Next up was Oklahoma, which had routed Utah State, 50–39.

No problem there, either, for the Ducks. They cruised past the Sooners, 55–37.

Summing up the Ducks' crushing win over the Sooners, one basketball annual noted: "Oregon's fast break, zone defense, and phenomenal one-handed shooting was just too much for Oklahoma. After a cautious first quarter, the Oregonians pulled away steadily."

The Ducks had more problems with the physical makeup of the court than they did with their opponents. The Treasure Island court proved to be no treasure for the Ducks.

"It was a dead floor, and it affected our dribbling," said Dick of the Sports Coliseum on Treasure Island. "We had to pound the ball a lot harder on that surface, but we got used to it after a while."

Along with the makeup of the court, the Ducks also faced a travel disadvantage, first in the PCC playoffs and then in the NCAA tournament.

"We had to play Cal on a Thursday and Friday in Eugene, Oregon (in the PCC playoffs), then we had to get on a train and go to San Francisco, play there Monday and Tuesday, then get on a train to Chicago and be ready to play on Monday," Dick said.

The final destination actually was Evanston, Illinois, and the campus of Northwestern—Big Ten territory—for the championship game against Ohio State.

The big game between Oregon and Ohio State didn't exactly inspire passionate national interest. It was held in a rickety old gym with a raised floor and lost $2,531.

"They said they had 5,500 people there," Hobson said. "I think they gave half the tickets away."

Among the reported 5,500 watching the national basketball championship game was James Naismith, inventor of the game.

Ohio State was led by Jimmy Hull, an All-American guard.

"When we came out and looked at him," Gale said, "he was about six feet. No problem."

The Ducks got off to a 6–0 start and led, 21–16, at the half. Even with just a five-point lead, the Ducks felt totally in control.

Going into the locker room at halftime, Arnet asked Hobson, "Do you want us to lay off?"

The message was clear: Did Hobson want to keep the score down?

"He was pretty cocky," Gale said of Arnet.

He had a right to be. In its report of the game, the *New York Times* noted, "The Webfeet delighted the 5,000 spectators with their splendid handling of the ball. On defense, they were just as alert, seldom giving Ohio State more than one shot at the basket before regaining possession."

Still, it was a while before the Ducks completely put the Buckeyes away. Reported the *New York Times*: "Ohio State remained in the running until ten minutes from the end, when the Webfeet had a 34–29 lead. Thereafter Oregon stalled, precluding any sustained rally by (Ohio State)."

Dick led the Ducks with 13 points, followed by 10 apiece from Arnet and Gale as Oregon routed the Buckeyes, 46–33. Hull, who had led the Big Ten in scoring, was the only one in double digits for the Buckeyes with 12.

Hobson was exceptionally proud of his team's accomplishment, and for good reason.

"We beat Ohio State on a Big Ten floor with Big Ten officials in front of a Big Ten crowd," he said.

On the way to the championship, Arnet provided the crowd with some extra excitement.

The championship trophy, adorned with the small figure of a basketball player at the top, stood on the media table at courtside.

Dick recalled the action: "Bobby dove for a loose ball going out of bounds and hit the trophy. He knocked it over and broke the man off as he went barreling into the sportswriters' laps.

"When they presented the trophy to us, they had to hold the figure on top. It was a two-handed presentation."

Then it was time to board an express streamliner train for the long ride home. It was 1939, with America still affected by the Great Depression. Basketball mania helped fans forget their troubles, at least for a little while. But they didn't forget their returning basketball heroes. The people of The Dalles, Dick's hometown, started a 25-cent donation to buy Dick a gold watch for $75.

It was a generous tribute to the highly popular Dick. Most Oregonians earned less than $700 a year, gasoline sold for 10 cents a gallon, and a postage stamp was 3 cents. Now that they had raised the money, they wanted to have a ceremony at the train stop. But the train wasn't stopping. The train only stopped for water and had a tight schedule.

The fans were undeterred. After threatening to barricade the tracks, they got their wish. The railroad president gave them 10 minutes.

It was just before 6:00 a.m. when the train stopped, and light was barely creeping into a new day. The Oregon players could hardly believe what they saw as the train came to a screeching halt. A crowd of 2,500 spilled out of the small station into the adjoining area, with the fans cheering their homecoming heroes.

When the adjoining areas heard about the tribute to Dick in The Dalles, they wanted to do the same. In Astoria, hometown of four of the players, it became an expensive proposition.

The players were representative of fierce geographical pride because most of the Ducks were from within the state. Astoria, for one, had been a source of great player contributions to the Oregon basketball program over the years.

When a team talks about local pride, this one had it in numbers. Among the starters, only Wintermute was not from Oregon. But he was close. He came over to Oregon from Longview, Washington, a close neighbor separated by the Columbia River.

The locals were out in numbers as the streamliner rolled through towns and villages.

The last stop was pure bedlam, the start of March Madness in the Northwest.

"They were literally hanging from the lamp posts," Hobson remembered of the greeting they received in Eugene.

It was one of the few times during the season that the "Tall Firs" were stopped in their tracks.

4.

Great Performances

With 11 NBA championships in 13 years, Bill Russell had a remarkable career with the Boston Celtics. It's easy for that to overshadow the fact Russell also had a brilliant college career, turning the NCAA tournament into his own personal playground. With Russell, the San Francisco Dons won two straight national titles in the 1950s and helped establish a dynasty that recorded 60 straight victories.

Also, who could forget Bill Walton's near-perfect show in the 1973 title game? Or Magic Johnson vs. Larry Bird in 1979? Or Austin Carr's lights-out shooting in the 1970 tournament. That's only for starters.

Here are ten of the NCAA playoffs' greatest performances.

Bill Russell, 1955

"We just can't let that big guy get the ball."

Before La Salle took on San Francisco in the 1955 championship game, Explorers coach Ken Loeffler issued that warning to his team.

The "big guy?" Why, that was Bill Russell. The 6-foot-10 center was the reason the Dons had turned around their program and advanced to the NCAA championship game.

Russell did it all for San Francisco: score, rebound, block shots, intimidate. Man, did he intimidate.

Before UCLA began to dominate basketball on the West Coast (and elsewhere) in the mid-1960s, Phil Woolpert's Dons had established a dynasty with Russell's help.

"With the rules as they were at that particular time," noted UCLA coach John Wooden, "it made it almost impossible to beat them."

It was an era favoring the big man in basketball, featuring a tight free throw lane only six feet wide that allowed extra-tall players to congregate near the basket, where they exerted full control of play. That would change. Following the 1955 NCAA tournament, which was dominated by Russell, the coaches' rules committee widened the lane to 12 feet.

Another rules change came in response to Russell: players would not be allowed to touch the ball on its downward arc toward the basket. This became known as "goaltending."

Talking about the widening of the lane, Oregon State coach Slats Gill told the Associated Press on March 22, 1955, "It will mean the big boys will have to develop more timing in getting shots after free throws now that they'll be further back from the basket."

The rules changes didn't seem to hurt Russell's game in any way. There were no statistics kept on blocked shots at the time, but no doubt Russell was among the country's leaders in that category.

"He permitted their other four defensive men to gamble because he was the best I have ever seen of the shot blockers," Wooden said. "It didn't mean that he would block every shot, but he'd be blocking a few and then you'd be looking for him, and it seems that teams would invariably not shoot well.

"Against Russell, you're going to get a shot over that long left hand of his, and he's going to slap it back in your face. You started looking for him and wouldn't even take a shot when you had it."

Russell had virtually come out of nowhere to make his mark at USF. A native of San Francisco, the gangly Russell was a slow starter on the McClymonds High School basketball team in Oakland, California. Putting in extra time on his game, the dedicated Russell worked hard enough to earn a scholarship offer from the Dons, a longtime college basketball doormat.

Russell changed all that once he rounded into his firm, 6-foot-10 form in his junior year in 1954–55. The Dons' longtime image as a loser was suddenly reversed. Now they charged into the NCAA playoffs, winning 23 of 24 games. The previously anonymous Dons were suddenly known from coast to coast as they knocked off their first four opponents in the playoffs.

La Salle, with its All-American forward Tom Gola, was expected to be more of a challenge.

"That Gola would really give (Coach Woolpert) an ulcer," Russell said of the 6-foot-6 La Salle star.

It was nothing, however, like the ill effect Russell had on La Salle, one of Philadelphia's "Big Five" basketball teams.

"He clogged the middle to keep La Salle from driving in, snared 25 rebounds, and batted away several shots by the Explorers," *Sports Illustrated* reported in its March 28, 1955, issue.

But it was on the offensive side that Russell really hurt La Salle.

"Operating from the post position right by the basket, the long fellow from San Francisco pocketed 18 points during the first half. Loeffler's boys simply could not keep Russell's hands off the ball," *Sports Illustrated* said.

"Particularly deadly were Russell's tap-ins. Timing his leaps perfectly, Russell would soar into the air just as a shot by a colleague floated in toward the basket and tip the ball into the basket while La Salle defenders impotently stretched and strained beneath."

Russell finished with 23 points as San Francisco beat La Salle, 77–63. Although K.C. Jones scored a game-high 24 points and held Gola to 16, it was really Russell's show.

The following year, Russell put on another great performance with 26 points and 27 rebounds as the Dons repeated as champions with an 83–71 victory over Iowa in the title game.

After watching the astonishing Russell work his magic, Kansas coach Phog Allen quipped, "I'm for the 20-foot basket."

Bill Walton, 1973

How do you stop an irresistible force on a basketball court?

In other words, how do you stop Bill Walton? That's what UCLA's opponents were asking in the 1970s.

"He's the best collegiate player I've ever seen," Memphis State coach Gene Bartow said. The UCLA star all but personally dismantled Bartow's team in the 1973 finals: 44 points, 13 rebounds, and numerous blocked shots. The Bruins won the national title with an 87–66 blowout of the Tigers.

The most remarkable number: Walton was a near-perfect 21-of-22 from the floor.

And to think, Walton did all this in serious foul trouble.

"He did so many things so well that we just couldn't stop him," Bartow said.

Walton's points total shattered the finals record of Gail Goodrich, another star UCLA player from a different era who had scored 42 in 1965.

Walton, a nationally prominent California high school star, had arrived with the same kind of big-man hype afforded Lew Alcindor several years before. It was well deserved, according to Wooden.

"Alcindor was the most valuable player I've ever coached," Wooden said. "Bill Walton is the second most valuable player, and you can put up a pretty good argument that he was as valuable as Alcindor."

While causing pain to his opponents, Walton learned to live with pain on the court. He played with inflamed knees that needed constant medical attention. It didn't seem to affect the quality of his play.

Few big men in college basketball were able to pick off a rebound and get a fast break going as efficiently as Walton.

Against Memphis State, Walton dominated inside play as the Bruins took a 33–24 lead. Memphis State would not go down easily, though. The Tigers rallied behind Larry Kenon and Larry Finch to tie the game at 39 at intermission, then took the lead in the second half.

With the game tied at 45, Walton took over. He scored a number of easy baskets on lob passes from Greg Lee.

Walton also took over the defensive boards despite being saddled with three fouls, four by game's end.

"Relentlessly he carried the champions from a 45–45 tie to a 57–47 lead with 12 minutes left and Memphis was done," reported *Sports Illustrated*.

And thanks to Walton, UCLA won its seventh straight national championship.

"(It) was just another UCLA bullfight," said Abe Lemons, the Pan American coach. "You gore the matador all night. In the end he sticks it in you and the donkeys come on and drag you out."

Waving the cape, of course, was Walton, who really stuck it to Memphis State that night.

Bob Kurland, 1945–46

In the 1940s, he was the big story on sports pages across America—with the emphasis on big.

Before Wilt Chamberlain, Bill Russell, Lew Alcindor, and Shaquille O'Neal made headlines, there was Bob "Foothills" Kurland, the first 7-footer in college basketball and the first player to bring the dunk shot to national attention.

A player of that size was sure to be conspicuous, especially on a basketball court. Seven-footers, particularly seven-footers as well-coordinated as Oklahoma A&M's star center, were virtually nonexistent at the time. It may sound laughable today, but Kurland was praised in an article by *Life* magazine for being "balanced and coordinated in spite of his height."

The same could be said for George Mikan, a 6-foot-10 giant of the times who challenged Kurland for national attention. A couple of inches shorter than Kurland, Mikan starred at DePaul before going on to professional glory with the Minneapolis Lakers.

Kurland took a different route when he left college. Turning down an $11,000 offer from the New York Knicks of the fledging NBA, Kurland continued to play amateur basketball with the famed Phillips Petroleum Amateur Athletic Union team, the Phillips Oilers.

Kurland played six years with the Phillips Oilers, winning three AAU titles. He worked for the company for 40 years. As a result, a potential individual rivalry with Mikan never developed to equal the great rivalries that would sprout between Wilt Chamberlain and Russell, Johnson and Bird.

On the rare occasions Kurland and Mikan did hook up, they were always the center of attention. In 1945, after Kurland's Oklahoma A&M team won the first of two national championships, the Aggies played in a Red Cross benefit game against Mikan's powerful DePaul team.

Playing Mikan head-to-head, Kurland quickly got the DePaul star into foul trouble and sent him to the bench. Kurland, eventually playing with four fouls, outscored Mikan, 14–9, as Oklahoma A&M won, 52–44.

Because of his amateur status, Kurland was able to compete in the Olympics and twice won gold medals, in 1948 and 1952.

He led the Aggies (since renamed Oklahoma State) to two straight national championships, in 1945 and 1946. It was the first time any college basketball team had won consecutive NCAA titles. In both finals, Kurland was superb.

Kurland's teammates on the Olympic teams were in awe of the big fellow.

"Bob was great," said Ray Lumpp, who played with Kurland on the U.S. team that beat France, 65–21, in the gold medal game in 1948. "He had a head and knew what he was doing. He did it all and was a first-class fellow."

At the start of his career at Oklahoma A&M, Kurland never could have imagined such success.

"I was only 17 and a big, clumsy kid," recalled Kurland, a Missouri native. "But Coach Iba had the confidence that I could do the job and had the patience to work with me."

Henry Iba, one of college basketball's coaching greats, was a primary reason why Kurland had selected Oklahoma A&M from among a number of other offers.

"Oklahoma A&M was a good engineering school, and I was interested in engineering at the time," Kurland said. "Also, I had heard a lot of wonderful things about Iba from my high school coach."

Kurland went through a three-day tryout before Iba handed him a scholarship. After playing as a reserve in his freshman year, Kurland came into his own in his sophomore season, 1943–44, providing a powerful presence exemplified by his patented dunk shot, then known as a "duffer."

In the midst of the Second World War, Kurland gave sports fans something to talk about other than the travails of American troops in Europe and the South Pacific.

Kurland led the Aggies to a sparkling 26–4 record in 1944, losing only to service teams, and a place in the final of the National Invitation Tournament. The Oklahoma A&M star was selected for the All-American team.

It was the following season, when the war was winding down and college teams were building up their rosters with talented young men who were returning home, that Kurland took Oklahoma A&M to higher levels. With all the great players now spread across America, the Aggies faced stronger opposition. It didn't matter to Kurland.

With his great height, Kurland could virtually score at will. His defensive talent also drew rave notices, particularly his shot-blocking ability. Soaring high off the court, Kurland had the ability to change the direction of a ball that was about to drop through the hoop. Many an opponent's basket was nullified by Kurland's sudden intervention.

A goaltending rule obviously directed at Kurland and other exceedingly tall players with a huge height advantage would eventually be introduced into college basketball.

In the 1945 NCAA final, Kurland rose to the occasion, leading Oklahoma A&M to a 49–45 win over New York University for the national championship. The following season, the Aggies beat North Carolina, 43–40, in the 1946 final, with their star center showing the way.

Reported the *New York Times*: "Horace (Bones) McKinney, the darling of the gallery, was assigned to defend against the tallest man in the sport, but did not fare too well. McKinney, at 6 feet 6 inches, is no midget. But the six inches that Kurland towered over him made the Tar Heel appear like a pygmy."

Kurland outscored McKinney, 23–5, in Oklahoma A&M's triumph. Kurland's value to his team in the '46 playoffs was all too obvious: he scored 72 of the 139 points the Aggies collected in three games, more than 50 percent of their total.

Now that's what they call going out on top.

Gail Goodrich and Bill Bradley, 1965

It's hard to believe there was a better college basketball player in America in 1965 than Princeton's Bill Bradley. Unless it was UCLA's Gail Goodrich.

At the time, Bradley was generally regarded as the best basketball player in Ivy League history—and still is.

Like Bradley, Goodrich handled the ball most of the time for his team, doing double duty as a point guard and scoring guard.

Both were All-Americans, each leading his team into the 1965 Final Four.

UCLA, Princeton, Michigan, and Wichita gathered for the championship round at the Portland Coliseum, a shiny modern building nicknamed "The Glass Palace."

Michigan was the nation's top-ranked team, favored over UCLA's defending national champions. Although the Bruins had lost player of the year Walt Hazzard to graduation, they still were good enough to make the Final Four in the 1964–65 season. Goodrich, a Los Angeles native whose father played at Southern Cal, was the main reason for that.

At the start of the season, Wooden made Goodrich the Bruins' main ball-handler in his senior year. The UCLA coach had good reason to have faith in Goodrich.

"Goodrich really made an amazing improvement for us," Wooden said. "As a sophomore, he was individually oriented and had some trouble accepting the team concept. As a junior, he began to accept it very well. And in his senior year, I let him handle the ball more."

Not that the star guard neglected his scoring responsibilities. He was the Bruins' leading scorer in 1964–65 with an average of 24.6 points.

At his tallest, Goodrich was generally regarded to be almost 6-foot-1, but played "a lot bigger," according to Wooden. The UCLA coach often talked about Goodrich's long arms that made him exceptionally good in the Bruins' pressing defense.

At an awards dinner at the end of Goodrich's senior year, Wooden praised him as the greatest all-around player ever under his tutelage at UCLA.

"I felt Gail did as much as any player that I had up to that particular time," Wooden said. "For his size, he did as well as any player I've ever coached."

In high school, Goodrich was generally listed at 5-foot-9, one of the main reasons scholarship offers from colleges were limited.

That couldn't be said of Bradley, who chalked up more than 3,000 points at Crystal City High School in Missouri. He received 70 scholarship offers, including one from Kentucky's Adolph Rupp. He preferred Princeton, a smaller, prestigious school with an extremely high academic standard. The Ivy League wasn't in the habit of giving out athletic scholarships. So guess what: Bradley paid his own way.

It didn't take long for Bradley to start dominating the Ivy League—or the rest of the country, for that matter. Playing both small forward and shooting guard, Bradley had a great touch.

His performance in the 1965 NCAA tournament was stunning. Bradley led the Tigers to victories over Penn State, North Carolina State and fourth-ranked Providence. Against the Friars, he scored 41 points, pulled down 10 rebounds, and dished out nine assists in a 109–69 rout to set the stage for a battle against powerful Michigan.

Scouting reports on the Princeton superstar were scary for the Wolverines. How does one prepare for one of the two best players in the country playing at his best?

"I'll just tell them that he's the greatest that ever lived," Michigan scout Tom Jorgenson told *Sports Illustrated*, "because they won't believe anything else I tell them."

As it turned out, it was Goodrich that Michigan should have feared most. His 28 points led UCLA over Wichita in the national semifinals, while Michigan advanced with a win over Bradley and Princeton.

Then Goodrich scored a finals-record (at the time) 42 points as the Bruins beat the Wolverines, 91–80, for the national championship.

The third-place game, soon to disappear entirely from the tournament, normally was a low-profile contest between two teams with little incentive. But there was some attention paid to this consolation game, won by Princeton. Bradley scored a record 58 points to lead the Tigers to a 118–82 win over Wichita.

Bradley made 22 field goals in 29 attempts, sank 14-of-15 free throws, and grabbed 17 rebounds.

"It's just too bad that this all didn't happen a night sooner," Bradley said, referring to Princeton's 93–76 loss to Michigan in the national semifinals.

Nevertheless, Bradley's scoring explosion capped an extraordinary tourney for the Princeton star, who scored a record 177 points in five games. That earned him the tournament's most outstanding player trophy, even though he didn't play in the title game.

Wooden thought the wrong player received the award.

"When Goodrich scores 42 points in the championship game against Michigan and 28 points against Wichita in 24 minutes (in the national semifinals), it seems that offsets what a man might do in a consolation game that doesn't count," Wooden said.

Wooden was happier when Goodrich and Bradley were selected co-winners of the college basketball player of the year award in 1965.

Even at the end of the year, it was hard to separate the two.

Lew Alcindor, 1967–69

OK, which of Lew Alcindor's performances in the national championship game was the greatest?

The 20 points and 18 rebounds against Dayton in 1967? The 34 points and 16 rebounds against North Carolina in 1968? The 37 points and 20 rebounds against Purdue in 1969?

Hard to pick? You bet. Alcindor always was at the top of his game against the toughest competition in the most crucial times.

And all three years that UCLA played with Alcindor as its leading man, from 1967–69, the Bruins won the national championship. In two of those seasons, the Bruins didn't lose a game.

Wooden described Alcindor as "awesome. At times, he even frightens me."

Think how scary it was for UCLA's opponents during Alcindor's three-year domination of the NCAAs.

Alcindor, who later changed his name to Kareem Abdul-Jabbar, was the most heralded freshman to ever play at UCLA— and maybe anywhere in the history of college basketball. In an era when freshmen couldn't play for the varsity, Alcindor was clearly the most notable sports name on campus when he arrived in Westwood.

A New York City high school superstar, Alcindor was unusually coordinated for a big man. One of his major weapons: a dunk shot.

When the dunk was ruled illegal during Alcindor's time at UCLA, in large measure due to his domination in the paint, he simply took his game a few feet outside.

His famed "skyhook," which he could deliver from medium range with either hand, was a devastating and feared weapon. Alcindor said he learned the shot in fifth grade because it was "the only shot I could use that didn't get smashed back in my face."

So much was expected of this young giant from New York City, and he didn't wait long to deliver. In his very first varsity game as a sophomore, Alcindor scored 56 points to lead the Bruins over their crosstown rival, Southern Cal. Averaging 29.7 points and 15.5 rebounds a game, Alcindor was the main cog in a UCLA machine that roared through the season undefeated.

It's hard to imagine UCLA's domination in today's well-balanced college basketball world, but think of this: In the 1967 NCAA tournament, the Bruins won all four games by no fewer than 15 points, including a 49-point blowout of Wyoming. Even more impressive was UCLA's 15-point victory over a powerful Houston team, which featured Elvin Hayes, vying with Alcindor for national player of the year honors.

In this one, Hayes actually had better individual stats than Alcindor with 25 points and 24 rebounds in one of the classic performances in NCAA tournament history. But with 19 points and 20 rebounds, Alcindor made his own statement. The biggest statement of all: UCLA 73, Houston 58.

In the 1968 NCAA tournament, UCLA simply annihilated Houston, 101–69, in the national semifinals.

It was sweet revenge for the Bruins, who had lost a two-point decision to the Cougars during the regular season and slipped out of the No. 1 ranking. Alcindor was clearly not at his best at the time, having suffered an eye injury the previous week. But he was seeing things better when the bitter rivals next met in the national semifinals.

With 19 points and 18 rebounds, Alcindor outplayed Hayes. The Houston star, saddled with foul trouble, could only manage 10 points and five rebounds. And UCLA won by 32 points in the Bruins' most emotional game of the season.

Led by Alcindor, UCLA beat North Carolina by 23 points in the 1968 finals.

It was business as usual for the Bruins in 1969, beating Purdue by 20 points as Alcindor dominated once more.

While Alcindor was unlacing the net for a souvenir and rejoicing with his teammates, his father was celebrating in his own way. Ferdinand Lewis Alcindor Sr., a New York musician, had left his seat in the stands and moved into a seat in the band to play first trombone. You couldn't blame him for blowing his own horn after watching his son finish his college career at UCLA in style.

David Thompson, 1974

Here's one for trivia fans: Which team did North Carolina State beat to win the national championship in 1974?

No, it wasn't UCLA.

Although North Carolina State and UCLA went toe-to-toe like two heavyweight fighters in one of the most memorable NCAA tournament games in the national semifinals, the answer is Marquette.

"Nobody seems to remember that," said David Thompson, North Carolina State's sky-walking forward of the 1970s.

Small wonder. NC State and UCLA were the two best college basketball teams in the country in 1974, both ranked No. 1 at various points of the season.

Their meeting in the semifinals would decide the national championship. At least, most everyone thought so.

On the eve of the semifinals in Greensboro, North Carolina, Marquette coach Al McGuire noted his team was playing in the "B class division" against Kansas. Jayhawks coach Ted Owens said he was just happy to be in the Final Four and playing in the "preliminary."

Thompson, actually, was also happy to be playing in the Final Four, but not for the same reason.

He had suffered a horrific head injury against Pitt in the final of the East Regional, leaving doubts as to his ability to play at full force, or play at all.

Midway through the first half against Pitt, Thompson was racing downcourt and left his feet to block a shot near the foul line. His legs tangled around a teammate's and he crashed headfirst onto the court.

"When his head hit the floor it sounded as if a bowling ball had fallen off the top of the backboard," said *Sports Illustrated*.

Thompson was carried off the court on a stretcher while everyone in the arena held their breath. North Carolina State coach Norm Sloan expected the worst.

"I was numb," he said.

Then, a miracle.

A hospital examination of Thompson revealed he had suffered deep lacerations but no neurological damage. He was stitched up and bandaged, and soon returned to the arena to watch his teammates completely dominate the Panthers.

Doctors soon cleared Thompson to play. They were amazed at his quick recovery.

"To have a blow knock him out for four minutes and not even leave him with so much as a headache is remarkable," said one doctor.

Thompson's amazingly quick recovery from his head injury became part of Wolfpack lore in North Carolina State's most memorable basketball season to that point.

But first, rewind to the early part of the season, when Thompson and his Wolfpack teammates were destroyed by UCLA, 84–66.

It would be the only loss in two seasons for the Wolfpack. They went undefeated in 1972–73 but were not allowed to participate in the NCAA tournament because of recruiting violations.

The Wolfpack's 18-point loss to UCLA was shocking. Not that UCLA wasn't a great team with Walton and Keith Wilkes, but the Wolfpack had some comparable players of their own in frontcourt stars Thompson and Tom Burleson.

"We know they aren't 18 points better than us," North Carolina State forward Tim Stoddard said. "But what's more important is that they know it."

Following seven straight national championships, the Bruins started out the season ranked No. 1. Despite returning many of their starters, most importantly the ubiquitous Walton, they struggled to attain the same level of play they had reached in two previous perfect seasons. Yet they continued to win, carrying a record 88-game winning streak into South Bend to meet Notre Dame.

The Bruins looked like they were on their way to win No. 89, holding a 70–59 lead with 3:30 remaining in the game. But UCLA failed to score a point the rest of the way and lost a shocker, 71–70. Although UCLA would crush Notre Dame in a rematch in Los Angeles later in the season, that streak-breaking loss to the Irish was a sign of vulnerability.

Another telling sign: UCLA lost two games in its own conference, on the same road trip, at Oregon and Oregon State. The Bruins finished the regular season with a 23–3 record.

"I did feel that we would lose some ball games," Wooden said. "When a team does extremely well for two years in a row, to have the same personnel the third year, it's been my experience that that's the most difficult year. I found the junior year to almost always be the best year."

UCLA nevertheless extended its record playoff winning streak to 38 as it headed into the national semifinals to face a North Carolina State team eager for revenge. A courageous Thompson was showing the way for the Wolfpack. Before his accident in the Pitt game, Thompson had dropped 40 points on Providence. Certainly no one expected him to duplicate that kind of production against powerful UCLA, particularly in the aftermath of his scary injury. But Thompson shrugged off his injury. Playing with a large white bandage covering a good portion of the top of his head like a hat, he attacked the basket without fear.

Many times rocketing above the rim with his patented "alley-oop" shot, Thompson scored 28 points. He also picked off 10 rebounds and led a rally when all seemed hopeless for the Wolfpack.

Twice trailing by 11 points, North Carolina State came back to tie the game at the end of regulation with the help of backcourt sparkplug Monte Towe. The teams were still tied after one overtime before UCLA streaked to a seven-point lead at the start of the second OT.

Game over. Surely UCLA's highly disciplined team could never lose a seven-point lead with 3:27 remaining in overtime. At least that had to be the thinking at the Greensboro Coliseum that night.

But back came the Wolfpack—again. Appropriately, Thompson banked in a jump shot over Wilkes with about a minute left to put the Wolfpack ahead to stay. Final: North Carolina State 80, UCLA 77.

"It was a great ball game," Wooden said. "Two fine, outstanding offensive ballclubs, each one holding the other to 65 points in regulation. But in that second overtime, we had a seven-point lead and lost the ball game. It seems inconceivable that we could dissipate a seven-point lead."

Oh, yes, North Carolina State beat Marquette, 76–64, for the championship as Thompson scored a team-high 21 points. Memorable, but not as memorable to Thompson as the victory over UCLA.

"Beating UCLA is my number one highlight in sports," said Thompson, who later played nine years in the pros with Denver and Seattle and once scored 73 points in a game.

Austin Carr, 1970-71

Sixty-one.

Think of that number. The first thing that comes to mind for a sports fan is Roger Maris' home run total that broke Babe Ruth's single-season record.

But it's not the only 61 with special significance in sports. Another is the 61 points Austin Carr scored for Notre Dame in an NCAA tournament game.

"He could flat-out score," teammate Collins Jones told the *Akron Beacon Journal*. "He was 6-3, or 6-4 with his Afro, but if an opponent was the same height, Austin was usually much stronger."

Carr's record scoring spree, against Ohio in the 1970 NCAA tournament, was hardly an anomaly. Carr scored 52 points against Kentucky in the same tournament and averaged 52.7 points in the playoffs that season.

One year later, Carr also scored 52 points against TCU, giving him three of the top five individual scoring outputs for the NCAA tournament. (The others: Princeton's Bill Bradley with 58 against Wichita State in the 1965 tournament and Cincinnati's Oscar Robertson with 56 against Arkansas in 1958.)

"I remember one of TCU's players saying after the game that he thought he had done a good job," Jones told the *Akron Beacon Journal*. "He had held Austin to 52."

Imagine if the three-point line were in vogue when Carr was playing. No telling how many points he would have scored.

"With that short three-point line in college, that's a layup," Carr wistfully recalled many years later. "I would have loved to have played with that line."

Carr, a legendary playground player in Washington, D.C., was a Parade All-American at Macklin High School in the district. He arrived at Notre Dame in 1967 as part of one of the best recruiting classes in Irish basketball history, featuring Carr and Jones.

The freshmen came into South Bend with an attitude, whipping the varsity seven times in eight practice games before the season started.

"I had warned the (varsity) guys, even before we played them," freshman coach John Tracy told the *Kansas City Star*. "I told them,

'You're not going to believe this guy (referring to Carr).' He was amazing."

Teammates remembered Carr with awe, and not only for his scoring proficiency.

"He was the first one to practice, he was the last one to leave," Jones recalled. "He practiced harder than anyone else."

It was a regular-season game in 1971 that provided Carr with one of his most notable moments—a 46-point performance to help Notre Dame whip a powerful UCLA team, 89–82. But it was his performances in the playoffs that truly defined his greatness.

First and foremost, his game against Ohio University in the 1970 NCAA tournament.

"Ohio's Mid-American Conference champions tried four players at stopping Carr," reported the Associated Press.

No luck. By halftime, Carr had 35 points to lead Notre Dame to a 54–35 lead. Amazingly, all by himself, Carr matched the output of the entire Ohio team for 20 minutes.

Ohio had no answers for Carr in the second half, either. He continued to score at will as the Irish rolled up the score.

Early in the game, Irish coach Johnny Dee threatened to pull Carr off the floor because of poor defense. Now realizing that Carr was edging closer to Bradley's tournament-record 58 points, Dee left him in longer than normal in such a blowout.

"I started out on fire right away," Carr told the *Kansas City Star.* "The last basket, which put me over 60, I'll never forget. It hit off the back of the rim, went way up, and came right back down. It must have been my night."

In scoring his historic 61 points, Carr connected on 25-of-44 shots from the floor as the Irish rolled past Ohio, 112–82.

At his postgame press conference, Ohio coach Jim Snyder was almost speechless. Asked by one reporter how to stop Carr, he simply said: "Deflate the ball."

Larry Bird and Magic Johnson, 1979

It was a match made in basketball heaven: Larry Bird vs. Magic Johnson.

And it came in a college game, before the two became fierce NBA rivals and helped to save a league gone sour.

The date: March 26, 1979. The occasion: the NCAA championship game.

No two players could be more different, both on and off the court. The star of the Michigan State team, Johnson played basketball with uninhibited enthusiasm. Bird, Indiana State's top player, was more businesslike in his approach, playing with indefatigable determination.

The name on Johnson's birth certificate was Earvin. He was dubbed "Magic" during his days at Everett High School in Lansing, Michigan, because of his basketball wizardry.

"It didn't really hit me until I got in the backcourt with him, on the first day of practice," teammate Terry Donnelly told the *New York Times*.

Donnelly was running down the floor, trying to stay ahead of players racing right behind him. For a split second, he managed separation from his pursuers. Magic spotted him open and threaded the needle with a bullet pass.

"All of a sudden the ball's in your hands and you have a layup," Donnelly said.

In college, Magic's magical passes were an integral part of his game. He played all aspects with similar skill but especially loved dishing off to teammates for baskets.

"When you make a pass that leads to a basket . . . the pass is more important than the basket. Earvin has proved that," Spartans coach Jud Heathcote said.

A 6-foot-8 guard—most college players that tall were forwards or even centers at the time—Magic did it all. He was a multipurpose player who could overpower shorter opposing guards or challenge centers for rebounds.

Bird, one of the country's top forwards, could fill the net with long-range jump shots or set up an opponent with a beautiful pass.

"My feeling about passing is that it don't matter who's doing the scoring as long as it's us," Bird said at a news conference on the eve of the NCAA championship game. "I just think when a man is open, he should get the ball whether it's 30 feet out on the wing or underneath."

That Bird was talking to the press at all was a revelation. He had avoided interviews since his freshman year, when he faced a crush of media wanting only to know about the kid from French Lick, Indiana, a town renowned as the birthplace of ketchup.

"My first year all they wanted to do was talk to me," Bird said. "That's the way it should be. But we got seven guys who play. They deserve to be talked to, too."

But finally, as the college player of the year preparing for the biggest game of his career, Bird had no choice but to talk to the media. Recalling his days at Springs Valley High School, Bird revealed how he had developed his style: "I was a guard my sophomore year. I was little then. I had to get the ball to the big guys. I found out that a two-foot shot by the basket is better than a 14-foot shot any day."

In the 1977–78 season, Bird starred on an Indiana State team that went 23–9 and played in the National Invitation Tournament. In 1979, he was the only returning starter on a Sycamores team that advanced to the Final Four. With a 32–0 record and No. 1 ranking in the country, the Sycamores were the talk of the tournament.

A showdown between Bird and Magic seemed inevitable. It almost didn't take place.

While Johnson had a triple-double against Penn (29 points, 10 rebounds, and 10 assists) to lead a 101–67 rout, Bird also had a powerhouse game against DePaul with 35 points, 16 rebounds, and nine assists. But Indiana State still struggled to pull out a 76–74 thriller with the help of last-minute heroics from Bob Heaton.

Next up: the 1979 NCAA tournament final.

Indiana State became the eighth undefeated team to reach the finals and the first to ever win 33 games in a season. The 6-foot-9 Bird led the way in the tournament for the Sycamores with 22, 29, 31, and 35 points.

Bird, it turned out, had already done his best work by the time the finals came around. He averaged more than 30 points a game for his entire three-year career at Indiana State. But he was held to only 19 by a stiff Michigan State zone defense.

Johnson, meanwhile, was still looking magical. Despite playing with three fouls in the second half, Magic scored 24 points as

Michigan State beat Indiana State, 76–64, for the national championship.

"I feel a combination of relief and elation," Heathcote said. "The players have accomplished so much. And they saved their best play for the tournament."

The game generated so much national interest, including record TV ratings, that it brought the NCAA tournament to a new level. It was, in fact, a turning point for college basketball, leading to the heightened awareness of the playoffs and billion-dollar TV contracts.

In other words, pure Magic.

The Top Ten Tournament Single-Game Scorers

Austin Carr, Notre Dame: 61 points vs. Ohio, 1970
Bill Bradley, Princeton: 58 vs. Wichita State, 1965
Oscar Robertson, Cincinnati: 56 vs. Arkansas, 1958
Austin Carr, Notre Dame: 52 vs. Kentucky, 1970
Austin Carr, Notre Dame: 52 vs. TCU, 1971
David Robinson, Navy: 50 vs. Michigan, 1987
Elvin Hayes, Houston: 49 vs. Loyola (Illinois), 1968
Hal Lear, Temple: 48 vs. SMU, 1956
Austin Carr, Notre Dame: 47 vs. Houston, 1971
Dave Corzine, DePaul: 46 vs. Louisville, 1978

5.

The Coaching Giants

It took 16 years for John Wooden to win his first national championship at UCLA. After that, he could hardly lose.

By the time he retired in 1975, Wooden had rewritten the playoff records book with 10 national titles in 12 years.

How's that for making up for lost time in a hurry?

The staggering stats place him in the throne room of college basketball coaches with more titles than the next two *combined*: Kentucky's Adolph Rupp with four and Duke's still-active Mike Krzyzewski with four through 2011.

Then there's Indiana's Bobby Knight, who not only won three national championships but also was the first Division 1 coach to win more than 900 games. Coach K was on track to replace Knight as the all-time winner at some point during the 2011–12 season.

Connecticut's Jim Calhoun was the latest to join the exclusive club of triple winners, posting his third in the 2011 NCAA tournament.

North Carolina's Dean Smith, who was replaced by Knight atop the all-time victories circle, made 11 trips to the Final Four and won two titles.

Here, then, are the stories of some of college basketball's greatest coaches.

The Wizard of Westwood

On a Mount Rushmore of coaching giants, you figure John Wooden has to be a slam dunk. No one else even comes close.

From 1964–75, the Bruins won an unprecedented 10 national championships and came close to winning another.

No wonder he was called the "Wizard of Westwood."

Maybe it was because he prepared his teams so well that he rarely had to do much coaching during a game. Sitting on the bench with his legs crossed and a rolled-up game program tightly wound in his hand, all Wooden usually had to do was watch his well-schooled players carry out their assignments. On those rare occasions when they weren't blowing out an opponent, Wooden would step in and make the necessary adjustments.

Not that Wooden was always, well, wooden. When he wasn't being quiet, he could be quite intimidating to both players and referees—on the court and behind the scenes. When he wasn't happy with the referees' performance, there were stories of Wooden's practice of face-offs with them as they walked to their dressing room at halftime.

"On the coast, we call him, 'Saint John,'" former Southern Cal coach Bob Boyd told a sportswriter with a hint of sarcasm.

Then there was Wooden's fastidious attention to detail, right down to the way sneakers were laced. Discipline, always discipline.

And along with his discipline, Wooden had fashioned a "Pyramid of Success" for his basketball players to adhere to: "The cornerstones of success to me, in anything, are hard work and enjoy what you're doing. So one cornerstone is industriousness and the other is enthusiasm."

To make his point, Wooden could be heard quoting some of his favorite homilies. He especially liked one from Cervantes: *The journey is better than the end.*

Also, these from other writers and philosophers:

Winning takes talent; to repeat takes character.

You can't live a perfect day without doing something for someone who will never be able to repay you.

UCLA, meanwhile, was just a dirty word to opponents. The Bruins ruled the sport under Wooden as no other college basketball team had in history.

Another legendary basketball dynasty, the Boston Celtics, won 11 NBA titles with basically the same core of players who returned year after year.

UCLA, on the other hand, kept reinventing itself with the constant graduation of players—and, yes, as a former English teacher, Wooden was exceptionally strict in the area of academics. That came first in his book.

On the hardwood, Wooden won with short teams (1964–65 with Walt Hazzard and Gail Goodrich), tall teams (1967–69 with Lew Alcindor and 1972–73 with Bill Walton), and medium-size teams (1970–71 with Curtis Rowe and Sidney Wicks).

Stringing together championships in a neat row as he did, it seemed Wooden had been capturing national titles forever. Actually, it took him 16 years to win his first national championship at UCLA.

Wooden was hired to replace Wilbur Johns, the third coach in UCLA basketball history since the sport started there in 1919. Johns had posted a mediocre 93–120 record over nine seasons.

A Midwesterner who had starred at Purdue and later coached at Indiana State, Wooden at first wasn't so sure he had made the right choice by coming to UCLA in 1948.

"When I came here, I was very disappointed with the looks of the basketball material," Wooden said. "I thought the weaknesses I saw in my first year at UCLA weren't physical weaknesses, but background weaknesses as far as natural reaction to the game of basketball. I thought we played too mechanical. I wanted a fast break and a more pressure defense."

The popular style of play then on the West Coast was a ball-control game.

"Most of the teams were using it," Wooden said.

Everyone, it seemed, but Howard Hobson's Oregon Ducks. The so-called "Tall Firs" won the NCAA's first basketball championship in 1939 with a speed-oriented game featuring a ferocious fast break.

Coming out of a basketball hotbed in the Hoosier state, where he had coached Indiana State to the NAIA finals, Wooden couldn't help but make comparisons.

"Basketball wasn't held in the highest esteem here," Wooden remembered of his early years at UCLA. "There were very few what I would term adequate places to play on the coast. That in itself doesn't make it very comfortable for fans to come."

In those days, the UCLA basketball team played in an old men's gymnasium. Because of a fire department restriction, capacity was limited to 1,200 fans for basketball. The gymnasium had earned a sorry reputation as the "B.O. Barn."

"We had to practice on the same floor with gymnastics and wrestling," Wooden recalled. "It was an open floor with trampolines on the other side of the floor."

As a result, the UCLA basketball team looked for other facilities off campus to play its games. The Bruins went wherever they could to play home games: the LA Sports Arena, Pan Pacific and Long Beach auditoriums, Venice High School, Santa Monica Junior College, and Long Beach City College, among other places.

"One time we even played Santa Clara in Bakersfield because we had a number of alumni there," Wooden recalled.

At that point, UCLA basketball was almost a second thought in Los Angeles.

"The Rams were hot, Southern Cal was outstanding in football, and UCLA had done well in football," Wooden said. "Basketball here had not done well. There were so many other things that basketball wasn't too much in the limelight at that time."

Even when the UCLA basketball team made the NCAA tournament, it was no big deal at the school, as Wooden recalled.

"I'm not even sure if our athletic director went along on the trip to the tournament," Wooden said. "I know we couldn't take our official scorer who had scored all our games. So there wasn't much particular interest."

Wooden aimed to change that.

"The fact that I was new and trying to establish myself (was significant)," Wooden said. "I was on a three-year contract. I hoped to do well in a strange, new place. Coming from the Midwest, the town of Los Angeles was so different from any situation to which I had become accustomed."

In an exclusive 1977 interview covering his career at UCLA, Wooden said he found great satisfaction from the start. He listed the 1948–49 squad, his first at UCLA, as one of a group of teams that gave him the most personal satisfaction.

The team was picked to finish last and ended up winning the Southern Division of the Pacific Coast Conference. With 22 victories, the Bruins won more games than any UCLA team had ever won. They also took the conference tournament title.

With such players as Eddie Sheldrake, Alan Sawyer, Karl Kraushaar, George Stanich, Ralph Joeckel, and Jerry Norman, the Bruins reached the NCAA playoffs in Wooden's second year at UCLA, 1949–50.

With Willie Naulls a key player in the 1955–56 season, Wooden had what he considered his best UCLA team to that point. "It was a good, sound basketball team—a very good team. I think in many years it could have gone all the way."

Not that year, with Bill Russell and the University of San Francisco standing in the way.

"We were in the same regional with USF, and USF was just better than we were."

Before UCLA became dynastic, San Francisco was an early juggernaut in NCAA play. The Dons set a record of 60 straight victories (before UCLA later surpassed them with 88) and won two straight national titles.

In chronological order, Wooden's favorite squads: the 1961–62 team, the 1963–64 team, the teams with Lew Alcindor as one group (1967–69), the 1969–70 team, and the 1974–75 team.

In 1962, UCLA competed in its first Final Four. In 1964, the Bruins won their first national championship. In the Alcindor years, UCLA won three straight national titles in 1967, 1968, and 1969, posting an 88–2 record along the way.

"Most everyone expected us to win with Alcindor, and we did," Wooden said. "But people don't realize how difficult it is to do when everyone expects you to win. You know, they expected Kansas to win the championship (in the 1950s) with Wilt Chamberlain, and they didn't."

The year after Alcindor graduated, the 1969–70 team had many close, tough games but still won the championship with such players as Wicks and Rowe.

Wooden's other favorite was the 1975 national title team, "which wasn't expected to win, but did a tremendous job and won."

It was also Wooden's final year as the UCLA basketball coach, capping his 10th championship season and completing his career record at an extraordinary 620–147.

The "Wizard of Westwood," indeed.

The Man in the Brown Suit

Adolph Rupp.

How would you describe one of college basketball's legendary coaches?

A winner.

How about controversial?

A battler.

How about colorful?

A basketball genius.

How about a bully?

Depending on whom you ask, Rupp was composed of all these qualities—and was both revered and feared.

His record speaks for itself: His Kentucky Wildcat teams won four national championships (and finished as runners-up twice), and 27 Southeastern Conference titles. He won an amazing 879 games, at one point the most by any college basketball coach in history.

A measure of stunning success by anyone's standards. Nothing compared, however, to the innovations and impact he made on the sport.

Rupp's arrival at Kentucky signaled a renaissance in basketball in his region and, eventually, nationally. To say that he entered the Southern Conference (later renamed the Southeastern Conference) in a rush would be an understatement. Rupp introduced fast-break basketball, the likes of which had not been seen in the region before. In his very first season at Kentucky, 1930–31, Rupp's Wildcats posted a 15–3 record.

They were off and running, literally. Rupp never had a losing season in his four often-tumultuous decades in the Bluegrass State.

Rupp built winning programs at Kentucky despite a tight athletic budget.

"I never had more than $10,000 a year to recruit," he once said. "But at first I didn't need much money because everyone in the state wanted to come to Kentucky. We were winning and we got all the best boys out of the state high school tournaments each year."

Rupp's teams reached their zenith with the so-called "Fabulous Five" of the late 1940s, featuring Ralph Beard, Wallace "Wah Wah" Jones, Alex "The Nose" Groza, Kenneth Rollins, and Cliff Barker.

The unit actually didn't stay together very long—only a total of 28 games. But those players started a run of three championships in a four-year period from 1948–51 and became Rupp's most famous team. No fewer than 14 different players would wear the blue and white of Kentucky during this dynastic four-year reign.

During this time, the Wildcats posted a stunning 125–12 record. And in 1948, the "Fab Five" as a group joined forces with the famed Phillips Oilers of the Amateur Athletic Union to help the United States win a gold medal at the Olympic Games.

The 1948 NCAA championship game was typical of Kentucky's play during this time. Taking on Baylor, the Wildcats simply toyed with their opponent and wound up beating the Southwest Conference champions, 58–42.

"Kentucky played smart and classy ball from the very start," said the report in the Converse 1948 Basketball Yearbook.

The star of the day, as usual, was Kentucky's star center, Groza, "whose head seems to threaten the mezzanine," wrote *Time* magazine in its April 5, 1948, issue. "He sucked in rebounds like a vacuum cleaner. He was swift afoot and deadeyed."

Groza led a balanced offense, and all scorers, with 14 points. Rebound totals weren't kept back then, but by all reports, Groza picked up more than his share.

Before the game, Baylor coach Bill Henderson was warned by coaches not to try to run with Kentucky. But the Bears missed several shots and fell behind early, 13–1. By then it was too late to catch up to the lightning-quick Wildcats.

"They had a great team," Henderson recalled.

Rupp was a man of many faces, and appellations.

Try the "Baron of the Bluegrass," for one. "Old Rupp and Ready" for another. And, of course, the "Man in the Brown Suit."

Rupp, a slave to superstition, had a closet of double-breasted brown suits that became part of his legacy. As long as his Kentucky teams were winning, Rupp would wear the same suit. Lose a game, change a suit.

"I wear other colors, as long as it's not a basketball game," the jowly Rupp once said in his familiar gravelly voice.

Rupp came from modest beginnings, his young life mostly revolving around schoolwork and farmwork in Kansas. Reflecting on his youth, he once said:

"We never heard of anything out there. The only thing we knew on the farm was that we chopped wood and piled it high so that we had enough to burn for heat. When the chores were done at night, we had our evening meals and our devotions. We headed for bed around eight o'clock and got up in the morning to do our chores and go to school."

He did manage to play some basketball, though. The ball he used was hardly official—a homemade ball "which was just a gunny sack stuffed with rags. Mother sewed it up and somehow made it round. You couldn't dribble it. You couldn't bounce it, either."

Rupp and his pals, wearing long underwear beneath their overalls, played on hard-packed, frozen ground in the harsh Kansas winters. It didn't take much to wear out basketballs on that type of playing surface.

Things got better equipment-wise when Rupp started playing high school ball in Halstead (population 1,110). Basketballs were still in short supply, though. Each year, Rupp and his teammates held a box supper to raise money for a new ball. Rupp's leadership characteristics were starting to become obvious at this point. Remembered high school teammate Glen Lehman: "Once I had a nosebleed and the coach was going to put in a sub. Adolph wouldn't let him."

At Rupp's urging, his teammate went ahead and finished the game, nosebleed and all. It was this kind of presence that put Rupp at the forefront while playing on state championship teams in 1908 and 1909.

"He was a pretty determined sort of guy," teammate Eugene Thornhill recalled of Rupp, the high school player. "He was always ambitious. He was a pretty good politician; he knew how to work things and get things done."

His teammates figured that Rupp would go into coaching at one point or other.

"He seemed to know more about it than any of us," said Thornhill, including the coach in his assessment.

Rupp was never more than 6-foot tall in high school. But he played bigger than his height, making about 10 baskets a game, according to another teammate.

Rupp later played for the legendary Phog Allen on the undefeated Kansas team of 1923. He put in a solid coaching stint at Freeport High School in Illinois before replacing Johnny Mauer at Kentucky.

The coaching change was immediately noticeable. Like many other coaches in college basketball, Mauer had been teaching a deliberate, ball-control style of game. Then in came Rupp with his fast-breaking ideas on a team that stressed speed and good rebounding.

Rupp wasn't hesitant to play the best. He loved bringing his team to Madison Square Garden in New York to face local powers there. He figured the Wildcats would gain national attention in the media capital of the world. He also scheduled Notre Dame on a regular basis, as well as the Big Ten's strongest teams and the Missouri Valley Conference champions.

Some of the biggest changes came within the program, where Rupp was a feared disciplinarian. He made certain his players knew the rules and stuck to them. No casual dress, and no more practices such as stealing towels from hotel rooms and playing cards on train trips.

"We are not packing around a bunch of tramps, gamblers, and thieves," Rupp said.

The remark dripped with irony in the wake of the nationwide gambling scandals of the 1950s, when players throughout the country were involved in fixing games.

Upon initially hearing of the scandal, Rupp had boasted that gamblers "couldn't touch my boys with a 10-foot pole." However, Rupp was stunned—and dismayed—when three of his former players admitted to accepting $1,500 in bribes to deliberately lose a game in the National Invitation Tournament in New York in 1949.

Things couldn't get worse, Rupp thought.

They did.

In the summer of 1952, the Southeastern Conference suspended Kentucky from basketball competition. The NCAA followed up that punishment by canceling the Wildcats' entire 1952–53 season because of the point-shaving scandal.

The Wildcats came back with a vengeance, winning all 25 of their regular-season games in 1953–54. They were invited to play in the NCAA tournament, but declined because three of their players were ruled ineligible for the event. The lost season had cost them their eligibility.

The following year, Rupp was back at the same stand, ruling the basketball court with an iron hand and cruel, cutting remarks that often dripped with sarcasm.

As one story goes, Rupp once had a 6-foot-9 center who deliberately shied away from contact. Rupp preferred forceful, aggressive players, particularly those inside, who weren't afraid to toss an elbow or two.

At one point in practice, Rupp spotted the center lingering at the free throw line while his teammates were staging a brutal battle under the boards.

Rupp blew his whistle and glared at the offending player.

"What's a nice boy like you doing in a place like this?" Rupp asked plaintively.

Rupp's practice sessions were anything but kind.

"A lot of people think we run a Marine Corps outfit," Rupp said, insisting he never wanted to be a fatherlike figure or friend to the players. "If they think that, that's fine. I knew when I came here that the only way I could be successful would be to go out and win these basketball games."

Win, he did.

He maintained that it was the only reason he was in the game: to win.

"If winning isn't so important, then why do you keep score?" he asked.

The heavyset Rupp went about producing some of the most brilliant basketball teams in college history—teams that were noticeably all white, from the top player to the last reserve. For most of his coaching career, until he was forced to do so by school officials and the trending times, Rupp simply refused to open his roster to a black player.

A racist? Yes, but also the product of an era when most schools, particularly major colleges in the South, refused to use African American players on their sports teams. Many of these schools simply believed black players were inferior athletes. Rupp wasn't the only coach who thought this way, but he was the most prominent.

This illogical thinking finally came to a head in the 1966 national championship game. It was then that Rupp's all-white squad lost to Texas Western, a team whose five starters and top two reserves all were African American players.

"We heard before the game that Mr. Rupp didn't believe that five blacks could beat his team," remembered Nevil Shed, one of the Texas Western (now Texas El Paso) starters. "Well, we showed him just how tough five (blacks) could be."

In Rupp's defense, Groza put in a vote for his old coach many years later.

"People said he didn't like blacks, or Jews, or Catholics," the former Kentucky star said. "But I'm Catholic and he never showed me any prejudice."

The face of basketball was changing in America. Although black players began dotting the rosters of major schools throughout the country, it wasn't until the late '60s that Rupp made any serious effort to recruit them. He was one of the South's last holdouts among coaches.

By then, Rupp was on the downside of his coaching career, battling to stay relevant after reaching the supposedly mandatory retirement age of 70. He fought retirement just as hard as he had battled opponents on the basketball court.

"If they don't let me coach, they might as well take me to the Lexington cemetery," said Rupp, who coached into the 1970s.

He remained at Kentucky through the 1971–72 season before failing health caught up with him.

Rupp was a dying man in 1977 when he visited New York to present a trophy in his name to the Associated Press College Basketball Player of the Year, UCLA's Marques Johnson.

"Have you seen the trophy?" Rupp asked an Associated Press sportswriter, puffing out his chest and pointing to a copper-colored piece standing in the corner of a crowded hotel room. "They're going to have to have four guys carry it back for Marques. It's too heavy for any one man."

But certainly fitting for a coaching giant who was larger than life.

A Dark and Stormy Knight

First things first: by the time he retired, Bobby Knight had won more games than any college basketball coach in Division I history.

Also true: at every stop he made along the coaching circuit, Knight dramatically raised his team's level of play—most notably at Indiana, where he won three national titles.

This, too: he ran one of the cleanest programs in the country without a hint of trouble with the NCAA, never facing major sanctions of any kind.

Another plus for Knight: his players (most of them, anyway) expressed a lionhearted loyalty to the tumultuous coach whose heroes included the tough-minded general George S. Patton. Knight's militaristic coaching style, patterned after Patton, earned him the obvious nickname, "The General."

Then there is Knight's charity work and the countless number of lives he has impacted individually in a positive way away from the basketball court. Among coaches, he had just as many deep-seated friendships as enemies.

And, no small thing, Knight's players usually were near the top in graduation rates for athletes.

Now for just a sampling of the lowlights:

- During the 1979 Pan American Games in San Juan, Puerto Rico, Knight was accused of assaulting a policeman.
- In February 1985, Knight threw a chair across the court to protest a referee's call during Indiana's game against Purdue.
- During an NCAA regional tournament game against LSU in March 1987, Knight slammed his fist on the scorer's table to protest a referee's decision. It cost Indiana University $10,000 in fines and earned Knight a reprimand.

There were also numerous incidents of physical and mental abuse involving players, coaches, sports information directors, sportswriters, and office workers that ultimately cost Knight his job at Indiana. One of his most infamous moments occurred during a tense game against Michigan, when Knight reached out and grabbed the jersey of reserve guard Jim Wisman and hauled him off the court.

Another time, in a game against Kentucky, Knight was embroiled in a running feud with Wildcats coach Joe Hall. The Hoosiers were way ahead in the game. Still, it didn't stop Knight from a constant barrage of berating the officials.

At one point, Hall yelled across the court, "Way to go, Bobby."

Later, when both their tempers were shortened considerably, the two coaches at odds drifted toward each other at the scorer's table. After exchanging some words, Knight reached out and hit Hall on the side of the head. After the game, Knight explained it as "only a playful tap."

Hall wasn't of the same opinion.

"He personally humiliated me," Hall said, "and I'll never forget it."

Once, in one of his more passive moods, Knight sheepishly made a general apology for his prodigious temper.

"I do dumb things sometimes," Knight confessed.

He has been called a bully by opposing coaches, and a maniac and obnoxious by his critics. His running war against sportswriters became legendary during his godlike rule at Indiana. Knight rallied against criticism in the press with curses, physical threats, and questions about the journalists' ethnic backgrounds.

Knight took umbrage at his reputation as a referee-baiter. One season, he had a friend help him research the number of technical fouls he had accumulated versus the number given to other coaches in the Big Ten.

"Indiana had the fewest in the Big Ten," Knight's friend said. "The next team had almost twice as many."

On occasion, Knight showed he could be as charming as anyone, that he was only part monster. The day before Indiana faced Michigan in March 1976 for the national championship, Knight faced his sworn enemies in the press.

"I made myself some promises this year," Knight told the gathered assembly of sportswriters. "I figured March 28 would be 'Be Kind to Press Day.'"

That day, Knight was positively lovable but still couldn't resist flinging a jab at his longtime adversaries, expressing his general distaste for sportswriters.

"All of us learn to write in the second grade," Knight said. "Most of us go on to other things."

Knight would be just as charming the following night. He had good reason, after his Hoosiers beat Michigan for the NCAA title, his first of three in a 12-year period. Knight went on to win national titles in 1981 and 1987, to say nothing of 11 Big Ten championships and a gold medal at the 1984 Olympic Games.

There has never been a more complicated and controversial coach in the history of college basketball. No coach has polarized the sport like Knight.

As a high school player in Orrville, Ohio, Knight was not particularly likable or easy to get along with.

"Not only was he the team's superstar, he was a self-proclaimed superstar," said Bob Gobin, who coached Knight at Orrville High. Or was it the other way around?

Knight was a senior during the 1957–58 season, when Gobin took over the team with a new approach. He didn't want to rely on just Knight to provide the offense, preferring to spread the scoring around for a more balanced attack. Naturally, the "self-proclaimed superstar" was not too thrilled with the new arrangement.

"Bobby didn't take kindly to the new coach—me—and the changes (I) wanted," Gobin said. "He subsequently did not hustle on the floor and was causing dissension on the team."

At one point, Gobin said he overheard Knight bad-mouthing him to fans. The eventual result was a one-week suspension for Knight. He came back with a vengeance, helping his team make the playoffs with an 18.6 average in his final season.

At Ohio State, Knight had a lesser role as a reserve, playing behind the likes of John Havlicek and Jerry Lucas, two future Hall of Famers. It was one of the strongest Buckeyes teams in history, winning the national championship in 1960.

Knight started his coaching career as an assistant at Cuyahoga Falls High School in Ohio, where he spent one season. He then enlisted in the U.S. Army and joined the coaching staff of the basketball team at West Point. Before long, he was the head coach, turning out compelling, aggressive teams despite a relative lack of talent. Like their coach, the West Pointers were brash and businesslike.

Marquette coach Al McGuire likened Knight to an army general with his "charge up the hill at the machine gun" approach to basketball: a rugged, uncompromising style of tough defense and a conservative, hard-nosed offense that kept mistakes to a minimum. When mistakes were made, the young soldiers heard about them loud and clear. Oh, boy, did they ever.

"Bobby is a disciplinarian but he has a genuine interest in his players' welfare and he has a real affection for them," longtime Indiana swimming coach Doc Counselman once pointed out. "In return, he has their respect."

Noted John Laskowski, who played for four years under Knight: "He used basketball to make us better people."

Knight's 102–50 record at West Point and four appearances in the National Invitation Tournament in six years were quite remarkable, given that Army and other service academies were at a disadvantage in recruiting top players. Military schools required a minimum of four years of service upon graduation, making it difficult for their players to pursue a professional basketball career.

In 1971, Knight moved on to Indiana and quickly established the Hoosiers as a national power. By 1975, they looked like a good bet to win the national championship. But with star Scott May playing at less than full strength with a broken arm, the Hoosiers lost a two-point decision to Kentucky in the regional playoffs for their first defeat of the season.

The following year, in Indiana's second appearance in the Final Four under Knight, May was clearly at his best, scoring 26 points and picking off eight rebounds as the Hoosiers destroyed a good Michigan team in the finals, 86–68. Other big contributors: Kent Benson with 25 points and nine rebounds and Quinn Buckner with 16 points and eight rebounds.

The triumph was historic. With a 32–0 mark, the Hoosiers matched North Carolina's 1957 team for the best record by an NCAA champion.

It was only the beginning of high times for Knight and his Hoosiers. With Knight sporting a noisy plaid jacket or bright red sweater while parading up and down the sideline and berating officials, the Hoosiers were the team to beat in the Big Ten and usually found themselves in the running for the national championship.

On campus and throughout most of the state of Indiana, Knight and the Hoosiers were followed by fans with cultish fury. On game nights, representatives in the state legislature dismissed themselves early so as not to miss a second of an Indiana game. Movie theaters were all but empty whenever the Hoosiers played, and men's and women's clubs knew better than to hold their meetings on such nights.

Before Knight arrived on the scene in Hoosierland, Branch McCracken had been the most famous and popular coach in the school's history, with national championships in 1940 and 1953. McCracken would also be remembered for breaking the color barrier in the Big Ten by recruiting Bill Garrett to be the first African American to play in the league.

During his tenure at Indiana from 1971–2000, Knight overshadowed McCracken's accomplishments with an amazing run: three national championships (1976, 1981, and 1987), visits to five Final Fours, one NIT title, 11 Big Ten Conference championships, and an Olympic gold medal. Knight was selected national coach of the year four times and was easily the most popular figure in the state of Indiana, sporting or otherwise. He might have run for governor and won in a landslide—if only he had been able to control his violent temper. An anger management class, or a course with Dale Carnegie, might have done Knight a world of good.

During his time at Indiana, there had been bullying incidents involving the sports information office, but those were nothing compared to the explosion that occurred at the 1979 Pan Am Games. Knight was accused of assaulting a police officer before a practice session with his U.S. team. Convicted in absentia, Knight was sentenced to six months in jail. Extradition efforts by the Puerto Rican government were not successful. Knight blamed the media for keeping the story alive and making him look bad, which, in turn, fueled an adversarial relationship with sportswriters that continued to sour over the years.

"I'm going to read forever about how I slugged a Puerto Rican policeman, and it didn't happen," Knight said.

Puerto Rico aside, Knight could do no wrong at Indiana—as long as he was winning. In 1981, a powerhouse team featuring Isiah Thomas led the Hoosiers to the national title with a 63–50 victory over North Carolina. In 1987, the Hoosiers won again, beating Syracuse, 74–73, on a shot by Keith Smart in the final seconds. Steve Alford, the Indiana native who was one of Knight's most prized players, was the star of that 1986–87 team.

Only a three-point loss to Duke in the national semifinals in 1992 prevented Indiana from advancing to yet another national championship game. Coaching Duke that day was Mike Krzyzewski, who had played for Knight at West Point. Coach K would become a successful coach in his own right, one of many who had developed in the Hoosier Hotbed.

Off the court, Knight continued to have his troubles, which culminated with an incident on September 8, 2000. This time a "disrespectful" remark by a student walking around on campus set off Knight. According to the student, Kent Harvey, the Indiana coach roughly grabbed his arm and lectured him on manners and respect. Knight later admitted to putting his hand on Harvey's arm and talking to him but denied raising his voice.

Two days later, an era ended at Indiana when Knight was fired. His record with the Hoosiers was 661–240. A remarkable stat: in 30 seasons under Knight, the Hoosiers missed postseason play only one time.

After sitting out a season, Knight took over the Texas Tech basketball program. At first, not everyone was happy he had been hired to coach the Red Raiders. That thinking changed some when Knight quickly improved the team.

The Red Raiders had not been to an NCAA tournament since 1996. In Knight's first four years at the school, the team went to the postseason four times, with three trips to the NCAA tournament and one to the NIT. Along the way, Knight extended his victory total to 902, breaking Dean Smith's all-time record.

Off the court, Knight made more friends at Texas Tech by contributing money to a school library fund.

Ten years after Knight was fired by Indiana, he traveled to Hammond, Indiana, for a roast to benefit Chicago's St. Joseph High School. Celebrities from the sports world joined in the fun at Knight's expense. On a night filled with laughter and good-natured ribbing, Thomas struck a serious chord.

"He never cheated anyone," the Hall of Fame guard said. "He gave his all to all of us."

Loved or loathed, Knight was always topical.

Dean Smith and Coach K

As the state that produced the Wright Brothers, North Carolina boasts more than its share of icons. In the world of sports, try two high-flying basketball coaches, Dean Smith and Mike Krzyzewski.

At the University of North Carolina, Smith took the Tar Heels to unprecedented heights. You can say the same for Krzyzewski at Duke University.

Remarkably, these two southern superpowers coexist roughly 12 miles apart, making theirs one of the most unique rivalries—and some say the best—in college basketball. The rivalry was the most passionate when these two coaches were on the sidelines.

As Krzyzewski continued to produce competitive teams year after year, it grew apparent it would only be a matter of time before the Duke coach passed Smith for second place on the all-time victories list. When that mission was accomplished, Coach K took aim at Knight's all-time record of 902 victories at the Division I level.

That Coach K would be in line to break Knight's record was only fitting. After all, Krzyzewski had played for Knight at Army, coached under him at Indiana, and professed a great love for his longtime mentor.

Smith could say the same for Frank McGuire, another legendary coach who had emphatically put his stamp on the North Carolina basketball program before falling out of grace.

As different as they were in many ways—Smith arrived on the big-time basketball stage from the plains of Kansas; Krzyzewski was a big-city kid from Chicago—Smith and Krzyzewski each had similar stories to tell in regard to putting their respective teams on the national basketball map.

Both were great motivators. Noting their differences in personalities, one sportswriter said, "Krzyzewski was more confrontational, Smith more calculating."

Smith's basketball lineage traces back to the very beginnings of the sport. At Kansas, he played on Phog Allen's national championship team in 1952. Allen had actually played for James Naismith, the inventor of basketball.

After an assistant coaching stint at the Air Force Academy from 1955–58, Smith joined North Carolina as an assistant to McGuire. At the time, McGuire was one of the most celebrated coaches in America. His 1957 Tar Heels had won the national championship with a 32–0 record. That team had closed out a remarkable season with consecutive triple-overtime victories over Michigan State and Wilt Chamberlain's Kansas team in the Final Four. At that time, no Division I college basketball team had ever won as many games in securing the national title.

So Smith hooked up with McGuire, unaware he would soon be taking over the North Carolina basketball program. But in 1961, McGuire resigned in the midst of a point-shaving scandal involving North Carolina players and an NCAA investigation of recruiting violations.

In handing the job over to the little-known Smith, the school's administration told him, in so many words, *We don't care if you don't win—just don't cheat.*

"That's the only thing he was told to do, don't cheat," recalled longtime Tar Heels sports information director Rick Brewer. "They didn't tell him to have a winning program. The impression was the administration here didn't care about having a great winning basketball tradition anymore. They just wanted to have a basketball program, period."

Considering Smith's hands were tied in respect to recruiting and scheduling as a result of the program's transgressions under McGuire, there wasn't that much optimism to spread around, anyway. As a result of the scandal, the Tar Heels cut their regular-season schedule to 17 games and withdrew from the Atlantic Coast Conference tournament. In addition, they were barred from the 1961 NCAA tournament.

The Carolina tradition not only included McGuire's once-in-a-lifetime unbeaten team, but also the fabled "White Phantoms" of the 1920s. In 1924, the Phantoms went 26–0 and staked a claim as the mythical national champion.

No such luck in Smith's first season as head coach at Carolina. Not even close.

"I thought, 'Oh, my gosh, this is going to be tough,'" Smith said.

He was right—the Tar Heels posted an 8–9 record in 1961 under their new coach. You couldn't blame Smith for having second thoughts about taking the head coaching position. Students were unkind, hanging him in effigy.

Things were about to change, more quickly than imagined. Known as a brilliant game coach, Smith showed how good he could be as a recruiter, as well. Welcome, Bob Lewis and Larry Miller, known as the "L&M Boys" in deference to a well-known southern tobacco firm. By 1966–67, the potent pair had led the Tar Heels to a 26–6 record and Smith's first of 11 visits to the Final Four.

Building on that team's success, Smith had no problems recruiting other great players to North Carolina, almost too many to name. Charlie Scott became the first African American to play at Carolina—thanks to Smith, who lent himself to great social causes—and earned a gold medal as a member of the 1968 U.S. Olympic basketball team. There was Bob McAdoo, a future NBA great. And Phil Ford, who skillfully ran Smith's controversial "Four Corners Offense."

Before there was a shot clock, Smith won many games using the "Four Corners," one of his numerous innovations, which featured players spread out in the four corners of the court and a main ball-handler in the middle to distribute the ball. Though the strategy brought Smith great success in many instances, allowing his team to maintain possession while running down the clock once it had a lead, on occasion the slowdown offense backfired, such as in the 1977 finals against Marquette.

The Tar Heels had rallied from a 39–27 halftime deficit to take the lead against the Warriors. At this point Smith ordered his team to go into his patented slowdown offense.

Rather than helping the Tar Heels, the maneuver wiped out their momentum and allowed Marquette to walk off with a 67–59 win for the national championship.

It wasn't until 1982 that Smith finally won his first national championship with the help of Michael Jordan, who was on his way to superstardom.

Like many of Smith's other great players, Jordan played within a tightly constricted ball-control system that featured a selfless, team-first attitude. There were no "stars" at Carolina; Smith saw to that. In his three years at Chapel Hill, Jordan averaged only 17.7 points, way below his record-tying 30.1 career average as a pro.

That prompted a popular joke on the North Carolina campus:

Question: Who is the only one to hold Michael Jordan under 20 points?

Answer: Dean Smith.

Never mind. Smith has a Jordan shot to thank for his first national championship. With 17 seconds left against Georgetown in the title game, Jordan hit a jumper to give the Tar Heels a 63–62 victory. The win was a relief for Smith, who had taken teams to the Final Four on six previous occasions, only to go home without the title.

Jordan, a freshman at the time, has described that shot as one of the greatest of his career, college or pro. He also remembered something else about his time at North Carolina—Smith's revulsion of cursing.

"You had to run the steps if you cursed," Jordan said. "I had to run the steps a couple times."

Smith added a second national championship in 1993, beating Michigan in the finals.

By that time, Krzyzewski had already established his place among the premier basketball coaches in America. His Blue Devils were not only challenging the Tar Heels for state supremacy but also making a name for themselves on the national stage.

Coach K brought a rugged, defense-first philosophy to Duke, thanks to his days at Army and the lessons he had learned from Knight.

Krzyzewski had faced two rough assignments at West Point: first training to become an officer in the U.S. Army, and then playing for Knight on the Cadets basketball team. Krzyzewski didn't know which was tougher.

Playing for Knight and his in-your-face coaching style was no picnic. During his time coaching the Army basketball team, he had developed a style that *People* magazine writers Frank Martin and Ralph Hovak called "a cross between Simon Legree and Father Flanagan." Whether you believe he was a brutal taskmaster or a kindly father figure, Knight became a role model for Krzyzewski, as well as a lifelong friend.

Krzyzewski became a standout on the basketball court and one of Knight's all-time favorite players. The coach thought highly enough of Krzyzewski to select him team captain in 1968–69, and the senior went on to lead the Cadets to the National Invitation Tournament.

After completing his Army service and coaching the Cadets team for five years, Krzyzewski took over the Duke basketball program in 1980.

Until that point, you had to go back to the 1960s, when Vic Bubas was the coach, to define Duke's greatest basketball glories. With players such as Art Heyman, Jeff Mullins, and Steve Vacendak, the Blue Devils went to the Final Four on three occasions in that decade—1963, 1964, and 1966. On each trip, they returned home without a championship.

When Krzyzewski was first introduced to the press covering Duke basketball, he was pretty much off the radar screen.

"Three thoughts crossed almost every mind that night: How do you pronounce (his name), how do you spell it, and who is this guy?" remembered one sportswriter.

Like Smith at North Carolina, Krzyzewski had a tough time turning around the Duke basketball program in the beginning. He dealt with two straight 17-loss seasons and was booed by the Duke fans. One day, it was reported, Coach K was spotted crying in the shower.

All of that was soon to change—dramatically. In 1985–86, Duke won an NCAA-record 37 games before losing to Louisville by three points in the national finals.

The Blue Devils also made appearances in the Final Four in 1988, 1989, and 1990, only to be thwarted each time in their bid for a national championship. Shades of the North Carolina Tar Heels.

Soon, the wait was over for Coach K. With Christian Laettner, Bobby Hurley, and Grant Hill showing the way, the Blue Devils won the national title in 1991. They repeated in 1992.

When Krzyzewski won national championships in 2001 and 2010, he joined the Mount Rushmore of basketball coaches, becoming only the third coach in college basketball history to win at least four NCAA titles. The others: John Wooden and Adolph Rupp.

Moving past Smith for second place on the all-time wins list with his 880th victory was inevitable. Every seat was taken at the 23,000-seat Greensboro Coliseum to watch the Blue Devils' dismantling of North Carolina-Greensboro in December 2010.

"When I walked out and saw it was a full house, and so many Duke fans, I did take a moment to reflect back to when I first got to North Carolina and there weren't very many Duke shirts," Krzyzewski said.

Winning does that for a basketball program, and it could be argued that Krzyzewski's mission had been tougher than most.

For one thing, the Blue Devils had to challenge the Tar Heels within the state of North Carolina, no doubt pushing the other to higher achievements through the teams' titanic basketball battles.

Smith had a head start on Coach K, having arrived at Chapel Hill several years before Krzyzewski made his way to Durham. And as the tension built between them, a natural rivalry developed between the two coaches—at times turning bitter, insulting, and spiteful.

Smith, known to be fair-minded with strong religious principles, stood for so many good things at Carolina. When it came to Duke, however, it was a different story. One day during the 1988–89 season, the normally noncontroversial Smith woke up the media with the remark that Duke's two stars, Danny Ferry and Laettner, had lower SAT scores than Carolina's J. R. Reid and Scott Williams. Whatever had prompted Smith to make the remark wasn't clear, but Krzyzewski clearly wasn't pleased. Nor were Duke's rabid supporters.

Back came the Blue Devils with a response from their fans. When Duke next played Carolina, the Tar Heels were greeted by placards in the stands that said, "J.R. Can't Reid."

The taunting didn't seem to bother the play of the Tar Heels. Nor did it matter that they were playing in Cameron Indoor Stadium, which under Krzyzewski's watch had become one of the most notorious college basketball arenas in the country, a place where Duke was nearly unbeatable. Dismissing the hostility and Duke's home-court advantage in the noisy and cozy arena, the Tar Heels whipped the Blue Devils, 91–71. Duke had only been ranked No. 1 in the country at the time.

By the week of the Atlantic Coast Conference tournament in 1989, it was inevitable Duke and North Carolina would meet for the conference championship. Tensions rose to new heights between the two coaches.

Duke was ranked No. 7 in the country and Carolina No. 9.

The Tar Heels led for most of the game and held a 39–35 advantage at the half. The teams took the game down to the wire, trading shot for shot like two great fighters.

In the end, North Carolina defeated Duke, 77–74, in one of the most intensely played games in their storied history. Ironically, it was none other than Reid who helped pull Carolina through by outplaying Ferry, the tournament MVP. A total of 49 fouls were called in the rugged game.

It was just one of many tremendous battles between Duke and Carolina over the 17 years in which Krzyzewski and Smith faced off against one another. Almost always, there was something on the line in those battles, whether within their conference or on the national stage. During that time, the two schools produced four national championships and visited the Final Four 18 times between them. They met a total of 38 times from 1980–97, although never in the NCAA tournament. Smith held a 24–14 advantage before he retired prior to the 1997–98 season.

With the two schools' proximity to each other and the stakes usually so high, it was only natural that some strong feelings would exist between the coaches who not only battled each other on the court but also battled for recruits from basically the same area.

Coach K softened his stance as the years went by and both men developed a great respect for each other's accomplishments. If there wasn't any love between them, there was certainly admiration.

Together, they left their mark on college basketball in America.

Jim Calhoun

No matter that Jim Calhoun became just the fifth coach to win three national basketball titles with his championship in 2011.

He may have been number one in the country, but was still number two on his own campus.

Calhoun continued to play catch-up to Geno Auriemma, who has coached the Connecticut women's basketball team to seven titles and set a record of 90 straight victories at one point.

Not that Calhoun's accomplishment was anything to disparage, considering the company he was now keeping in the men's game: Wooden, Rupp, Krzyzewski, and Knight.

And with 855 victories at the end of the 2010–11 season, Calhoun also stands very tall among all college coaches.

Calhoun has led the Huskies to the Final Four on four occasions, winning the national title in 1999 and 2004 prior to his stunning triumph in 2011.

It's probable the 2011 championship was Calhoun's greatest coaching job. The Huskies were coming off a frustrating 16-loss season in 2009–10 that had ended with a defeat in the NIT. With a young roster in 2010–11, Connecticut was picked to finish 10th in the Big East Conference. For a while it looked like that prognostication was right on the money.

However, UConn pulled itself together behind junior point guard Kemba Walker and had a spectacular second half of the season.

The Huskies, who finished ninth in the Big East during the regular season, won the conference tournament title and then the national championship with an unlikely run in the final month. They finished with 11 straight victories, including a triumph over Butler in the NCAA final.

Long before he took over UConn and turned the onetime doormats into a national power, Calhoun had already sharply upgraded the basketball program at little-known Northeastern University.

The Massachusetts native wasted little time doing the same at Connecticut, winning the NIT in 1988 just two years after taking over the coaching job.

Under Calhoun, the highly competitive Huskies didn't miss postseason play too often after that. He became a New England icon, rivaling any of the region's most celebrated faces.

His most talented team may have been the 2004 national championship squad that featured Emeka Okafor and Ben Gordon, the number two and number three picks, respectively, in that year's NBA draft.

Calhoun's rise to the top was not without negative implications. In 2011, the men's basketball program was cited by the NCAA for recruiting violations. Among the penalties handed out was a three-game suspension for Calhoun during the 2011–12 season, which was generally regarded as "a slap on the wrist."

Some media members were appalled by what they thought was the NCAA's relatively light punishment shortly before the start of the playoffs in February 2011.

"(Calhoun) shouldn't have been allowed anywhere near the gym," said Joe Nocera, a *New York Times* columnist, on the op-ed page.

Nocera called the NCAA "an organization that bends over backward to accommodate big-time basketball schools like Connecticut that drive TV ratings, and marquee coaches like Calhoun, who, with his $2.3 million salary, is the highest paid state employee in Connecticut. March Madness was right around the corner, so Calhoun's suspension was (of course!) deferred until next season, allowing him to coach the team during the tournament."

Before the Final Four, Calhoun had insisted that, in a season of parity in college basketball, none of the teams in the championship round was great.

"If you take all four of us, all four of us are capable of winning a national championship," Calhoun said.

Yes, and in the end, it was none other than Calhoun who was holding up his third national championship trophy.

A rundown of the other multiple-championship coaches:

- Henry Iba won NCAA titles in 1945 and 1946 with Oklahoma A&M (now Oklahoma State), becoming the first coach to win consecutive championships. The Aggies' hallmark: ball control and defense—and a brilliant center by the name of Bob Kurland.

- Forrest (Phog) Allen once played for James Naismith, basketball's inventor. In time, he made his own impact coaching the Kansas Jayhawks. A pioneer of recruiting, Allen won 771 games. Among his many highlights: an NCAA championship in 1952, and Helms national titles in 1922 and 1923 in the years before the NCAA tournament.

- Phil Woolpert won consecutive national championships at San Francisco in 1955 and 1956. Bill Russell, the Dons' outstanding big man, described Woolpert as "an excellent technician." Woolpert emphasized defense, and the Dons drilled for hours on play patterns and timing.

- Branch McCracken was only 31 years old when he led Indiana to the national championship in 1940. McCracken did it again in 1953. An obsessive recruiter, McCracken continuously drove thousands of miles around the state of Indiana hunting for talent.

- Ed Jucker coached Cincinnati to consecutive national titles in 1961 and 1962. The Bearcats had lost All-American Oscar Robertson to graduation when Jucker took over for George Smith in '61. "Defense was really the key," Jucker said. "I put in a man-to-man pressing defense I felt our players could use."

- No one had a better mentor than Denny Crum, who learned basketball as a player and then an assistant coach under Wooden at UCLA. When Crum took over the Louisville program in 1971, he was well prepared to win championships. He did, leading the Cardinals to national titles in 1980 and 1986.

- While coaching at Kansas, Roy Williams won 80 percent of his games. But it was only when he took over at North Carolina in 2003 that he began winning national championships. He led the Tar Heels to the national title in 2005 and again in 2009. He ranks No. 2 in career victories at both Kansas (behind Allen) and North Carolina (behind Smith).
- Billy Donovan led the Florida Gators to three national championship games, winning the title in 2006 and again in 2007. In the process, he became an NCAA rarity as only the fourth man to play in the Final Four and win the title as a coach. The others: Smith, Knight, and Joe B. Hall. Donovan also became another rarity by winning consecutive championships.

Two of a Kind

Bob Knight is lauded for his 902 career victories, as well he should be.

Herb Magee? If you haven't heard of him, here's something every college basketball fan should know: Magee, not Knight, holds the NCAA career victories record.

Easy to see why Magee flies under the radar. His basketball program at Philadelphia University, a Division II school, is fairly anonymous when compared to Knight's celebrated career on the Division I level.

But there it is, nevertheless—Magee's small college teams have recorded more NCAA victories than anyone at that level, 922 at the end of the 2010–11 season.

Magee joined Philadelphia University when it was known as the Philadelphia College of Textiles & Science. He deserves some kind of medal for consistency. He starred as a player for the Rams and remained as a coach. He has stayed throughout the years despite offers to coach at higher-profile schools and even in the NBA.

In a way, he did make it to the NBA. Magee has worked with pro players as a "shot doctor." Some of his most prominent "patients": Charles Barkley, Sebastian Telfair, and Malik Rose.

"This is where I live, where my kids are, my family," Magee told *Sports Illustrated* in 2006, explaining why he has stayed put for more than 50 years. "Coaching is coaching. Being where you're comfortable is more important to me than millions of dollars."

The same could be said for Glenn Robinson of Franklin & Marshall.

(continued)

Two of a Kind *(Continued)*

With 805 wins at the end of the 2010–11 season, Robinson has the most victories of any coach in Division III basketball history.

Robinson's Diplomats have been consistent visitors to the NCAA Division III playoffs with appearances in 15 Sweet Sixteens, nine Elite Eights, five Final Fours, and one national championship game. Another number to be considered: He has been named National Association of Basketball Coaches (NABC) coach of the year 12 times.

There's a small college coaching giant in the Badlands, too: Don Meyer.

Meyer's career record of 923 victories makes you do a double take. The majority of his victories came in the National Association of Intercollegiate Athletics (NAIA), at Hamline University and David Lipscomb University. He finished his career at the NCAA's Division II Northern State University in Abderdeen, South Dakota.

With 44 successful years as a coach, including a national championship in 1970 and 25 visits to the NCAA Division II tournament, it was inevitable Magee would break Knight's NCAA record of 902 victories. The historic moment came on a February night in 2010 when Magee's Rams beat Goldey-Beacom College, 76–65.

Magee was 68 at the time, with no plans to retire.

"It's really hard to win games," Magee said in an interview with the Associated Press.

This basketball magician somehow has mastered the trick better than most.

6.

TV Lights the Way

If there was one thing that made college hoops fans mad (as in angry) about March Madness, it was how the coverage of the tournament regressed on television.

Complaints throughout the years ranged from poor production, to a lack of continuity during broadcasts, to the network switching from one game to another without any decipherable pattern or philosophy.

Mainly, though, the loudest cries came because not every game was made available on live TV to the entire nation.

So the announcement in April 2010, just weeks after Duke had won the national crown, was greeted with enthusiasm: the NCAA's new 14-year contract with CBS and Turner Sports would guarantee live coverage of every game. This made every fan of the NCAA playoffs happy—particularly those more interested in winning their office pools than in seeing their alma mater walk off with the title.

True, some games would air on truTV, a fairly anonymous cable network, but better-known networks such as TNT, TBS, and the over-the-air CBS affiliates were also in on the deal, which made it big news. *Very* big news.

It was the latest and greatest step in the evolution of the NCAA tournament on the tube.

How great?

How about $10.8 billion?

That meant a payoff of roughly $740 million annually for the NCAA's member colleges.

And it came at a crucial time—when the networks and sponsors they so heavily rely on for revenues to defray costs were just beginning to recover from the recession.

"In this economy, think about how many things have gone backward," said Chris Plonsky, women's athletic director at the University of Texas. "The fact that this is a positive move forward is attributable to some really hard work at the negotiating table. . . . And when you're talking about opportunities for young people, it's a blessing."

More than 95 percent of the NCAA's revenue comes from the contracts for March Madness.

How did TV become such an integral part of the tournament?

Rewind to the 1970s, and we get a glimpse into the symbiotic relationship about to develop.

NBC owned the rights to the NCAA men's basketball tournament—it paid a mere $1.165 million in 1973 for those rights—but didn't even televise every game; the NCAA playoffs still were something of a quaint gathering on the sporting schedule, more March Meekness than Madness. Wisely, the network chose to move the championship game, which previously had been played on a Saturday night and primarily shown on regional outlets, to Monday evening.

ABC had established Mondays as a hot night for sports with its NFL telecasts, so NBC was not breaking new ground.

Fortunately for NBC, UCLA's dynastic run still was intact. With the sensational Bill Walton dominating the court and the legendary John Wooden on the sideline, the Bruins had transcended the game. They seemed unbeatable as they pursued a seventh consecutive NCAA championship, and their appeal as either record-setting heroes or omnipotent villains was virtually unmatched in college sports.

In the 1973 final, Walton made 21 of 22 shots and ravaged Memphis State for 44 points as UCLA cruised to another title. NBC's numbers jumped off the screen: the audience of 13.5 million homes was the largest for a college basketball game.

NBC was hooked, at least for a while, and so was much of America. The following year brought the end of UCLA's string of national championships with the Bruins' epic semifinal loss to North Carolina State. The "Peacock Network" now was synonymous with college hoops, and suddenly the term Final Four meant must-watch television.

But NBC wasn't nearly as committed to the tournament as it needed to be to remain the NCAA's partner for very long. The network tended to feature the big-name players and high-profile teams in its tournament coverage. There was no wall-to-wall telecast of all the rounds.

After Marquette won the national title in 1977, its bombastic coach, Al McGuire, took his Rockaway witticisms and accent behind the microphone. He combined with smooth play-by-play man Dick Enberg and knowledgeable, edgy analyst Billy Packer to form a dream team to rival ABC's *Monday Night Football* crew of Frank Gifford, Don Meredith, and Howard Cosell.

As Enberg chronicled the action, Packer broke down the ins and outs of the game and McGuire brought the terms "aircraft carrier," "French pastry," and "Dunkirk" to the audience. They became an iconic trio. In McGuire's language, "aircraft carrier" was a big center, "French pastry" a showy move, and "Dunkirk" an extremely poor performance.

About McGuire, the *New York Times*' Frank Litsky wrote: "McGuire liked toy soldiers, seashells, balloons, clowns, and nostalgic country songs. He also dismissed talk that he was a basketball genius. 'I wasn't different,' he said. 'I was ahead of my time.'"

Packer had his own sense of importance that he brought to the broadcasts.

"I have a passion for the history and the value of the game and its direction. I will say this, not to be in a bragging fashion: I do understand the game. I would not be averse to debate the status of basketball with anybody."

Legendary Indiana coach Bob Knight would side with Packer in any debate—except, perhaps with Knight himself.

"I think Billy can be very comfortable knowing the tremendous role he played in college basketball," Knight said.

As for Enberg, Packer summed up the consummate sportscaster, one who has never been matched by subsequent lead announcers in college basketball: "He was a teacher by trade, and, consequently, he knows what it is like to prepare for and take a test. His interest as a former teacher in acquiring knowledge and not overburdening you with his knowledge is the ultimate preparation."

That trio got to broadcast the ultimate matchup of individual college stars in 1979. In that year's NCAA final, Magic Johnson led Michigan State past Larry Bird and Indiana State. The game drew the highest-rated TV audience in the history of the tournament, which mainly had been televised through regional coverage, not on the networks, for decades.

By the end of the 1970s, the size of the tournament was expanding, too. So was the interest other TV networks had in the playoffs. When the NCAA—never an organization to discourage a bidding war—again attempted to sell the television rights for the tournament, there were interested parties.

CBS paid top dollar—$48 million over three years, which tripled NBC's fees—and then pirated away Packer from NBC; Enberg and McGuire remained with NBC and handled regular-season games with the same engagement and flair as they had before Packer left.

Packer became more than an announcer for CBS: he helped set policy on college hoops coverage. After all, CBS was a novice at this sport; Packer was the expert.

Through Packer's contacts and the enlightened guidance of producer Len DeLuca, CBS turned its newest property into one of its most valuable. It ranked up there with the Masters and U.S. Open tennis, even with the NFL (CBS lost the rights to broadcasting NFC games to FOX in 1994 before wresting away the AFC from NBC four years later).

DeLuca determined that a buildup to the NCAA tournament would make for a natural crescendo. Devoted fans would regularly watch games through the winter, but drawing in other viewers was crucial. His plan was to get more casual watchers interested by taking them on a four-month journey leading up to the big payoff.

Thus, "The Road to the Final Four" was born.

"It was a brilliant idea, just the right touch," *USA Today*'s television sports columnist Rudy Martzke said. "Get fans familiar with the key players, the best teams, during the season, and build the anticipation for the tournament."

Meanwhile, a startup network called ESPN was itching to become a force in TV sports. Among the people it hired was Bill Fitts, who developed the groundbreaking *NFL Today*, the daddy of all pregame shows, for CBS.

Fitts also had worked at NBC, and his boss there, Chet Simmons, had become president of ESPN.

"When I got there in 1980," Fitts recalled, "Chet handed me two projects. One was the NFL draft, to make a show out of it. Then, the other was to do sort of the same thing they had experimented

San Francisco's Bill Russell getting carried off the court by fans after winning the championship game against LaSalle in 1955.
Rich Clarkson/Sports Illustrated/Getty Images

North Carolina Coach Frank McGuire with his 1957 NCAA champion Tar Heels. *John G. Zimmerman / Sports Illustrated/Getty Images*

MARCH 30, 1964   30 CENTS

Sports Illustrated

UCLA IS THE CHAMP

WALT HAZZARD DRIVES
THROUGH DUKE

This *Sports Illustrated* cover shows UCLA's Walt Hazzard in action against Duke during the 1964 NCAA national championship. *Rich Clarkson/Sports Illustrated/ Getty Images*

Kentucky coach Adolph Rupp tossing the ball for Thad Jaracz and Cliff Berger during a practice in 1965. *Lee Balterman/Sports Illustrated/Getty Images*

University of Kentucky, 1966 NCAA National Championship: (L–R) Kentucky's Thad Jaracz, Tommy Kron, Cliff Berger, and coach Adolph Rupp sit on the bench during the awards ceremony after losing the championship game against Texas Western. *Rich Clarkson/Sports Illustrated/Getty Images*

UCLA Coach John Wooden entering the court before a 1972 NCAA Finals game against Florida State. *George Long/ Sports Illustrated/Getty Images*

Indiana coach Bobby Knight on the sidelines during the 1976 NCAA finals game against Michigan. *Rich Clarkson/Sports Illustrated/Getty Images*

Michigan forward Chris Webber grabs a rebound during a 1993 Wolverines game against the Badgers. *Todd Rosenberg/Getty Images*

Old Dominion v. Butler: Old Dominion forward Kent Bazemore, right, tries to drive past Butler guard Shawn Vanzant in the second round of the thrilling 2011 NCAA men's basketball tournament. *Harry E. Walker/MCT via Getty Images*

Connecticut Huskies center Stefanie Dolson drives between Purdue Boilermakers center Chelsea Jones and Purdue Boilermakers guard Courtney Moses during the second round of the 2011 NCAA women's basketball tournament. *Richard Messina/Hartford Courant/MCT via Getty Images*

with at NBC on a show called *Grandstand*, with cut-ins to live events.

"He decided we would do it at the NCAA tournament. I reminded him that we had no contact to the (production) trucks at the games in those days. So Chet said, 'I guess that can be a problem.'"

Fitts laughed when he recalled his boss' response—and the challenge the assignment presented.

If nothing else, ESPN was willing to think outside the box, or in this case outside the lane.

"We started with doing only one game that the NCAA couldn't get anyone else to do early in the tournament," he said. "We did cut-ins on the fly, from one game to another. We found out what games were coming in on satellites, taping them but trying to get into the live action as soon as we could."

Early on, the anchor was Bob Ley, who remains with the network and is considered by many to be ESPN's best host and journalist. Ley did his best to keep track of all the action, and there was plenty of it going on throughout the country. When he'd get instructions in his earpiece, often very loud instructions, Ley would throw the studio broadcast to that game; CBS was not covering the early rounds yet.

"Some of it the first year was blind luck," Fitts said. "We were not going to that many homes yet, but we got good reaction. So we started to do more games, the early rounds that CBS was not handling, and our ability to cut in and know what was happening strengthened each year, the cut-ins to the other games maintained an interest in our broadcasts on a national basis, and our number of homes went up each year."

So much so that Fitts was "100 percent sure CBS picked up the whole (tournament) and the cut-ins" because of the success ESPN had been having with the early games.

"CBS realized they needed to do this to have a full product," Fitts said.

Another part of the full product would be televising the selection show rather than leaving coaches and players to find out via telephone whether they were in or out.

The entire approach, from the regular-season buildup to the selection show, from the combination of ESPN and its wraparound endeavors to CBS' handling the later, more meaningful—if not necessarily dramatic—contests, worked immediately. The 1982 championship game between North Carolina (with Michael Jordan) and Georgetown (Patrick Ewing) earned a 21.6 rating, which reportedly intimidated another network. In 1983, ABC moved the Academy Awards from its traditional Monday night spot to the previous evening, avoiding a matchup with the NCAA title game.

While CBS was prospering with the package, it didn't have nearly as much riding on the success of its college basketball presentations as ESPN did. Plain and simple, ESPN needed a calling card to hand to viewers, to legitimize the network as a place for fans to tune in and get turned on by sports.

The NCAA tourney provided it.

"The basketball games were not really hard for us because of all the sports we did," Fitts said. "It is probably one of the easier ones to cover."

In the very beginning, ESPN had only three cameras on the game, only one of which was handheld. Thus, viewers would only see close-ups at the foul line and under the basket at one end of the court.

Needless to say, ESPN quickly increased the number of cameras covering the games. It added some other technical improvements, particularly in terms of graphics, through the years. The amount of information ESPN provided during its early years of tournament coverage—as opposed to nowadays, when information is secondary to entertainment for the network—became impressive.

"Early on, when we had some of our own trucks, the complexity in the broadcasts was not having a lot of info to produce," Fitts said "We got a whole lot better in getting the info on all these teams—and there were some teams we had to dig a lot to get that info—and then making satellite feeds.

"We figured out how to adjust the cut-ins; you can't just keep bouncing around. You have to make sure you don't shortchange that game you jump from to the people who are wanting to see it."

Indeed, as Fitts pointed out, mastering the cut-ins was the foundation of ESPN's coverage. Among the problems CBS encountered as the tournament—and office pools that revolved around it—grew in size and popularity was that so many viewers identified with specific teams or games. Those fans didn't want any switching between contests.

Plus, the network's awkwardness in its cut-ins, such as going to games just as they hit a timeout or getting there too late for viewers to see a critical basket or blocked shot, drew the ire of critics and fans alike.

"A lot of things that hurt CBS in the beginning was because they couldn't figure out how to make the jumps," Fitts said. "They still play it very conservatively. Their switches mostly occur at halftimes and not cutting away from the main game action. It's a judgment thing.

"I think it is harder to do the whiparounds and cut-ins. Technology has gotten better, but the decisions have gotten harder. Technology was changing the demands (of viewers) to a point it was hard to keep up with. Take split screens. A lot of people can't watch split screens. Some people would want three or four multiple screens."

By 1991, the NCAA tournament, particularly the Final Four, had become one of the elite events of American sports. Wisely, CBS recognized that and agreed to increased rights fees by 160 percent, to $143 million per year for six years. All games would be carried live, as opposed to the dozen that had been in 1990, but not on a national basis.

Of special significance, CBS opted to preempt its lucrative afternoon soap operas lineup on the first Thursday and Friday of the event.

From there, the affiliation between CBS and March Madness grew on all fronts. Advertising the tournament during other CBS sports telecasts, not just regular-season hoops games, became common. The network signed deals with several conferences to televise their in-season and tourney games.

And the price for rights kept rising.

In 1996, CBS secured the tournament for $247 million per year, nearly a 73 percent jump. Eight years later, the fee soared by almost 84 percent, to $545 million per year.

"The tournament delivers terrific entertainment and each year, you can rely on stories that will develop," Neil Pilson, former CBS Sports president, told *USA Today*. "It comes with the great coaching personalities and the colleges themselves are legendary, so you never have to work extremely hard to sell Kentucky, Duke, North Carolina, or a UCLA."

But CBS worked hard at it, in marketing both the tournament and the sport itself. March Madness and CBS seemed to belong together.

And their latest deal, that $10.8 billion monstrosity that brought Turner Broadcasting into the fold, too, is further proof the Madness will continue.

"Sports fans got swept up into this," Fitts said. "My son, when we were doing this at ESPN in the early going, would stay up to watch all those games, even ones we replayed at three a.m. Some were even live from out west.

"It fits so well because you are having all of this action, a lot involving unseeded teams you never heard of, and last-second buzzer-beaters, trying to keep up with it, and the pools going—blowing my bracket apart—all the behind-the-scenes stuff. You can't throw out the gambling aspect, either.

"TV certainly encouraged all that with the talk about upsets, the brackets, the early-round matchups, and talking 64, 65, 68 different teams. It's Madness."

"My biggest asset at the time was my ability to teach defense and fundamentals," Woolpert said.

Woolpert attributed much of that knowledge to Jimmy Needles, his coach in college, who grounded him in "good, solid basketball."

"I was never a chess player as far as coaching was concerned," Woolpert said. "During a game I was aware of situations but did not have the facile ability to make quick adjustments as some coaches are able to do. I attempted to overcome this by having our players so well grounded in fundamental basketball that we could adjust to any situation. And we did that reasonably well."

One of the main reasons was Bill Russell, an agile, sky-walking center who was mostly responsible for a record 60-game unbeaten streak that stood until it was surpassed by UCLA in 1973. Russell was a shot-blocking marvel and brilliant rebounder who made an impact in just about every game. His success with the Dons offered only a hint of the impact he would make in the pros, where he used his shot-blocking technique to scientific perfection. Not only did Russell block shots, but he very often redirected those shots into a teammate's hands for a quick break downcourt and an easy basket.

In his very first varsity appearance in 1953, Russell blocked the first shot by California center Bob McKeen, drawing an awed response from Bears coach Newell.

"Now, where in the world did he come from?" Newell said in astonishment.

Woolpert put Russell on a different level than any other player he coached.

"He had fantastic pride and as much heart as anyone I've seen," Woolpert said in a 1970s interview. "He did not feel anyone could beat him and that washed off on the other players, the coaches, the rooters, and anyone associated with the team."

In high school, no one would have thought Russell would be a basketball player, and certainly not a star. At McClymonds High School in Oakland, California, he initially was so awkward and so little schooled in basketball fundamentals that when he came on the court he was subjected to jeers and catcalls. Supported by the faith of his coach, George Powles, Russell spent hours upon hours practicing the fundamentals. He chose USF because it was close to home and not too big: Russell didn't want to get swallowed up in the crowd.

"He had awesome physical talents but always wanted to improve," Woolpert said.

The same could be said for K. C. Jones, who complemented Russell with his great play at guard.

"He was one of the underrated players in all of basketball," Woolpert said of Jones. "He was a tremendous leader and scored only when needed. He was one of the finest pure passers it was ever my pleasure to see. Along with Russell, he was the heart and soul of the (Dons') team."

Jones would go on to play for the Boston Celtics with Russell and help establish one of pro basketball's greatest dynasties. The Celtics won 11 championships in 13 seasons. Just like in college, Russell was the star attraction for the Celts. Along with the titles, most notable were Russell's spectacular battles with Wilt Chamberlain in the paint.

Other key USF players from this era who complemented the "Big Two" perfectly: Stan Buchanan, Jerry Mullen, Hal Perry, Mike Farmer, Gene Brown, and Carl Boldt. The Dons boasted teams full of talent—and surprises. Every one of their players came from California, and each made a contribution to the team's success.

Buchanan started at the forward spot, opposite Mullen.

"He was 6-2 and did not have great physical skills, but he was one of the smartest and most effective players anyone could imagine," Woolpert said of Buchanan, whom he felt often flew under the radar against opposing teams.

"When we played at Oregon State, they didn't guard (Buchanan), figuring he couldn't hurt them," Woolpert said. "It was an insult. Then he hit two shots from the sidelines and they had to stop double-teaming Russell."

Mullen had played solely zone defense in high school. He developed his game while at San Francisco, and by the time he was a senior, he was second only to Russell as a defensive player.

Perry, a 5-foot-11 guard, was, in Woolpert's words, "the gadfly on our team."

"He was continually needling everybody on the ballclub, demanding better and better performances," Woolpert explained.

Farmer was a defensive terror who usually matched up against the opposition's top scorers. Brown, meanwhile, was a terror in practice sessions.

"(Brown) gave K.C. as much trouble as anybody he played against," Woolpert said.

Boldt had played a considerable amount of ball while serving in the military, and like Buchanan, was considered to be a "smart ballplayer" by his coach.

"This team had great defense at all times," Woolpert said. "Their pride in defense was amazing."

The Dons were orphans in a sense. They didn't have a permanent home court during the Russell era. They practiced and played their home games at either nearby Kezar Pavilion in Golden Gate Park or St. Ignatius High School in San Francisco. When big-name teams came to town, the Dons rented out the Cow Palace. It wasn't until 1958 that, fueled by the excitement of the Russell era, proud San Franciscans took up a collection to build a home-court gym for their team. The War Memorial Gym opened its doors for the first time in 1958.

The seeds for San Francisco's success were planted early in the 1954–55 season, when a 47–40 road loss at UCLA proved to be a turning point for the Dons.

"We went in there expecting to be beaten by 20 or 25 points," Jones said.

Instead it was a competitive game, and the Dons came away from it with a new awareness of their potential—and a new backcourt combination. Woolpert inserted Perry into a starting guard spot opposite Jones.

"From that time on, that group did not lose a basketball game," Woolpert said.

Another highlight of the Dons' 1954–55 season was their stunningly easy victory over a strong Wichita team in the All-College tournament in Oklahoma City.

"They were equal favorites, yet we ran away," Woolpert said.

Indeed, the Dons led, 53–26, in the second half before putting on the brakes. Woolpert pulled his starters and inserted the reserves—a move that elicited some complaints.

"The first string was upset because the reserves allowed too many points," Woolpert remembered.

Final score: San Francisco 94, Wichita 75.

At that point, the Dons really knew they had something special. They went on to win the national championship in 1955 with a

28–1 record, capping the season with a victory over La Salle and All-American Tom Gola. They repeated in 1956 with their unbeaten masterpiece.

The 1955–56 team had three holdovers from that championship squad: Russell, Jones, and Perry. The new faces included Farmer and Boldt.

"The distinguishing characteristic of this team was that it was more poised and more efficient than the 1955 team, a smart team as we moved into the heart of the season," Woolpert said.

By the time the 1956 playoffs rolled around in March, the Dons had yet to lose a game. However, they lost a key player when Jones was declared ineligible by the NCAA to play in the postseason. The basis of the NCAA ruling: Jones had already used up his eligibility, thanks to a brief appearance in his sophomore year in 1953 before sitting out the rest of the season with an appendicitis attack.

"His own conference, the California Basketball Association, wrote the game off the books and voted to allow Jones a fifth varsity season," *Sports Illustrated* reported. "Not so the NCAA."

Woolpert appealed the NCAA's ruling but was turned down.

"We felt that since he had played for only one minute of his sophomore season during which he burst an appendix and had been out for the remainder of the season that he should be allowed to play (in the playoffs)."

Later events proved this ruling was not totally disastrous. Brown substituted artfully for Jones as a starter in the playoffs.

"Gene played swing man all season long and he never did anything but contribute (positive) situations for us," Woolpert said.

If the 1955–56 Dons had a weakness, it was that they tended to let Russell handle most of the rebounding.

"Consequently, we were putting too much of a burden on him, but it was being done subconsciously," Woolpert said.

The Dons had a desire to prove the previous season's championship was not a fluke. And this encore season had a few highlight games that defined the Dons.

One of them was a victory in the Chicago Invitational over a powerful Marquette team that had won 22 straight games.

"It was a tough basketball game, but we didn't appear to be playing our normal game," Woolpert said in an interview with Earl Luebker of the *Tacoma News Tribune*.

There was a reason for that. Woolpert wasn't aware of what had happened the day before. The entire San Francisco basketball team had gone on an exhausting excursion, touring a Chicago museum. "They were gone for four and a half hours, up and down stairs and everything that goes with touring an outstanding museum," Woolpert said. "It was understandable why they were a little below par in their play."

Even so, the Dons won by nine points, tied for their smallest margin of victory during the entire 1955–56 season.

Another nine-point victory brought attention to the Dons, this time over a solid California team coached by Newell, Woolpert's onetime teammate. The Dons coach called it "an outstanding highlight of the season."

The game was played at Berkeley, a basketball hotbed at the time. (Newell himself would coach the Bears to a national championship in 1959.)

As it was, the Dons were gunning for their 40th straight triumph, which would break the record for consecutive victories.

"We knew it was going to be tough," said Woolpert, whose team fell behind by 10 points early in the game.

"I called a timeout and went into a full-court press and finally managed a lead," continued Woolpert, remembering his team was leading by "four or five points early in the second half" when Newell called a timeout.

"His team held the ball for nine straight minutes," Woolpert said. "We held the lead and made no attempt to go after the ball. People were sitting on the floor. It wasn't one of the more enjoyable games to watch. In any event, we did win the game by nine points, 33–24."

In the NCAA tournament, Brown did a pretty good imitation of Jones with 69 points in four games, actually outscoring Russell in an opening-round, 72–61 win over UCLA. Overall, Russell was at his best throughout the playoffs with 91 points.

San Francisco's 83–71 victory over Iowa in the championship game was not as easy as the 12-point margin indicated. The Dons suffered breakdowns on defense early in the game, and Iowa couldn't miss the basket.

The Hawkeyes grabbed an 11-point lead, 15-4, at the start of the game. Woolpert called a timeout and inserted Warren Baxter, a 5-foot-8 guard who had considerable playing experience as a substitute.

"When Warren moved in, we moved Brown to defensive forward, and we ended up by not only overcoming Iowa's lead but going into a substantial lead of our own," Woolpert said.

As usual, Russell took care of most of the scoring chores. The Dons surged to a 13-point lead at 50–37 before the second half was five minutes old. It was enough to hold off a late comeback by Iowa.

With about three minutes left, the Dons' reserves were having a tough time putting the ball in play because of a stiff Iowa defense.

"I had benched our starters and not only were we having trouble getting the ball into play, the ball was being taken away from us and Iowa was scoring," Woolpert recalled. "I had to reinsert our starters to ensure the victory."

With Russell leading the way with 26 points, the Dons' first string finished with a flourish.

"During the playoffs there was speculation that we would be missing K. C. Jones, his leadership and his great floor play," Woolpert said.

As it turned out, the Dons didn't miss Jones at all.

"Brown was truly outstanding," Woolpert said, "and he had a steady running mate in Perry."

Brown scored 16 points and Perry had 14.

Upon their return home, the Dons were treated to a big reception that included a ticker-tape parade.

"The support was considerably greater than the previous year," Woolpert said. "The acceptance of the team was heartwarming."

So was a gift from Stan Watts, then coach of the Brigham Young basketball team. Following the championship game, Watts handed his present to Woolpert in a brown paper sack: a fifth of bourbon.

"For a gentleman as abstentious as Mr. Watts to give me a bottle of bourbon was a highlight of that victory," Woolpert said.

Actually, Woolpert didn't need any extra stimulants to celebrate. He was already high enough.

"It is something that has to be experienced to be believed," Woolpert said of his perfect championship season.

Perfect Teams

No Adolph Rupp. No Mike Krzyzewski. No Dean Smith.

In fact, many of college basketball's most illustrious Division I coaches have failed to go through a season from start to finish without a loss.

The list of those who have made it is an exclusive club. Only four coaches in college basketball history can boast of perfect seasons, with UCLA's John Wooden topping the list with four.

The others: San Francisco's Phil Woolpert, North Carolina's Frank McGuire, and Indiana's Bobby Knight.

Rupp's 1953–54 Kentucky team actually went 25–0, but the Wildcats coach turned down the NCAA's tournament invitation after his three top players were ruled ineligible in the wake of a gambling scandal.

In 1972–73, North Carolina State streaked to a 27–0 record in the regular season, but the Wolfpack was shut out of the playoffs because of recruiting violations.

Also, in 1939–40, Seton Hall went 19–0 but was not invited to play in a limited tournament field. Same for the 1943–44 Army team, which fashioned a 15–0 mark.

Over a 20-year period beginning with the San Francisco Dons in 1956 and ending with the Indiana Hoosiers in 1976, men's college basketball produced seven unbeaten national champions. By 2011, the sport was still looking for number eight.

Rundowns of the "Magnificent Seven":

- San Francisco Dons (29–0), 1955–56. The '56 title was the second straight for Woolpert's Dons. San Francisco managed to complete its perfect season without All-America guard K. C. Jones, who was ruled ineligible for the '56 NCAA tournament. The Dons did have Bill Russell, though.
- North Carolina (32–0), 1956–57. After 18 years without an undefeated national champion, the playoffs produced one in two consecutive years when the Tar Heels won it all in '57. Just about all of McGuire's players had been recruited from the New York area, giving rise to the expression, the "Underground Railroad." Leading the way was Lennie Rosenbluth and his magnificent scoring touch.

(continued)

Perfect Teams *(Continued)*

- UCLA (30–0), 1963–64. This undefeated title season marked the start of an incredible run by the Bruins under Wooden, the "Wizard of Westwood." This was Wooden's smallest championship team, featuring Walt Hazzard, named the national college player of the year that season, and the ubiquitous Gail Goodrich, a playoff scoring machine, in the backcourt.
- UCLA (30–0), 1966–67. Led by Lew Alcindor (later known as Kareem Abdul-Jabbar), the Bruins rode roughshod over opponents, including a 79–64 win over Dayton in the tournament final. Alcindor's impact on the college game was unmistakable. Following the '67 finals, the sport's rules committee voted to ban the dunk shot, which had been the star 7-footer's major weapon.
- UCLA (30–0), 1971–72. This time Bill Walton, another All-American center, led the way for the powerful Bruins. After cleaning up rebounds, the irrepressible redhead was the trigger man on the fast break. Even though the Bruins struggled to beat Florida State in the championship game, during the season they whipped opponents by an incredible average margin of 32 points.
- UCLA (30–0), 1972–73. The Bruins finished in high style with a stunning performance by Walton, who had 44 points and 13 rebounds against Memphis State in an 87–66 victory in the final. The Tigers had no answer for Walton, who made a remarkable 21 of 22 shots. It marked the first—and only—time a national champion posted two straight perfect seasons.
- Indiana (32–0), 1975–76. With 32 victories, the Hoosiers matched North Carolina's record for most wins in an unbeaten season. Indiana closed out its year with an 86–68 championship win over Michigan. Led by Quinn Buckner, Scott May, and Kent Benson, the perfect Hoosiers ran over and around just about all of their opponents. "Take a look at these kids, because you're never going to see the likes of them again," Knight told the audience at Indiana University on Senior Day in March 1976.

He was absolutely right: the Hoosiers were simply perfect, a feat no team since has managed.

8.

Grand Slam Kids

It was late at night when the train pulled into the station. Nat Holman and his City College of New York (CCNY) basketball team, in the midst of the grinding 1950–51 season, were happy to be back in New York. Exhilarated and exhausted after a victory over Temple in Philadelphia, they were ready for some shut-eye.

As the team stepped off the train, Holman immediately knew something was wrong. A grim-looking welcoming committee stood on the platform.

In their hands, police detectives held arrest warrants for some of Holman's players.

The charges? Point-shaving.

Three of his players were taken "downtown" to the station house for questioning: Ed Roman, Ed Warner, and Al Roth.

Roman, Warner, and Roth were questioned all night. Exhausted from their trip to Philadelphia and the hot lights of the interview room, the trio finally broke down and confessed they had each received $1,500 for "fixing" three games at Madison Square Garden during the 1949–50 season.

The players were so good they had been able to control the games so the final score favored gamblers. In return for their illegal activity, they had received cash rewards.

A scandal erupted.

In just one year, the City College of New York basketball team had gone from fabulous to frauds.

In 1950, CCNY had pulled off the unique feat of winning both the NIT and NCAA tournaments. Unlike today, both tournaments then shared equal billing as crowning a national champion, the NIT pre-dating the NCAAs by one year. The double victories, both over Bradley, earned the Beavers the nickname "Grand Slam Kids."

Now it was the 1950–51 season. The investigation of point-shaving continued. Surprise after surprise followed, and more

"Grand Slam Kids" were implicated. Norman Mager, Floyd Lane, Irwin Dambrot, and Herb Cohen admitted to taking bribes from gamblers.

The basketball world was shocked. So was the unsuspecting Holman. Though only college kids, his players were the personification of modern-day rock stars. They challenged the New York Yankees and Brooklyn Dodgers for public relations supremacy in New York City. At the time, Holman himself was a high-profile sportsman, as popular as any of the famed national sports figures in America.

Holman had been well respected and idolized in college basketball circles for many years. He drove his players unmercifully while establishing the "City Game," a highly disciplined style of play built on guile, finesse, and smart passing.

Dambrot described the "City Game" as "constant ball movement, screens, backdoors, pick-and-rolls. We got a lot of easy shots."

Holman's teams were usually all homegrown. Their talent was a sublime mixture of black and white, unlike most all-white basketball teams at major colleges around the country at the time.

There was plenty of talent to go around in New York, and such schools as CCNY, Fordham, Long Island University, Manhattan, New York University (NYU), St. John's, and Brooklyn College took advantage of the rich local pool. Players had their choices of top college programs, all within a subway stop. They didn't have to leave the city to play top-flight basketball, as the case would be in later years.

With CCNY playing a major role, college basketball was king in New York. The NBA was just starting to get a foothold and was many years away from becoming a national passion. Attractive college doubleheaders were played before sellout crowds at Madison Square Garden, featuring local powers against big-name teams from around the country. The Garden was the mecca of college basketball.

The CCNY saga started with Holman, who had been coaching basketball at the college since 1919. He grew up on the Lower East Side in New York and played basketball with a ferocious intensity. He learned his early lessons on the streets and schoolyards of New York. Somehow, life didn't seem natural without a basketball in his hands.

An all-star athlete at NYU, Holman soon made the jump to professional ball with the Germantown (Pennsylvania) team. From 1920–27, Holman played for the Original Celtics, the most celebrated barnstorming team of the era. At the same time, he served as the CCNY coach.

Not much older than his college players, Holman was a tough competitor, unafraid to dive into practice sessions and show his boys how things were done. During one of these practices, a scout for an opposing team showed up to watch the Beavers work. He was duly impressed with Holman, who, in fact, could very well have been mistaken for any of his players.

The scout alerted his team that the Beavers were going to be tough because "they have the greatest forward I've ever seen on a college team."

Due to his frantic schedule, Holman had little time for anything but basketball.

"I was one of the few men able to play pro basketball and coach a college team at the same time," Holman remembered.

His experience with the Celtics was eye-opening, and included an exhausting travel schedule and brutal opponents.

"If the teams beat the Celtics in those days, it would make the season for them," said Holman, remembering how opponents went to great (and illegal) lengths to take down the Celts.

"There were basketball courts with wooden or wire fences about as high as your hips," he continued. "And when you came down and took your shot and were jammed into those things, you saw blue. Many a time, really, I went to the foul line with tears in my eyes. There was a lot of contact in those days."

While scrambling around in tiny gymnasiums—even dance halls filled with smoke and spiked with beer—the Celtics remained triumphant. Holman was toughened by the experience and translated it to the way he coached the CCNY team.

"It was brutal," Holman recalled of his basketball-playing days. "You had to be quick on your feet and fast with your fists."

At least Holman was paid well for his troubles. His salary of $1,500 a month with the Celtics was reputed to be the highest in the world for a basketball player.

Despite dividing his time between pro ball and the college game, Holman continued to turn out some stunning CCNY teams.

During one three-year period in the 1920s, the Beavers posted a 36–4 record. Another time, during a three-year period in the '30s, CCNY went 43–3.

Also during the 1930s, Holman's pro playing career was winding down. He had done it all, playing for 14 pro teams in 17 years. That included the Chicago Bruins of the old American Basketball League, the forerunner of the NBA.

Following his retirement from the pros in 1933, Holman focused his attention full-time on the CCNY basketball team. Coaches in New York, and across the country, admired Holman's success, which continued through the '40s.

The 1949–50 Beavers team topped them all. But while it was Holman's most successful season—one never equaled by another coach or team—eventually it proved to be his most troubling.

When training camp opened for the 1949–50 season at CCNY's concrete campus in upper Manhattan, Holman had to be pleased with his player personnel. Dambrot, a 6-foot-4 forward, and Mager, a 6-foot-4 scoring threat off the bench, returned from a team that had gone 17–8 the previous season. In addition, the Beavers were flush with a solid group of sophomores—the 6-foot-2 Roth, the 6-foot-4 Lane, the 6-foot-3 Warner, the 6-foot-6 Roman, and the 5-foot-11 Cohen—all of whom were products of the gritty New York playgrounds.

Roman would win the starting job at center, Roth and Lane were guards, and Warner and Dambrot played forward. Among the top seven players, Cohen and Mager were sparkplugs off the bench. These players, among the cream of the crop in New York, had been recruited by Holman's assistant, Harold Sand, who had outmaneuvered all other top basketball recruiters in New York to land these young gems.

The other reserves included Mike Wittlin, Ronald Nadell, and Joe Galiber.

During the season the Beavers lost five games, quite possibly one or more the result of the deal the players had made with game fixers.

Gamblers had been working such deals, it seemed, since the beginning of time. And basketball wasn't the only sport smudged by them.

In 1920, eight players of the Chicago White Sox were convicted of throwing the 1919 World Series to the Cincinnati Reds in the most notorious case of cheating in baseball history. Many of the White Sox players, including the great "Shoeless Joe" Jackson, a surefire Hall of Famer, were promised money for losing the Series. But most of the money ended up in the gamblers' pockets.

By the 1940s, gamblers had added a new twist to an old game: the point spread. Now the final score—or spread between the teams—was more important than just winning or losing.

A team could win a game, but a gambler could still lose a bet unless the point spread fit within a certain number. Thus, gamblers dangled large amounts of money in front of teams' star players—more than many had seen in their lifetime—in an attempt to get them to control the point spread.

The CCNY kids probably heard a pitch like this from the gamblers:

You don't have to lose, just make sure that you win by less than eight points.

And this:

All you have to do is miss a few baskets, throw a bad pass, don't try too hard for a rebound. And don't stink up the joint!

However the gamblers had approached the seven CCNY players, it was likely Roman and Warner were among the first sought out. They were the Beavers' two top offensive players and could more easily control the ebb and flow of a game.

The 1950–51 CCNY basketball guide had noted of Roman: "Ed can hook with either hand or move out and display one of the best one-handed set shots in basketball."

The versatile center usually played under the basket, scoring many of his points inside. But he also was comfortable shooting from the outside. Holman had no problem switching Roman and Warner. When Warner moved under the basket, Roman moved out and scored just as easily from there with his long-range shot. They were known as "Mr. Inside" and "Mr. Outside," nicknames loosely borrowed from Army's football greats Glenn Davis and Doc Blanchard.

While only 6-foot-3, Warner successfully challenged pivotmen many inches taller.

"He has wonderful timing and a deceptive fluid body motion that enables him to feint defensive men out of position," the CCNY guide said.

Much was made of Warner's oversized hands that helped him control the ball. And of his ability to outjump players many inches taller, enabling him to play center as well as forward. Opponents sometimes double- and triple-teamed him, to no avail. Frank Mc-Guire, then the coach at St. John's, noted that Warner had "hands like an octopus—fine, educated hands."

On defense, Layne was the stopper for the Beavers.

"Floyd is a ballhawk and one of the best defensive players in the country," the CCNY guide said. "A long, wiry fellow with stooped shoulders, Floyd is in constant motion on the court with his arms churning windmill fashion. He steals the ball and keeps the heat on the opposition."

Roman, Warner, and Layne were starting for the first time with the varsity as the Beavers opened the 1949–50 season with five straight victories: a 46-point blowout of Queens, a 32-point win over Lafayette, a 14-point win over SMU, a 54-point trouncing of Kings Point, and a 27-point win over Brooklyn.

The rest of the season wasn't as easy. After putting together a seven-game winning streak at one point, the Beavers dropped three games during a five-game stretch, including an 83–74 loss to Syracuse.

"It looked like another case of sophomores playing over their heads and blowing up when the pressure was applied," noted the CCNY basketball guide.

The Beavers wound up with a 17–5 record. But victories over St. John's, Fordham, Manhattan, and NYU earned them the unofficial title of "Subway Conference" champions, prompting the NIT to extend CCNY an invitation to play in its prestigious tournament.

In setting up the tournament schedule, the NIT committee didn't do the Beavers any favors: CCNY opened with a game against San Francisco, the defending NIT champion. Awaiting the winner was Kentucky, the defending NCAA champion.

The Beavers, who had started out the season on such a high note as super sophomores, were now decided underdogs in postseason play.

"It looked like a short, quick tournament for City College," the CCNY basketball guide said.

Who would have expected what happened next?

How about a stunning 65–46 blowout of San Francisco in the opening round of the tournament at Madison Square Garden?

Warner led CCNY scoring with 26 points.

"The kids had grown up," Holman said.

Up next, Kentucky, another heavy favorite.

Adolph Rupp's Wildcats boasted a group of NBA-caliber players, including feared 7-footer Bill Spivey. Rupp was in love with this team, which he called quite possibly the best he had ever coached.

Holman and his players were fully aware of the Wildcats' NBA-caliber talent—and Rupp's racism. The Kentucky players followed their coach's lead by refusing to shake hands with CCNY's black and Jewish players before the game.

It was a fired-up group of CCNY players that took their positions on the court for the opening tip-off.

In what seemed like a statement to the Kentucky coach, the Beavers started three black players. One of them was a surprise addition to the lineup—6-foot-7 reserve Leroy Watkins, who started in place of the 6-foot-6 Roman, the Beavers' top scorer.

Not much was lost in transition.

"Leroy was a great jumper," Layne said. "He controlled the tip. I got the ball and gave it to Ed Warner, who went right down the court and scored, and we were off and running."

Perhaps Rupp couldn't help but notice that all three of CCNY's black players touched the ball on this particular opening sequence.

CCNY jumped to a 13–1 lead at the 4:30 mark. At 11:25, it was 28–9. Then 45–20 at the half.

The proud Kentucky team never had a chance. The Beavers bounced the Wildcats out of the tourney, 89–50—the worst defeat for a Rupp-coached team. Ever.

Chants of "allagaroo garoo gara," the Beavers' patented cheer, echoed throughout Madison Square Garden as CCNY thoroughly embarrassed the Wildcats.

Writing for the *New York Herald Tribune*, Everett Morris said a sellout crowd of more than 18,000 at the Garden yelled itself into hysterical acclaim for CCNY. It was "a team effort of such surpassing excellence that it defies description by normal adjectives."

The state of Kentucky was stunned and heartbroken.

Kentuckians showed how seriously they took their basketball when the state legislature ordered the flag be flown half-staff at the capitol building following the defeat.

The Beavers, meanwhile, celebrated by attending a Broadway show.

Noted Layne: "We were sky-high for Kentucky. We were above the rim all night."

The red-hot Beavers then swept past Duquesne, 62–52, to gain a berth in the NIT finals against Bradley. Another game, another underdog role for the Beavers, who still were trying to make believers of everyone despite their current hot streak.

The Braves were led by Gene Melchiorre and Paul Unruh, two of the country's best players, and were ranked No. 1 in the nation with a 29–3 record.

When the Braves jumped to a 29–18 lead in the first half, it looked like time was finally running out on CCNY. The Beavers were missing layups and foul shots. The usually energy-filled, sold-out Saturday night Garden crowd had little to cheer.

But hold on—not so fast.

Soon enough, CCNY cut into the Bradley lead. By the half, CCNY only trailed by three points, then outscored the Missouri Valley Conference champions by 11 in the second half.

The Braves had a hard time—as Kentucky had—keeping up with CCNY's brilliant fast-break offense.

With their fans roaring in support, the Beavers rushed to a 69–61 victory for the NIT championship. The players were carried off the court on the shoulders of their happy fans, as was Holman.

Next stop for the Beavers: the NCAA playoffs.

The NCAA committee had invited the Beavers to participate in its tournament after watching CCNY's demolition of the NIT field. Holman, who had climbed out of a sickbed with 103-degree fever to coach the NIT title game, had only five days to rest, and recuperate, before opening the NCAA tournament against Ohio State.

The Buckeyes, led by Dick Schnittker, had won the Big Ten championship and gave CCNY problems right away. Their zone defense bottled up Roman and Warner as the teams played to a 40–40 halftime tie. The Buckeyes took the lead in the second half as they continued to hold CCNY's top two scorers at bay.

They should have also kept their eyes on Layne and Mager, who suddenly started hitting from the outside. CCNY held on for a one-point victory.

Two nights later, CCNY beat North Carolina State, 78–73, to set up a compelling rematch with Bradley for the NCAA championship.

Arriving in New York following wins over Kansas, UCLA, and Baylor in the Western Regional, Braves coach Forddy Anderson boldly predicted victory for his team in the NCAA finals. No matter that the Braves were all but exhausted after playing an extra game to get to the championship contest. Bradley had been tied with Kansas in the NCAA's District 5, and a playoff game was necessary to decide the final tournament berth. Bradley survived a challenge from a strong Kansas team, 59–57, for the last NCAA berth. CCNY, meanwhile, only had to play two playoff games to get to the NCAA finals.

"Everything pointed to a thriller," wrote Louis Effrat in the *New York Times*, "and that is precisely what developed."

The game was tied six times in the first half, which ended with CCNY in front, 39–32. The Beavers had solved the Braves' tight zone defense. Roman led the way for CCNY with 12 points in the first 12 minutes. It was "one of the best nights of outside shooting seen that year," noted the CCNY basketball guide.

Other than Mager's collision with Bradley's Aaron Preece, which required five stitches in his forehead, the first half was going in the right direction for CCNY.

The second half was a little different. After falling behind by 11 points midway through the period, Bradley battled back.

Reported the *New York Times*:

"It looked like a romp, but the lads from Peoria—though six of them had to proceed cautiously because of four fouls against each—got their second wind, switched to a man-to-man defense, capitalized on an all-court press, picked misdirected passes out of the air and suddenly it was a contest all over again."

Not helping matters any for CCNY was the loss of Roman, who fouled out with nine minutes left. The Braves steadily cut into CCNY's lead but still trailed by five points, 66–61, with 57 seconds left.

"Ordinarily, a 66–61 advantage at this stage is monumental," the *New York Times* said. "But the Lavender was not up against an ordinary outfit, one that might succumb without a struggle, and what happened in the last minute almost defies description."

Joe Stowell hit a foul shot for Bradley.

Then Melchiorre, the smallest player on the court, intercepted a pass and drove in for two points. Another misdirected CCNY pass fell into Melchiorre's hands, and the Bradley guard went in and scored again.

In a matter of 20 seconds, Bradley had scored five straight points and pulled within one of CCNY, 69–68.

Then—incredibly—with 10 seconds left another wild pass by CCNY provided another chance for Melchiorre to drive for a basket.

"Melchiorre, digging toward the basket, attempted to go all the way," Effrat wrote. "However, as Gene tried to get his shot off from the key hole, Dambrot made the game's most vital 'save.'"

The players collided. Defensive or offensive foul? There was no whistle.

Remembered Unruh:

"I had fouled out and watched the whole thing from the bench. Melchiorre drove toward the middle and the entire CCNY team converged on him, like a hatchet job. The films showed him being ripped apart. We all felt he was fouled. And, of course, if the foul would have been called, Melchiorre probably would have made the free throws and there would have been a different champion.

"The irony of the thing is that the official who should have called a foul, Ron Gibbs, was from Springfield, Illinois, one of our home-state boys. We wondered how a local boy could let that happen."

The *New York Times* never mentioned the non-call in its game story. Neither did the CCNY basketball guide one year later.

"City took the ball out, but a wild pass gave Bradley possession," the guide said. "Melchiorre got the ball again and drove in, but an alert Dambrot blocked the shot and passed the length of the court to Mager."

Mager converted a layup to seal CCNY's 71–68 victory.

Champions again!

In winning the two titles, CCNY had beaten teams ranked Nos. 1, 2, 4, 5, 6, and 9 in the Associated Press poll.

Considering the level of competition and the closeness of the scores, not to mention the high stakes, it was unlikely any of the CCNY players had caved into gamblers' demands for any of the tournament games. It had been reported that gamblers approached CCNY players to fix games in the tournaments but had been rejected.

"They were a Cinderella team," Unruh said of the Beavers. "We had reached our peak and tried to hang on. They came on like a whirlwind. They had a mediocre season, but came on hot as a firecracker at the end. It's clear that when we played CCNY, they just played excellent ball. They jelled and we caught them at the wrong time."

CCNY's double victory set off celebrations all over New York, most notably at the school's uptown campus, where some 4,500 students turned out to toast the new basketball kings. Downtown, some 2,000 students from the business school marched up Fifth Avenue and tied up traffic for hours in Times Square.

"The whole school turned out," Roth said. "You couldn't walk through the crowds. We were toasts of the town."

One year later, the Beavers crashed from those heights when the point-shaving scandal broke. And they weren't the only ones involved.

Rupp had once boasted that gamblers "couldn't touch my boys with a 10-foot pole." He was soon saddened to know that they could.

Kentucky and Bradley, two of the nation's powers, were soon implicated in a widespread gambling ring that involved some 30 players from a half-dozen schools around the country.

CCNY's players might have been hit the hardest. Not only were potential NBA careers completely ruined, but the Beavers' elite basketball program was basically destroyed. The sport was de-emphasized at the school, and college basketball suffered a severe blow to its image nationally.

Big-city arenas, such as New York's Madison Square Garden, suffered in the wake of the scandal. The Garden, thought by many to be a hothouse for festering the gambling element, wore a tarnished image among the college basketball set. Fan support dwindled, and so did teams willing to compete at the world-famous arena. New York college basketball had clearly lost its luster, falling behind big-time programs in other parts of the country.

The NCAA replaced the NIT as the country's preeminent national basketball tournament, although the NIT did continue to hold postseason tournaments of its own in Madison Square Garden. In 1985, the NIT added a preseason tourney known as the Preseason NIT, which was later renamed the NIT Season Tip-Off. Both tournaments were operated by the Metropolitan Intercollegiate Basketball Association (MIBA) up until 2005, when they were purchased by the NCAA.

Holman, meanwhile, continued on his own path. In the midst of public outcry, he was suspended by the Board of Education of New York City on November 18, 1952, from his post as basketball coach and associate professor for "conduct unbecoming a teacher." The 21-man board suspended Holman for not reporting cash offers made to players on his team. He fought for vindication—and won. He was reinstated in September 1954 after missing nearly two years.

A goodwill ambassador for basketball, Holman, who had helped establish the game in Israel, remained the coach at CCNY until his retirement in 1960. His record in 37 years with the Beavers: 421–190.

Despite everything he went through, it's easy to see which team he favored the most.

"The team that won the double championship should be given credit as the best team I ever coached," Holman said. "Those fellows went into tournament play not ranked too highly. But they went in, gave all they had and did what they had to do."

Naturally, there were consequences for the players' illegal actions. Six of them received suspended sentences after pleading guilty to misdemeanor conspiracy charges. Warner, meanwhile, served six months in jail.

Many managed to turn their lives around: Warner as a counselor for youth recreation programs in New York, Dambrot as a dentist, Layne as a basketball coach at CCNY, Roman as a psychologist helping emotionally disturbed children, and Roth as an insurance executive.

Reflecting on his double-championship team, Holman noted, "That was my most satisfying season, no doubt."

But one with a bittersweet ending.

9.

Black and White

Harry Flournoy had attended many pregame meetings in his years with the Texas Western basketball team. This one was different.

It was 1966 and Texas Western (now the University of Texas at El Paso, or UTEP) faced a gigantic challenge. The Miners' opponent: Kentucky and its legendary coach, Adolph Rupp. The stakes: the national basketball championship.

It was right after the pregame meal, around 3:30 or 4:00 in the afternoon. Miners coach Don Haskins called his black players together for a meeting—only his black players.

Coach Haskins had just returned from a press conference and stood there for a second, composing his thoughts.

What followed might have been one of the greatest motivational talks in sports history. Also one of the shortest.

"Listen." He paused.

"Coach Rupp just said in his press conference there was no way that five African Americans could defeat his five white boys."

The coach stood there for a second to let the message sink in.

"I'm just going to play you guys," Haskins told the seven African American players on his team. "I'm not telling anybody else. The other players do not know. You can't say anything."

Haskins reiterated, his voice strong and clear: "I'm going to start you, and I'm going to play only the African Americans. It's up to you."

He turned and walked out of the room.

The black players were stunned.

For the record: it would be the first time in the NCAA Division I tournament that a basketball team started five black players in the championship game.

Five black players against Kentucky's five whites, another first. "Rupp's Runts," one of Rupp's favorite teams, were relatively small in size but large on talent. They were also white, from star performers to the last bench-sitter, and ranked No. 1 in the country.

"So we knew what was going to happen," said Flournoy, one of the Miners' tri-captains along with Orsten Artis and Jerry Armstrong. "The white players didn't."

Teammate David Lattin recalled, "It was a very powerful message. And I'm telling you, he didn't say anything else about it at halftime and didn't say anything during timeouts. He just said, 'You guys know what to do. Do what you do.'"

Of course, the players couldn't fully appreciate the significance of the moment, other than the fact it was a battle for the national championship. Only time would put the event in proper iconic perspective as a game for the ages. For now, it was just a high-stakes, emotional game against a hated opponent. Or at least, a hated opponent following Rupp's proclamation.

Rupp's racist beliefs were there for all to see, in black and white. The Kentucky coach simply refused to bring black players to bluegrass country, believing them inferior, and didn't mind who knew how he felt.

Black basketball players had already made their presence felt in other areas of America. Bill Russell had led the University of San Francisco to two national titles; Wilt Chamberlain had starred at Kansas, Oscar Robertson at the University of Cincinnati.

In 1962, Cincinnati won the national championship with four blacks in the starting lineup; in 1963, Loyola University Chicago won the title, also with four blacks starting.

But there had never been a team that started five blacks in the NCAA Division I finals. And for a team to play only African Americans in the same game was another first.

For many years, Rupp's racism reflected the bigoted attitudes of schools in the Deep South—most notably in the Southeastern Conference, Atlantic Coast Conference, and Southwest Conference. This, despite a Supreme Court ruling long in effect that segregation in public schools was unconstitutional.

Only four years earlier, in 1962, Mississippi State, the Southeastern Conference champions, refused an invitation to play in the NCAA tournament. The Bulldogs' school policy would not allow them to play against integrated teams.

Bulldogs coach Babe McCarthy finally broke the mold. The following year, he took a courageous stand against Mississippi's lawmakers. Defying an edict by the state's legislature, he sneaked his team out of town to play in an NCAA tournament game. Even though the Bulldogs lost to Loyola University Chicago in the Mideast Regional, McCarthy made a statement against racism.

And now Haskins' Texas Western team would be making another powerful statement against racism.

Haskins, in his sixth year of coaching, practically went to the ends of the earth to recruit his team. His budget was small, meaning he wouldn't be flying first-class any time soon. Or flying at all on recruiting missions.

Thus, his 2,000-mile car trip to Gary, Indiana. For Flournoy, Texas Western—located in a small border town some 2,000 miles from Indiana—was at first far off his radar screen.

"I had never heard of Texas Western College or coach Don Haskins coming out of high school," Flournoy said.

How did he manage to wind up there? One word: mom.

One day Flournoy was walking home from school on his lunch hour when a car pulled up alongside him.

"There were two white guys in it," Flournoy said. "You have to understand, I went to a school that was a majority white high school, and we were having a lot of racial tension at that time."

One of the men in the car introduced himself as Coach Haskins.

"He asks me to get in the car and he would take me home," Flournoy continued. "Well, I'm not getting in that car. No way I'm getting in that car."

Flournoy turned and hightailed it toward his house, taking a shortcut.

When he arrived, a familiar-looking car was sitting in front of the house. Flournoy walked in and found his mother having a cozy chat with Haskins and his assistant.

Coach Haskins was outlining his plans for the Texas Western basketball team, and how Flournoy would fit in.

"I really wasn't listening to him because even though I didn't have a lot of schools after me, that wasn't one of the places that I would want to go," Flournoy said.

His mother saw it differently.

"She liked Haskins—as a matter of fact, she liked him so much that she gave him my pie that I was going to have for dessert after I ate my lunch," Flournoy recalled. "Now I really don't like him, eating the last bit of my pie. And he's talking about how he's a disciplinarian and that really perked my mother's interest because that's what she was."

Flournoy's mother, Amy, overruled any preferences for college her son might have had. Next stop for Flournoy: El Paso, Texas, home of the Texas Western Miners. What sealed the deal for her was Haskins' promise to call her if her son had any academic problems.

It didn't matter to her that Flournoy would be missing an important track meet to go to Texas, even though he was the No. 2 half-miler in the state of Indiana.

"She made me quit the track team," a miserable Flournoy remembered.

Lattin's was an entirely different story. A star at Worthing High School in Houston, he had received hundreds of scholarship offers, but none from the Deep South.

Guy Lewis, the University of Houston basketball coach, had developed a close friendship with Lattin when he was in high school. Lewis wanted Lattin but was thwarted in his efforts to recruit him.

"I would have gone to the U of H if they were ready to recruit African Americans, but they weren't," Lattin said.

Lewis told Lattin to hang in there, maybe spend a year at a junior college. Times were changing at the school.

"I didn't want to wait," Lattin said.

Lattin presented a proposition to Haskins: If he would recruit four of his friends from the high school football team, he would consider going to El Paso. Otherwise, his friends didn't have a chance to go to college. It was a no-go with Haskins, but Tennessee State said OK.

Lattin's time at Tennessee State was short.

"I wasn't very happy," Lattin recalled. "I left at the end of the first quarter and came home. I started getting recruited again."

Haskins again was one of the interested coaches. Helping him recruit Lattin was Jim "Bad News" Barnes, one of the legendary players at Texas Western who had helped the Miners make the NCAA tournament in 1963 and 1964.

"I met 'Bad News' Barnes and was very impressed with him," Lattin said. "He challenged me to come back there and break all his records. That was the main reason I went to Texas El Paso."

Reporting for practice at Texas Western, Lattin soon had a nickname, courtesy of the sports information department.

"I was 'Big D' when I was in high school and the PR director named me 'Big Daddy,'" Lattin said. "We had 'Bad News Barnes' before me, so (the PR director) was always nicknaming somebody."

"Big Daddy" fit Lattin to perfection, even though he wasn't the tallest player on the team at 6-foot-6. Nevil Shed was a couple inches taller at 6-foot-8. But Shed weighed only about 185 pounds to Lattin's 235, a tall fir tree to "Big Daddy's" solid oak.

"He backed me up at the center position," Lattin said of Shed. "When I got into foul trouble, he moved over to center. He was very quick, but still only 185 pounds."

Lattin found life a lot more fun at El Paso than he had at Tennessee State. His classes included a stint as a disc jockey for the campus radio station.

Flournoy was among the first of the seven-man group of black players to arrive at El Paso. Lattin was the last piece of the puzzle, arriving two years later.

Flournoy first got to El Paso in 1962 along with Artis, both products of the Gary, Indiana, school system. Flournoy was a forward and Artis a guard.

One year later, in from Detroit came Bobby Joe Hill, a spirited, frisky guard who almost immediately became the team leader.

"Bobby Joe was the engine that drove that team," Flournoy recalled. "Bobby was a very quiet guy, but when he got on the floor, he was an entirely different person."

At 5-foot-10, Hill was one of the smallest players on the team but that didn't stop him from getting in the face of bigger teammates if they needed it. Unhappy with Lattin's performance one night against New Mexico's Mel Daniels, Hill challenged him to do better: "If you can't guard him, you sit down and I'll guard him."

New York City's schoolyards then produced Shed, Willie Worsley, and Willie Cager. Shed was a forward-center, Worsley a guard, and Cager a forward.

Then along came Lattin, a sturdy pivot man with broad shoulders who was considered one of the top high school players in Texas.

Meanwhile, Haskins made the players dance to his own tune with strenuous workouts.

"He was hard," Flournoy said. "He was an entirely different person away from the basketball court than he was on the court. During practice, he was demanding. He was extremely demanding."

The squad had long practices from October 15, when official practices started, until November 1, about a week prior to the first game.

"We had two-a-day practices and each one of them lasted about three hours each," Flournoy recalled. "We were practicing about six hours a day. And even when (Haskins) cut it down to one practice after the season started, we would practice about three, three and a half hours in that gym."

The day of a game, the Miners would have "walk-throughs" that seemed more like "run-throughs" to the players. Haskins' favorite words: "Get after it!"

"We'd be out there and he would say it, 'We're just going to walk through the play . . . kind of warm up, go through our defensive assignment,' and we'd get out there and the next thing you know, we're in a full-blown practice, and we were going to play in a few hours," remembered Flournoy.

And no drinking water until practice was over.

"In those days, there was a whole different mind-set (about dehydration)," Flournoy said. "They claimed that if you drank water while you're doing all the exercise that you would cramp up. That was just how they looked at it then. They later found out that it was different, you should hydrate yourself as much as you can."

Talk to Lattin and others on the team and the consensus was that Haskins was not that easy to know—or like. He wasn't nicknamed "The Bear" for nothing.

"We didn't have a personal relationship with him," Lattin said. "He was kind of standoffish. He was the kind of guy who didn't want to be friends with the players. He didn't talk to us that much. In practices, he was all about defense. And, you know, defense is hard work. That's what the practices were all about."

Added Flournoy, "I was captain in name only. He ran the team—it was his team. On that court, in that gym, that was his territory. He was a tyrant."

One day before the start of the season, Haskins called Flournoy into his office.

"He told me that the best players on the team were all African Americans, his seven best players," Flournoy recalled. "He asked me if I had any suggestions.

"I told him, 'No, you have to do what you think is right. You're the coach. What would I look like telling you how you should play these guys?' He played us like he wanted to."

Haskins started African Americans in every game, despite what many other coaches felt about black basketball players.

"The thinking in those days was if you could stay close to us, because of all the African Americans on the team, that we would break," Flournoy said. "If you were ahead of us, with five, six minutes left in the game, we would quit."

But Haskins displayed a tremendous amount of confidence at a preseason banquet. Lattin remembered:

"Coach Haskins was giving a speech and said, 'You know, these players are special. This is a special team.' He didn't say anything about winning the national championship. I don't think he knew we were that special. He just knew we had a lot of talent and we were going to be good."

Good, but completely under the radar from the start of the season.

"They didn't see us coming—it was like a giant freight train coming down the tracks," Lattin said. "It was barreling down the tracks and nobody saw it coming until it was too late."

Haskins, who had played for the legendary Henry Iba at Oklahoma A&M (now Oklahoma State), had coached an Amateur Athletic Union (AAU) team and some small-town high school teams before arriving at Texas Western in 1961. He took a pay cut to do so because he passionately wanted to coach in Division I. The Miners had long since broken the mold by recruiting African Americans. There were three blacks on the squad when Haskins pulled in to El Paso, including Nolan Richardson, who later would coach Arkansas to the national title.

Although the Miners had four straight winning seasons in Haskins' early years, including two straight appearances in the NCAA playoffs and another in the NIT, not much was known about their basketball program nationally. The Miners went 18–6, 19–7, 25–3, and 16–9 in those years.

El Paso was a border town known more as the "gateway" to Juárez, Mexico, than it was for basketball.

"They called us the 'Bandits from the Badlands,'" Lattin said.

Flournoy was now 2,000 miles from home, with no mother around to watch his every move. He went into a partying mode and let his grades slip.

"We were right next door to the border," he said. "I went crazy for a little while."

It was time for Haskins to call Flournoy's mom. She was on the next plane out from Gary. Flournoy was double-teamed by his mother and his coach in Haskins' office.

With his mother looking on, the coach "read me the riot act," Flournoy remembered. "I had to get my grades up. If I didn't get them up, I would be gone."

Once the Miners assembled for the 1965–66 season, the style of the team wasn't hard to figure out from the start: defense was the name of the game.

"Coach Haskins knew the kids from the inner city knew how to play offense," Lattin said. "He wasn't worried about that. But if he could teach good team defense, then they should be successful."

Unranked at the start of the year, the Miners just went about their business winning games.

"The first few games that we played at home weren't sold out," Flournoy said. "They weren't selling the place out until our (Sun Carnival) tournament. Iowa was in it and they were ranked nationally. The place was sold out because I think the fans wanted to see us lose to Iowa. There were people in El Paso who wanted to see us lose because they weren't used to seeing a team playing with that many African Americans."

The Miners had chalked up nine straight wins before meeting the sixth-ranked Hawkeyes in the Sun Carnival tournament.

Haskins knew a victory over Iowa would go a long way toward establishing a place in the national spotlight for Texas Western.

The Miners had failed to get much attention early in the season playing inferior opponents.

"Coach Haskins had said at the pre-tournament banquet before the Iowa game that we were going to meet them when they got off the bus, and we were going to be on top of them from the time they were in the locker room to the time that they went out to warm up to the time the game started," Flournoy said. "We were going to be on 'em. And that's what we did. We just completely dominated them."

Playing a "brilliant first-half defense," according to United Press International, the Miners held the Hawkeyes without a field goal in the first 11 minutes while rolling up a 21–4 lead. The Miners went up, 40–19, at the half and cruised to an 86–68 victory.

"(The Hawkeyes) didn't think they would be challenged before the NCAA playoffs," Lattin said. "We had to show them."

Lattin remembered that the more the Miners won that year, the tougher the practices became.

"We were winning easily and Coach Haskins was so afraid that we were going to get big heads and stop practicing hard, and then were going to lose. He was so afraid that we were going to lose our intensity, so practices got harder."

A couple of days after the Sun Carnival tournament, the Miners woke up to find their performance against Iowa had propelled them into the No. 9 spot in America.

All of the national attention, though, was focused on the battle for the No. 1 ranking between Duke and Kentucky.

"Duke's high-flying basketball team, riding the crest of a nine-game victory streak, maintained its No. 1 position," reported United Press International in the second week of January.

Little notice was taken of the Miners, who moved up a notch to No. 8 after winning their 12th straight game. By the end of January, Texas Western had moved to No. 6, and then No. 5 in early February after going to 16–0.

In one of its most impressive performances of the season, Texas Western rallied from a double-digit deficit at the half to beat bitter rival New Mexico, 67–64, in overtime. The Miners, in fact, played the entire second half and the overtime period without Lattin, who had fouled out before intermission. It was one of the Miners' sweetest victories of the season, according to Flournoy.

"Number one, we were rivals and we didn't like each other," he said. "It didn't make any difference who was going to play in that game, we didn't like each other."

The Lobos had one of their best teams, featuring Daniels, who went on to stardom in the American Basketball Association.

"We just buckled down in that second half, and it shocked people," Flournoy said. "When we came out of the locker room to go back to the bus, to catch the plane, there were a lot of people left in that field house because they couldn't believe that we had come back and beaten them."

Before the Miners pulled out the game, they had been taunted by the crowd. "Top Ten no longer," the crowd chanted, alluding to the national ranking.

While winning games, the Miners faced much hostility throughout the season.

"There were a lot of incidents where fans would throw things," Flournoy recalled.

And shout nasty words directed at the players and the coaching staff.

"There was a lot of tension," Flournoy said. "We would go into different cities and the phones in the players' rooms would be cut off. The coaching staff didn't want any of those people calling or threatening the players directly. When we had our pregame meals, the trainer would have to go into the kitchen and watch them prepare the meals so that they didn't tamper with the food."

There was sometimes a problem with accommodations when the team was on the road. Not every hotel allowed blacks.

"We had to find someplace where we could all stay together, not have the white players stay in one place and the black players stay someplace else," Flournoy said.

By the time the Miners traveled north for their final game of the regular season against the University of Seattle, they were still undefeated at 23–0. They were ranked No. 2 in the nation behind Kentucky, which also had a 23–0 record.

When Kentucky took its first loss, 69–62 to Tennessee in an afternoon game, the Miners had an opportunity to move into the top spot that night. But they failed to cash in, losing to Seattle, 74–72.

Kentucky nevertheless held on to the No. 1 spot, followed by Duke. Texas Western dropped to No. 3 going into the NCAA tournament.

Texas Western opened with an 89–74 victory over Oklahoma City, then beat Cincinnati, 78–76, in overtime. Lattin led all scorers with 29 points against the Bearcats, and Cager turned from goat to hero with six points in overtime.

"Cager missed a free throw with 11 seconds left in the regulation game that ended at 69-all," United Press International reported. "In the five-minute overtime, Cager twice drove in for layups and added two free throws."

The road got even tougher: another day, another overtime game. Actually, double overtime.

Texas Western and Kansas were locked in a 69–69 tie after regulation. It appeared Texas Western had lost in the first overtime, when Kansas' Jo Jo White hit a 32-foot shot with seven seconds left. But a referee ruled that White had stepped out of bounds, leaving the teams tied at 71.

"The teams stalled for most of the first five-minute overtime before White hit his shot that did not count," United Press International reported. "In the second five-minute overtime, Willie Cager of Texas Western hit on a jump shot and Bobby Joe Hill, Nevil Shed, and Orsten Artis made free throws."

This time, Texas Western's "rugged, quick five" overcame the Jayhawks, 81–80.

Recalled Lattin, who had a game-high 17 rebounds and 15 points: "Kansas, without question, was the toughest team we had to play. They were big, they were strong, they had everything. Our ears were pinned back the entire game. It was a very difficult game."

Artis scored 22 points as the Miners beat Utah, 85–78, to advance to the championship game against Kentucky, which had beaten Duke in the semifinals at Cole Field House in College Park, Maryland.

It was down to one game: an upstart coach and team against a legendary coach and program. Rupp's coaching genius had led the Wildcats to an unprecedented four national titles. The Miners, on the other hand, had never gotten past the second round of the NCAA playoffs under Haskins.

Until '66.

In the 1940s and 1950s, Kentucky basketball was at its zenith with the so-called "Fabulous Five"—Alex Groza, Wallace "Wah Wah" Jones, Cliff Barker, Ralph Beard, and Kenneth Rollins. These players helped Kentucky win three national championships in four years. The 1958 team, which Rupp called the "Fiddlin' Five," added a fourth title for the "Baron of the Bluegrass."

Explaining that team's nickname, Rupp said, "They fiddled around enough to drive me crazy. They weren't the greatest basketball players in the world—all they could do was win."

His 1966 team featured no "fabulous" players, no "fiddlers," and no starter over 6-foot-5. It was the shortest team Rupp had ever coached, but a high-scoring, speed-oriented squad.

The so-called "Runts" featured Pat Riley, who would go on to a brilliant NBA coaching career, Larry Conley, Tommy Kron, Louie Dampier, and Thad Jaracz.

"They weren't really big, but they were very quick, and they were smart and they were great shooters," Lattin said.

Many thought the Wildcats had already beaten their toughest competition when they knocked off Duke, the Atlantic Coast Conference champion and No. 2 team in the country. Kentucky, with its great basketball tradition and No. 1 ranking, was established as the favorite in the championship game.

Then along came Lattin to make a couple of early impact plays.

First he blocked a shot by Riley as he tried to drive to the basket on Kentucky's opening possession. Then Lattin threw down a ferocious dunk over Riley. Haskins had told Lattin to take the ball to the hole whenever he had his first opportunity. The intimidating shot made just the impact Haskins had desired.

"We talked about it the day before and we decided it was a good idea to go in and do that," Lattin said of the dunk shot. "That's basically what we did all the time anyway. It was the right moment for it."

Noted Haskins: "I didn't think they had seen many guys who could dunk it like David."

Haskins was correct.

"When David went up, Pat tried to contest him," Conley said, "but it was fairly awesome."

Noting the reaction from Kentucky's players, Lattin said, "They kind of scattered a little bit."

Lattin, who had 16 points in the game, made another statement shot in the first half to give the Miners a 16–11 lead.

An additional statement came from another Texas Western player. Hill made two steals within 10 seconds, turning each one into a basket. He finished with a team-high 20 points.

"The 5-foot-10 junior from Detroit dropped in some of the fanciest shots of the tournament," reported the *New York Times*.

Along with Lattin's devastating dunks, Hill's steals had an adverse effect on Kentucky.

"That really demoralized them," Lattin said. "That took the wind completely out of their sails."

Reported the *New York Times*:

"The Miners never lost their poise in the face of a strong comeback attempt by the team rated No. 1 in the nation. Their rebounding strength and fine shooting kept them ahead from after 9 minutes, 40 seconds of the first half until the end of the game."

Rupp gave Hill credit for providing the "turning point of the game" with his timely steals.

When the Miners seemed certain of victory in the final minute, their fans started chanting, "We're No. 1."

Final: Texas Western 72, Kentucky 65.

It was the first national title in any sport for the Miners athletic program and it had taken a superb effort, particularly on defense, to beat Kentucky.

"I remember they were very quick and every player on Kentucky was a good shooter," recalled Lattin, who led that great defense despite being in foul trouble. "I just remember that we didn't give them anything. Whatever they got, they worked for it."

The Texas Western-Kentucky game of 1966 was a turning point that led to complete integration of basketball in America.

"Within two or three years after we won it all in '66, teams throughout the country had black players," Haskins pointed out.

Including, eventually, Kentucky.

In time, the Texas Western players would appreciate the significance of what they had done, how their performance had changed the game and society in general.

"It was years later when you realize the impact the game had," Lattin said. "Then all that stuff came out, and it's always about history. Then, it was just another game to us."

Not to the students at Texas Western.

"Oh, boy, they went crazy," Flournoy recalled.

Bonfires broke out all over the campus following the victory.

"And then when we got back to El Paso and the plane circled the airport, you could see this sea of people, and we had a caravan back to the school. . . . It was at least seven, maybe ten miles from the airport back to the school. Those streets were lined all the way back to the campus . . . ."

Haskins started to get a sense of the significance of the game after returning home and facing the wrath of racists who sent tons of hate mail to the school.

"We filled up trash baskets with those letters," Haskins said. "People from all over were calling my players names that started with the little letter 'n.' White people were saying I used them to win games. Black people said I had exploited the players."

Good thing for basketball that Haskins, and Texas Western, were color-blind.

"I can tell you that, even if it was a great season, it was a hard season for me," Flournoy said. "It was because of all the negativity that was going on. It should have been a time when we were having the time of our lives, and it wasn't that way.

"It was the hardest season I went through—of the three seasons I played up there. And if it wasn't for my mother (staying) on me, if it wasn't for the loyalty I felt for Coach Haskins, I don't know if I could have done it. I really don't."

Haskins never took another team to the Final Four before retiring in 1999 with a 719–354 record. But once was enough for the trailblazing basketball coach.

10.

Tourney Blunders

Oh, the angst and anger.

Ha, the chuckles and derisive cheers.

Of course, it all depends which side of the equation you are on: rooting for the blunderers or pulling for the fortunate opponent that benefited from the gaffes.

Regardless, it wouldn't be March Madness without some weird stuff happening on and off the court, involving players, coaches, and administrators.

So here's a Dirty Dozen—if your team messed up. Or a Terrific Twelve if your guys were the beneficiaries.

Fab Five Flop: Chris Webber's Timeout Call with None Remaining Ruins Wolverines

There were several decisions Chris Webber could have made in the final moments of the 1993 NCAA title game. He could have driven to the basket, or hoisted up an outside shot. Webber could have passed to one of his talented teammates, then headed to the lane for a potential rebound.

The one thing he couldn't afford to do was ask for a timeout—precisely what the All-American sophomore forward did.

"I just called a timeout when we didn't have one," he told the Associated Press. "I probably lost the game. If I had known, I wouldn't have called one. Obviously, I didn't know or I wouldn't have called one. I probably cost our team the game."

Yep. But his blunder also earned Webber lasting fame. You see, plenty of players have hit last-second shots to win key contests during March Madness. Sometimes, the Lorenzo Charleses and Darrall

Imhoffs, the Keith Smarts and even the Michael Jordans can get lumped together.

Sure, that's very nice company to keep. Still, it's company, a group, a list.

Webber stands alone: the guy who called the timeout when his team didn't have any.

The beneficiaries of a big bungle in the Louisiana Superdome for the second time in 11 years: the North Carolina Tar Heels (more on the first incident later).

With 19 seconds remaining, UNC's Pat Sullivan missed a free throw, and Webber swallowed it up. He also dragged his pivot foot, something the entire Carolina bench noticed—and screamed about when no whistle was blown.

Webber hurried upcourt, making sure to stay close enough to the sideline to hear any instructions. None was forthcoming from coach Steve Fisher. Webber, surrounded by Tar Heels George Lynch and Derrick Phelps and feeling suffocated, stopped his dribble and opted for the good old timeout so everyone could discuss strategy with 11 seconds to go.

Instead of signaling the timeout, the referees signaled a technical foul.

"Heat of the moment, it happens like that," Fisher said.

Asked if the Wolverines had discussed the lack of timeouts once they'd used the last one trying to get the ball inbounds, Fisher shrugged and nodded his head.

Lynch wondered if the Wolverines really were so aware of the situation. He claimed the "whole Michigan bench" was yelling at Webber to ask for time.

Jalen Rose, another member of the "Fab Five"—the group of highly recruited freshmen who joined Michigan together and almost immediately became starters and stars—who went on to a solid NBA career, tried to downplay the significance of Webber's goof.

"Without the timeout, our offense might have just thrown up an airball," Rose said. "And Chris was trapped. They had a trap on him. Chris didn't lose the game, and we'll all just have to tell him that."

Forgotten is how Webber's 23 points and 11 rebounds kept Michigan in the game and put the Wolverines in position for their second title in four years.

"I don't think that timeout necessarily cost Michigan the game," Tar Heels coach Dean Smith said. "We only had three team fouls at that point, and we were going to keep fouling them to use up the clock."

No need to foul after the phantom timeout was taken. Donald Williams hit two free throws after the technical foul was called, then two more following another foul, and UNC had a 77–71 victory.

The "Fab Five" had nothing but some very bad memories.

I Thought He Was One Of Us: Fred Brown's Errant Pass Helps Seal North Carolina's Title Win Over Georgetown

If Webber's goof is No. 1 on the March Madness Oops Parade, Fred Brown's errant pass is a close second.

Brown was the leader of Georgetown's backcourt in 1982, a solid performer on a team featuring future Hall of Famer Patrick Ewing and such other college standouts as Eric Floyd and Eric Smith. They were up against perhaps the most formidable Tar Heels squad ever to take the court for Dean Smith, featuring James Worthy, Sam Perkins, and some guy nicknamed "MJ" (soon to be "Air" or just plain "Michael").

And the Hoyas not only were holding their own, they also were in position to win their first national championship and deny Smith his first.

The fans at the cavernous Superdome in New Orleans had been treated to an intense, sometimes physical, and always entertaining game. With a 62–61 lead, Georgetown hunkered down for a last-minute Tar Heels possession, confident its defense could protect such a slim lead.

Jordan was not yet the hoops (and beyond) icon he would become. In fact, he was just a skinny wing player, a freshman with the gumption to take charge regardless of the circumstances, but not even the best player on his team. That was Worthy, who would be selected the Most Outstanding Player of the tournament.

Yet when North Carolina worked the ball for a potential game-winning shot, it found Jordan on the left wing, open and ready to fire.

"How many freshmen back then were going to take that shot, let alone hit it?" Worthy asked. "But we all knew Michael would. We wouldn't have passed the ball to him otherwise."

Worthy laughed at that thought, then added, "Coach Smith wouldn't have had him on the court if he didn't think Michael would make it."

Which, of course, Jordan did.

Still, there were 15 seconds remaining, and now it was UNC's task to stop Georgetown from grabbing back the lead—and the NCAA crown.

Here's how Brown described the pivotal play to the *Washington Post*:

"I rushed the ball upcourt, and when I saw Eric Floyd open on the left baseline, I picked up my dribble. But the Carolina defense overplayed Floyd, so I looked to the middle for Patrick Ewing or Ed Spriggs. But both of them were covered.

"At that point I should have called timeout, because picking up the dribble had killed the play. But I decided to pass it to Eric Smith, who was on the right side of the lane. I thought I saw Smitty out of the right corner of my eye."

Except it wasn't Smitty. It was Worthy.

"My peripheral vision is pretty good," Brown continued. "But this time it failed me. It was only a split second. But, you know, that's all it takes to lose a game. I knew it was bad as soon as I let it go. I wanted to reach out and grab it back. If I'd had a rubber hand, I would have yanked it back in.

"It was just a standard guard to forward pass. I had made so many similar passes throughout the game, and someone from my team was always there. But not that last time.

"He didn't steal it. I gave it away."

The stunning turnover came as just as big of a surprise to Worthy, who then headed downcourt before being fouled as the clock ticked down. The damage had been done.

"I saw him pick up his dribble," Worthy said. "I saw him fake the pass. He looked back and I just stood there. I thought he would throw it over my head. I was pretty surprised when it landed in my chest."

None of Brown's fellow Hoyas, nor coach John Thompson—with whom Brown had a falling-out later in life—ever blamed him for the defeat.

"I feel bad for Fred," Thompson said. "But he's a tough kid. This is just part of growing up. We're not mad at Fred. And we don't feel like he lost the game."

Brown would go on to captain the Hoyas two years later, when they won their only national championship by beating Houston. He repeatedly said throughout the years that the pass to Worthy and the loss to North Carolina didn't haunt him.

Yet the play is among the most replayed highlights/lowlights associated with March Madness.

"It's part of life," Brown said, "and it's a part of me."

So You Think That Was a Bad Foul?
Butler vs. Pittsburgh, March 19, 2011

The Butler Bulldogs were the darlings of March Madness in 2010, a mid-major that fell a missed long-range shot short of winning it all.

Not nearly as much was expected of the Horizon League champions when they entered the 2011 NCAA tournament. Their best player from the previous year's squad, Gordon Hayward, had left for the NBA, and the Bulldogs had struggled for much of the regular season.

When they met Big East powerhouse Pitt, the top seed in the Southeast Regional, at the Verizon Center in the nation's capital, the eighth-seeded Bulldogs were decided underdogs.

But this was March.

"When you look at Butler, you definitely have to respect them a little bit more," Pitt forward Gilbert Brown said. "Look what they have done."

Brown would play a pivotal role in one of the most bizarre endings the NCAA tournament has seen.

A tight, back-and-forth contest came down to the final seconds. Andrew Smith somehow sneaked away from Pitt's defense and was wide open for a layup with 2.2 seconds remaining to give Butler a one-point lead.

As Brown took an inbounds pass and hurried up the left sideline for a desperation shot, Bulldogs guard Shelvin Mack—one of Butler's most intelligent players—stunningly ran into him as he heaved the ball. From midcourt.

Mack was called for a two-shot foul, virtually handing the game to the Panthers.

"Brain lock," he said.

Unless, of course, Brown missed one of the free throws.

He made the first to tie it, 70–70, as the Pittsburgh bench and fans throughout the arena saw their mood soar from devastated to delighted. On the Butler side, there was pure dejection.

Then Brown missed the second shot.

Overtime? Uh, no.

Butler's Matt Howard and Pitt's Nasir Robinson went for the rebound, which Howard easily grabbed, and—even more inexplicably than what Mack did—Robinson hacked Howard, just a few feet from the basket.

"I'm the one that people like to get on for making fouls 90 feet from the basket," Howard said. "But I can't imagine what was going through (Robinson's) mind. Maybe he thought they were still down instead of tied, I don't know."

Not at all, Robinson said.

"I knew how much time was on the clock. I knew what the score was. I just went after the rebound. It was a reaction," he said. "I wasn't thinking. It was just a reaction of me just playing hard. I tried to make a play."

Instead, his boneheaded play sent the teams to the other end, and Howard needed to hit one of two free throws with 0.8 seconds remaining to win it for Butler.

He did, canning the first, missing the second intentionally. No more silly fouls, either.

"I've never seen anything like that in 39 years of coaching," said Connecticut coach Jim Calhoun, whose Huskies would beat Butler in the championship game two weeks later. "Both plays."

Frieder's Folly is Fisher's Good Fortune:
Bill Frieder Leaves as Michigan Coach,
Steve Fisher Leads Wolverines to National Title

On the eve of the 1989 NCAA tournament, Michigan lost its coach.

A little more than three weeks later, the Wolverines were national champions.

Bill Frieder's awful timing was Steve Fisher's big break.

Frieder had been negotiating with Arizona State as the regular season was drawing to a close. When he accepted the Sun Devils' job on the Ides of March, Michigan athletic director Bo Schembechler—yes, that Bo, the great football coach—felt as if he'd been knifed in the back.

If Frieder expected to lead the Wolverines into the NCAAs, then head to Tempe, he was dreaming.

"I don't want someone from Arizona State coaching the Michigan team," Schembechler said after firing Frieder. "A Michigan man is going to coach Michigan."

That man would be Fisher, a somewhat nondescript and certainly semi-anonymous assistant coach.

Maybe that's exactly what the Wolverines needed, a change from Frieder's loud eccentricity to Fisher's laid-back, academic style. Frieder never was one of Schembechler's favorites, anyway.

Two of the players who led Michigan to the title with an 80–79 overtime victory against Seton Hall, Terry Mills and Rumeal Robinson, believed Frieder never got due credit for the Wolverines' run to the championship.

"He told us that we would understand his decision later on in life," Mills said. "And, as I got older and wiser, I know people make career moves and why he had to leave when he left."

Not that Frieder had a choice once Schembechler learned of the Arizona State connection.

"I was going to be upfront, and as it turns out, I was penalized for being upfront," Frieder said. "I could have lied, but I was going to be honest about everything."

Fisher, a seven-year assistant at the school, stepped in and wasn't overwhelmed. He gave his stars, particularly Robinson and sharp-shooting forward Glen Rice, just enough freedom to build their confidence.

"Being real honest, I was more than a little frightened taking over from Bill and so I set very modest goals," Fisher said. "I simply wanted to be able to eliminate the distractions to the point where we wouldn't be eliminated in the first game.

"Even before this happened, I understood that one man's disappointment is another man's opportunity. I'm not the first to say it and I won't be the last. That's life. I know Bill was happy and proud for me, but I also knew he was very, very disappointed."

Frieder would have only modest success at ASU. Many years later, he summed up his departure from Ann Arbor with no malice: "I have always said that if that's the worst thing that ever happens to me, then I am going to have a great life. And, I've had a great life."

No-No At Nova: Villanova Stripped of 1971 Final Four Appearance

"From ecstasy to an asterisk."

That's how guard Ed Hastings described Villanova's trip to the Final Four in 1971, a journey you won't find in the record books anymore.

Led by three-time All-American Howard Porter, one of the greatest players in school history, and versatile Chris Ford, the Wildcats of Jack Kraft stormed through the NCAA tournament. They reached the Final Four along with another longshot, Western Kentucky, led by Jim McDaniels. Also on hand were two blue-bloods: UCLA, seeking its fifth straight national title, and Kansas.

Coincidentally, you won't find Western Kentucky's name in the record books for that Final Four, either.

Porter led Nova past the Hilltoppers, 92–89, in the semifinals, while UCLA beat Kansas, 68–60. John Wooden's Bruins felt threatened by Porter and Villanova, but a staunch defense against the 6-foot-8 Wildcats star worked well enough for UCLA to win, 68–62, even though Porter won the Most Outstanding Player award.

But neither Nova nor Western Kentucky belonged in March Madness; both had ineligible players. Not just any players, either, but their respective stars, Porter and McDaniels.

Porter not only had signed with an agent while still in school, but he also had agreed to a contract with the Pittsburgh franchise of the American Basketball Association (ABA). McDaniels also had accepted money from the pros.

"It was such a sad thing," said Jake Nevin, Villanova's trainer for 56 years, including the 1971 season, and a member of various Philadelphia-area Halls of Fame. "The poor kid, he really did nothing wrong. They told him if he signed today they'd give him so much money, and if he waited until next week, it would go down."

Nevin, who died in 1985—the year Villanova won the championship and kept it—said Kraft and the players never held anything against Porter.

"We blame the men that were approaching these kids and flashing all this money in front of them," he said.

In his college career, Porter set the Villanova rebounding record with 1,317, an average of 14.8 rebounds per game. He also scored 22.8 points per game. His number 54 uniform was retired in 1997.

Away from basketball, his life wasn't as smooth.

"I took a ride with the devil," Porter told the *Minneapolis Star Tribune* in a 2001 interview. "And the devil picked me up and rolled me for a while. But I always knew, deep down inside, I felt God wasn't through with me yet."

After a spotty NBA career, Porter began using drugs. He had the funds, the leisure time, and access to cocaine, and after injuries limited his on-court skills, Porter's life spiraled.

By 1985, he was broke, living in his mother's house in Florida. Eventually, he found his way into rehab and back into the workforce. Porter became a probation officer in Minnesota in 1995, supervising former convicts or people on probation for various crimes.

Plus, he eventually was welcomed back into the Villanova basketball community by coach Jay Wright.

Porter became a role model for Villanova players, until his life was tragically cut short in May 2007 during a robbery attempt. He probably never will be remembered for his basketball talent.

"He was doing so good, helping his fellow people that were in a little bit of trouble," Kraft said. "That's the irony of it all—the fact that you're helping people and this happens."

Phi Slamma Bummer: Guy Lewis Coaches Right into the Wolfpack's Lair

North Carolina State's 54–52 victory over Houston in the 1983 NCAA final will forever be remembered for two iconic moments: Lorenzo Charles' last-second dunk off Dereck Whittenburg's 35-foot desperation shot that won the game, and coach Jimmy Valvano's desperate, delirious search for someone to celebrate with on the court.

On the other side of the result were the heavily favored Houston Cougars and coach Guy Lewis, whose ill-advised strategy was as responsible for grounding "Phi Slamma Jamma" as just about anything the Wolfpack had to offer.

Sure, Valvano's work was impressive. He coaxed his "Cardiac Kids" squad to a quick lead so they could slow the pace, keeping defenders between the Cougars and the basket at all costs, thus limiting the momentum-swinging dunks that had carried Houston into the stratosphere all season.

And when in doubt, what did Valvano order up? Fouls—fully knowing how Houston struggled at the free throw line.

Meanwhile, Lewis couldn't get his team back up for the NCAA title game after routing Louisville in a semifinal that many considered the championship contest. After that high-flying act, the Cougars fell flat.

"Perhaps we left a bit too much in that game," Lewis admitted.

Lewis also left one of his stars, Clyde Drexler, on the floor deep into the first half after the versatile All-American was called for a third personal foul. Late in the half, Drexler picked up No. 4.

After 20 minutes, NC State led, 33–25, and the Wolfpack's confidence had soared. Lewis implored his players to get back to their weaving, rollicking, sky-walking, and rim-rattling ways. They did, opening a seven-point edge for Houston with 10 minutes to play.

"They looked like they could run us off the court," Valvano said.

Instead, Lewis ordered up a slowdown, a format that went directly against everything his slam gang was about. Rather than utilizing the Cougars' athletic skills and flair for the dramatic to outscore NC State, Houston played the kind of style that befit, well, the Wolfpack.

And NC State climbed right back into the game.

Houston misfired from the outside, the only place where the Cougars were getting shots once they had slowed the tempo. And they couldn't hit their foul shots—again. They finished 10-of-19 at the line.

"I have confidence in that offense," Lewis said. "I wanted to pull State out on defense and then get some layups. We only got one.

"Just as everybody knew it might, our foul shooting caught up with us."

As did Lewis' coaching miscalculations.

Going Once, Going Twice: Two John Calipari-Coached Teams Disappear from Final Four Record Books

Lots of coaches have lots of college hoops records, from John Wooden to Dean Smith to Bob Knight to Tennessee women's basketball legend Pat Summitt. Only John Calipari, however, can be called the "Invisible Man."

Or, more fittingly, only his UMass Minutemen and Memphis Tigers can be called the "Invisible Teams."

Calipari is the only coach to have two Final Four appearances stripped: Massachusetts in 1996 and Memphis in 2008.

Yes, Valvano and Dick Vitale have carried "Coach V" tags, but so has Calipari: Coach Vacated.

Keep in mind—right up front, actually—that the nomadic Calipari never was implicated in either of the cases that led to NCAA action.

Calipari, now coaching at Kentucky, was in the NBA when the NCAA made its ruling on Massachusetts following its 1996 appearance in the Final Four. Because Marcus Camby was ruled ineligible for accepting money from an agent, the Minutemen were wiped from the NCAA tournament record books.

In 2008, Memphis lost its 38 victories and records as a Final Four squad for using an ineligible player throughout the season. Speculation always has centered on guard Derrick Rose and his academic transcripts. Rose nearly guided the Tigers to the championship (more on that in a moment) before Chicago made him the top overall pick in the NBA draft after spending only one year in college.

So it seemed fair when Calipari said:

"We will all be judged fifty years from now. The good news is, there will be no emotion to it where someone wants to be nasty and mean; it won't be here. It will be 'Here's the facts, here's what he's done.'"

Added Paul Dee, chairman of the NCAA infractions committee when Memphis was sanctioned: "Whenever you have a situation where you have a record that's vacated, that's a pretty strong indication that there was a problem. But because no allegations were brought concerning the coach . . . we did not consider any allegation against the coach and therefore made no finding (and) no penalty."

Ah, but there is a penalty: the "V" word in place of "runner-up" or "Final Four contestant."

At least UMass didn't come close to winning the title in 1996, falling in the national semifinals to Kentucky. But the Memphis team in '08 stood at the foul line for five free throws in the final 1:12 of the championship game against Kansas. Rose and Chris Douglas-Roberts went a combined 1-for-5.

Flaws at the free throw line? Certainly.

Exacerbating the situation: Calipari admitting the Tigers "spend no time worrying about free throw shooting."

The Tigers had only one close game on their road to the championship game, going 15-of-32 at the line in a 77–74 second-round win against Mississippi State.

"I thought that was an eye-opener," said Douglas-Roberts, who had an All-American season. "We felt a lot of games were going to be close this tournament, so we talked amongst each other and said, 'We have to make these free throws.' But they really haven't been close, so free throws really haven't been a burden."

Until the moment they counted most. Kansas tied the title game on Mario Chalmers' three-pointer—Memphis made another mistake by not fouling with a three-point lead—at the buzzer, then ran away in overtime.

Not that you'll find Memphis' name on the Final Four ledger.

The Gopher Ate It: Homework Scandal
Brings Down Minnesota Basketball

Nearly three years after their most successful basketball season and only visit to the Final Four, the Minnesota Gophers were slam-dunked by the NCAA. Over homework.

Apparently, the idea of Minnesota's basketball players actually doing their own schoolwork had escaped the team and its coaching staff.

In 1999, Jan Gangelhoff, who worked in the school's athletic/academic counseling department, claimed she completed more than 400 pieces of course work for at least 20 players during a five-year span in the 1990s. Not only had she done the assignments, Gangelhoff said, but head coach Clem Haskins was aware of it, and the school's academic advisor at the time, Alonzo Newby, had made the arrangements for 18 basketball players.

The cheating began earlier in Haskins' tenure as Gophers coach, and lasted from 1994 until Gangelhoff came clean—at significant risk to herself. She eventually pleaded guilty to a felony charge because, the *Minneapolis Star Tribune* reported her saying, "federal prosecutors said if she didn't, they'd charge her with 20 felonies and send her to prison."

As a reward—or, more accurately, to keep her quiet during the years she was doing the homework—the Gophers had taken her on road trips, including one to Hawaii. She also claimed Haskins once paid her $3,000 in cash to tutor a player, something Haskins repeatedly denied before finally admitting.

Haskins took a $1.5 million buyout to leave the school in 1999 and wound up paying back nearly half of that once a school and NCAA investigation determined his culpability. He didn't return to coaching, although he spent a short stint as a scout for the NBA's Minnesota Timberwolves.

"I never once asked a young man to do something wrong, to cheat or to protect me," Haskins told ESPN. "Never. I'm not perfect, but I never did anything that would embarrass or hurt the university, the community, or the program. If I did anything wrong, it was because I was trying to help an individual, someone who needed my help."

Presumably, one of those players was guard Russ Archambault, who told the *Saint Paul Pioneer Press*, "In the two years I was there, I never did a thing. Either Jan or Jeanne (Payer, Gangelhoff's sister) did everything."

Archambault also said Haskins gave him as much as $300 in cash.

Archambault was kicked off the team by Haskins in early 1998 for violating team rules and left the school.

"The coaches knew. Everybody knew," said Archambault, a freshman reserve on the 1997 Final Four team. "We used to make jokes about it. . . . I would go over there some night and get like four papers done. The coaches would be laughing about it."

No one was laughing when the NCAA stripped Minnesota of its 1997 achievement.

Orange Crushed: Derrick Coleman's Flop on Free Throw Dooms Syracuse

Syracuse coach Jim Boeheim was so close to his first NCAA crown he could almost taste it—with an orange flavor.

And with a future top overall NBA draft pick, Derrick Coleman, in his lineup, what could be bad?

Well, Coleman at the free throw line, all alone, with the game in the balance, that's what.

The freshman had been toying with Indiana's frontcourt, clearing rebound after rebound to help Syracuse take a late lead over Bob Knight's Indiana Hoosiers.

Syracuse's Howard Triche made one of two foul shots for a three-point lead, but when he missed the second, the entire Orange squad was caught flat-footed. Indiana's Keith Smart scooted downcourt for a quick basket that Boeheim called "the most damaging until then."

"If they have to set up for a shot," Boeheim said of Indiana, "they would lose a lot of time, maybe 10 or 15 (seconds)."

With the score of 73–72 favoring the Orange, Smart fouled Coleman, a 69 percent shooter from the line and, by the end of this intense contest, a tired teenager.

With 28 seconds remaining, Boeheim—fearful of another transition basket—ordered the other four Orangemen to back off the lane and defend as Coleman prepared for his one-and-one opportunity.

With the crowd at the cavernous Louisiana Superdome in a near frenzy as Indiana called a timeout, Coleman tried to steady himself, catch his breath—and hit the biggest free throw of his young life.

"I felt confident, there wasn't any emotion," Coleman said. "I wasn't nervous, I knew it could be the game."

Coleman missed.

"When I released it I knew it was off to the right," Coleman said. "Coach didn't want anyone on the foul line so we wouldn't get in any foul trouble."

Nor could they fight for the rebound. Indiana's Daryl Thomas grabbed it, and the Hoosiers set up their final play.

That play was made by Smart, whose corner jumper won Indiana its third title under Knight.

On the other bench, Boeheim felt the emptiness of last-second defeat. And he doubted his own strategy.

"I think I made a mistake," he said. "If I made a mistake, I think I made it on the earlier free throw. I think we should have kept guys back then, maybe they wouldn't have gotten the transition basket that Smart got. We had the lead and we weren't worrying about scoring more points. We had enough to win."

Not quite.

Crushed Seashells And Punctured Balloons: Al McGuire's Technical Foul Wakes up Wolfpack

Al McGuire was as much a colorful and entertaining personality as he was a brilliant tactician and understanding mentor. Even if he didn't invent the term "aircraft carrier" for hefty centers and forwards, he certainly popularized it. To him, every day brought seashells and balloons. The sun always seemed to be shining for the Marquette coach, and there was always a challenge to be met.

"I don't believe in looking past anybody," he said. "I wouldn't look past the Little Sisters of the Poor after they stayed up all night."

But he also had a tempestuous side that sometimes got the better of him. No, he was not a chair-tossing Bob Knight type. He didn't intimidate physically the way Bob Huggins, coach of Cincinnati and now West Virginia, might.

Still, McGuire was capable of just enough March Madness to spark his team—and ruin it.

His Marquette Warriors were the "other team" in the 1974 title game. North Carolina State was coming off its monumental overtime victory that ended UCLA's incomprehensible run of seven straight national crowns. Though not quite ignored, the Warriors generally were given about as much chance of knocking off the Wolfpack in the final as McGuire was of becoming NCAA president.

But his Warriors were not without talent, from All-American forward Maurice Lucas to freshman Bo Ellis.

Late in the opening half, Marquette's Marcus Washington scored on a drive but was called for a charge. McGuire went wild, drawing a technical foul protesting the call.

His tirade awakened the slumbering Wolfpack, which finally seemed to realize it hadn't won everything by knocking off UCLA. Superstar David Thompson scored four of NC State's 10 points in less than a minute, and the Wolfpack built a nine-point halftime edge. The Warriors never got close enough to threaten again.

After McGuire's technical foul, Marquette turned into "cream puffs," another of the coach's pet phrases.

When it was over, Lucas growled, "Thanks for losing the game for us, coach."

The response was vintage McGuire: "That makes up for all the games I won for you."

Three years later, McGuire and the Warriors won it all.

A Bengal Tigers Boo-boo: LSU's Dale Brown Helps Indiana Win 1981 Title

Dale Brown was the most successful coach in LSU basketball history. Long a football power—the Bengal Tigers have won two national championships—LSU had 18 winning seasons and 15 straight postseason basketball tournament appearances, including 13 in the NCAAs, under Brown. There were two trips to the Final Four, both ended by Brown's archenemy, Indiana coach Bob Knight.

Brown termed Knight "a bully" who intimidated officials, gaining an unfair advantage for the Hoosiers. Knight once quipped about Brown: "I was worried about losing until I looked down the floor and saw Dale Brown. Then I knew we had a chance."

Even though they had future Hall of Famer Isiah Thomas leading them in 1981, the Hoosiers struggled to seize on that chance in the national semifinals in Philadelphia. Brown certainly helped with a decision that backfired.

Brown's highly skilled Tigers rode the "Get Silly in Philly" motto to the Final Four in the City of Brotherly Love—not that Brown and Knight would display any love for each other. Nor would Knight show any adoration for LSU in general, to the point of depositing a heckling Tigers fan into a trash can.

City of Brotherly Love, indeed.

LSU survived a sizzling regional final against Wichita State at the Superdome before a frenzied crowd. The win sent the Tigers to their first Final Four since 1953.

At a price, though. Rudy Macklin broke a finger while trying to block a dunk and was severely hampered against the Hoosiers.

Brown started Macklin against Indiana anyway, but his star struggled. After his team blew a one-point halftime lead and got blown away in the second half, Brown admitted he shouldn't have used Macklin so much.

"Had Rudy not broken his finger, I don't think there's any doubt we would have won it all," Brown said. "I don't want to degrade any of my teams or any other great teams, but it's probably the greatest team in LSU history. I don't think anybody could have beaten us if Rudy had been healthy."

Perhaps. But Brown always will be fingered for his insistence on riding a subpar Macklin.

Imhoff's Hiccups And Heroics: Cal Overcomes Darrall Imhoff's Late-Game Goofs, Thanks to Imhoff Himself

If there's been a greater pure shooter, intelligent defender, and all-around college player than Jerry West, it's hard to imagine. West certainly was the centerpiece of West Virginia's only trip to the national title game, leading the Mountaineers to a meeting with California.

West, however, didn't decide the winner of the 1959 championship. A less-celebrated player did: Darrall Imhoff.

Imhoff wasn't an unknown in the sport, even though Cal didn't originally recruit him out of high school. He was a 6-foot-10 center who developed under Cal coach Pete Newell, perhaps the best mentor of big men in basketball history.

Imhoff was selected a second-team All-American in 1958–59 and would move up to the first team the next year. Twice, he would help the Golden Bears make the Final Four. In the '59 semifinals, his dynamic performance (22 points, 16 rebounds) lifted Cal past Oscar Robertson and Cincinnati.

He would even join West, Robertson, and Jerry Lucas on the 1960 U.S. Olympic squad, one of the original "Dream Teams." Imhoff followed with 12 productive NBA seasons; most of his pro career, he once said, was spent in "Wilt Chamberlain's armpits." Imhoff was the opposing starting center the night Chamberlain scored 100 points in 1962.

But that all came later in his basketball career. Early on at Berkeley, Imhoff was so uncoordinated "he could barely walk when he came to Cal," according to Tom Fitzpatrick, the leading scorer during Cal's run to the title.

Against West Virginia, Imhoff showed some of that clumsiness. And some clutch play, too.

The Golden Bears led by three points with less than a minute to go. Naturally, West had the ball in his hands, and when he drove and shot, Imhoff blocked it.

Goaltending. Mistake number one.

Still, Cal had the ball and there was no shot clock. But when the ball found its way to Imhoff, he was tied up. WVU got the ball back and took a 70–69 lead. Mistake number two.

Imhoff's blunders had cost the Golden Bears. Cost them, yes, but not critically, as it turned out.

Imhoff had a chance to redeem himself—finally.

He missed a hook shot but put in the carom with 17 seconds remaining, scoring the final points in the Golden Bears' 71–70 triumph.

Imhoff jumped from goat to glory.

"If Darrall didn't get his rebound and West Virginia got the ball, it would have been the end for us," Newell said. "We all knew West would score if he got his hands on the ball. It was a great play by Darrall."

It stunned West.

"I didn't think you should have beaten us then, and I still don't," West told Newell years later. "I never will."

Imhoff finished with only 10 points and nine rebounds, not one of his best games. But he could be forgiven. He had provided the winning basket—and Cal's only NCAA basketball crown.

"Nobody back there knew anything about us, except we were from the West Coast and played this defensive-style basketball," Imhoff said. "And I don't think it really hit us until we got back and saw the crowd at the airport."

A crowd he helped attract with his late-game hiccups and heroics.

11.

Classic Confrontations

Jim Valvano, in his words, was speechless. You might say the same for Rollie Massimino—a very rare occurrence.

Could you blame them? Their teams pulled off two of the greatest upsets in the NCAA tournament's history.

These David. vs. Goliath story lines happened just two years apart: Valvano's North Carolina State Wolfpack beat Houston in 1983, and Massimino's Villanova Wildcats downed Georgetown in 1985.

There have been many other stunning upsets in the NCAA tournament's history. But most basketball experts would find it hard to top these two classics in terms of sheer improbability.

And the games were eerily similar:

- In both cases, the underdogs faced 7-foot superstars, Akeem (later Hakeem) Olajuwon with Houston and Patrick Ewing with Georgetown. (Incidentally, both these players were born outside the United States—Olajuwon in Lagos, Nigeria, and Ewing in Kingston, Jamaica—bringing an international flavor to March Madness.) Both Olajuwon and Ewing would go on to Hall of Fame careers after they had each been selected No. 1 overall in the NBA draft.
- In both cases, Houston and Georgetown were ranked No. 1 in the country and playing their best basketball of the season. Houston had won 22 in a row and Georgetown 17, including a sweep through the powerful Big East Conference playoffs.
- Both the Cougars and Hoyas had a number of pro-quality players ticketed for the NBA.
- And both lost the final by two points, North Carolina State beating Houston, 54–52, and Villanova beating Georgetown, 66–64.

Pulling off memorable upsets in the NCAA tournament was nothing new for North Carolina State. Nine years earlier, the Wolfpack had stunned UCLA in the 1974 national semifinals to stop the Bruins' 38-game playoff winning streak, halting their championship run at seven. That shocker belongs near the top of anyone's list of classic tourney games.

Also not to be forgotten: Duke's upset of UNLV in the 1991 national semifinals, and UConn's stirring victory over Duke in the 1999 championship game.

Hard to argue that any of these games don't belong in a top five list of all-time tournament classics, considering their impact on the national scene.

The lasting image of the North Carolina State-Houston game, one seen as often in TV replays as any in the sport's history, is Valvano racing around the court looking for someone, anyone, to hug.

Always ready with a punch line or quick quip, Valvano was so excited and exhausted after that game that he was practically unable to express himself.

"I've got no funny lines," he conceded while facing a news conference after the game.

No matter. He could just enjoy the moment following his team's shocker.

How in the world did the Wolfpack do it? How did they beat Houston? After all, the Cougars were an overwhelming favorite with Olajuwon and Clyde "The Glide" Drexler in the lineup. They were part of a group of fabulous dunk-shot artists known as "Phi Slamma Jamma."

North Carolina State, which wasn't ranked higher than No. 15 all season, had finished only third in the Atlantic Coast Conference.

It didn't look like Valvano's team would survive the first round of the NCAA tournament. The Wolfpack trailed Pepperdine, 59–55, with 28 seconds left in overtime but pulled out a 69–67 victory in double OT.

On to the second round: another thriller, another heart-stopper. This time, the Wolfpack rallied from a 12-point deficit in the second half to beat UNLV, 71–70. Both times, North Carolina State won when its opponents failed to hit crucial foul shots in the final seconds.

After an uncharacteristic blowout of Utah, North Carolina State reverted to form with a nail-biting 63–62 win over ACC colleague Virginia that propelled the Wolfpack into the Final Four in Albuquerque, New Mexico.

With all of the close calls, the Wolfpack were building on their reputation as the "Cardiac Kids."

As the Wolfpack players watched the Cougars destroy Louisville in the semifinals, they were in awe. Not so Valvano. He figured out a way his team could beat the powerful Cougars.

"We will have to control the tempo, keep the score in the fifties and sixties," he said. "We want to be in position to win it at the end."

Valvano wasn't counting on any help from Houston coach Guy Lewis, but he got it. After a 17–2 lightning run put the Cougars ahead, 42–35, with about 10 minutes remaining, Lewis inexplicably slowed things down with his "locomotion offense."

"I was a little surprised," Valvano said later. "They were on a roll. I don't know what was going through Coach Lewis' head."

Just this: Lewis was hoping to pull North Carolina State away from the basket and get some easy layups, but the move backfired.

The Wolfpack, meanwhile, forced a series of turnovers and suddenly couldn't miss their outside shots. North Carolina State pulled even at 52 when Dereck Whittenburg drilled a 20-footer with 1:59 remaining.

Valvano's late-game strategy: foul the Cougars. For all their magnificent talent, Houston was a poor foul shooting team.

The strategy worked beautifully. The Cougars kept missing their free throws, giving the Wolfpack the chance of a lifetime.

Suddenly the ball was in North Carolina State's hands with 44 seconds left.

More late-game strategy from Valvano: hold the ball for the last shot. The precious seconds ticked away.

Thurl Bailey, trapped in the corner, tossed a shaky pass out to Whittenburg at midcourt.

"It wasn't the shot I wanted," Whittenburg said, "but I didn't want to go into overtime knowing I had the ball, but couldn't get the shot off."

The shot was way off the mark, but Lorenzo Charles was standing wide open under the basket. Olajuwon had missed his assignment, failing to cover his man in the lane.

"Akeem didn't see me," Charles said. "He just stood there. He didn't even go up."

Charles did, slamming the ball through the basket at the buzzer for the two-point North Carolina State win.

Then it was time for the emotional Valvano to start hugging anyone he could find, and later for his players to cut down the net—and for the coach to wear a strand of it around his neck.

Valvano's story didn't end there. He would be forced out of coaching when his program was investigated for a number of NCAA violations involving his players. He started a new career as a basketball analyst and became a media darling with his glib, quick-witted observations.

In 1992, Valvano went public with a very private disease. He was battling cancer, which eventually took his life on April 28, 1993.

Another lasting image: Valvano's speech at the ESPY Awards show in 1993, where he was presented with the Arthur Ashe Courage and Humanitarian Award.

"Don't give up," he told the audience, "don't ever give up."

Those words remained a rallying cry for a foundation set up in his name to fight cancer. A legacy that, as it turned out, became far more important than just a basketball championship. In the wake of Valvano's death, a number of sports events sprung up to raise money to continue the battle against cancer. One of the most prominent: the Coaches vs. Cancer Classic tournament (now known as the 2K Sports Classic benefiting Coaches vs. Cancer) played in Madison Square Garden every year.

Two years after North Carolina State had vanquished Houston, another huge underdog pulled off a stunning upset when Villanova beat Georgetown.

Along with Ewing, the Hoyas had four other players who were potential first-round NBA draft picks: David Wingate, Billy Martin, Reggie Williams, and Michael Jackson. The only Villanova player considered good enough to be a first-rounder was center Ed Pinckney.

Hardly anyone gave Villanova much of a chance against Georgetown. The Hoyas, gunning for their second straight national championship, were considered far and away the best team in the country. The Wildcats had played the Hoyas twice during the season, and lost both times.

After the Hoyas had knocked off St. John's in the Big East tournament finals to improve their record to 30–2, Redmen coach Lou Carnesecca called Georgetown a "really great team."

"They're not just physical," he said. "They are just good. They have such flexibility offensively."

The Hoyas charged into the national championship game with a 17-game victory streak.

"It Would Take an NC State-Type Miracle to Unseat the Hoyas Tonight," headlined the *Los Angeles Times*.

No way that could happen again, could it?

Well, yes.

The Wildcats, who had played the Hoyas tough in those two regular-season losses, led 29–28 at the half thanks to some sharp shooting. Nothing, however, like the shooting they did in the second half—some of it from an unlikely source, reserve guard Harold Jensen. He made all five of his shots, including a jumper that put Villanova ahead to stay, to lead an incredible outside shooting display. The Wildcats made nine of 10 shots from the floor.

"Ninety percent, that's unbelievable," said Georgetown's Jackson. "They hit their shots, hit their free throws, and kept coming at us."

The Wildcats were almost as good from the foul line, making 22-of-27 attempts for the game.

Their slowdown offense took care of the rest.

"We weren't afraid to lose," Massimino said. "We were playing to win."

Win they did, with a two-point margin before a disbelieving nation.

To mark the 20-year anniversary of the "Great Upset," the Villanova players had a team celebration. Massimino couldn't bring himself to watch a complete video of the game. Why?

"I still think we might lose," he said, continuing to pinch himself.

Like Massimino, Duke coach Mike Krzyzewski faced a daunting task when his team met UNLV in the 1991 national semifinals.

How do you convince a group of players they're as good as an opponent that whipped them by 30 points in the 1990 final?

This is what Coach K did: he pulled out a tape of the 1990 game and showed the first six minutes to his players. It wasn't a horror movie—well, maybe a little bit horrible—just a way to demonstrate why the Blue Devils lost so badly the previous year. It was a matter of emotion: UNLV had it, Duke didn't.

"This was one of the few games where we actually came back a year later and talked about a team to our guys," assistant coach Pete Gaudet said.

This was, after all, a UNLV team that had rolled up a 45-game winning streak and featured several NBA-quality players: Larry Johnson, Stacey Augmon, Greg Anthony, and Anderson Hunt.

It was basically the same team that had won the national championship in 1990.

The Blue Devils, meanwhile, had lost three senior starters to graduation and featured a youthful lineup that included freshman Grant Hill. The year before, when Jerry Tarkanian's UNLV team had run the Blue Devils out of the arena, Hill was a high school student.

This time, Hill got the Blue Devils off and running with a dunk, giving Coach K's team an early confidence boost. Hill's play against Augmon, a three-time national defensive player of the year, gave the Blue Devils even more of a boost.

Point guard Bobby Hurley made up for a poor performance in the previous year's loss to UNLV with 12 points, seven assists, and only three turnovers in 40 minutes of play.

Christian Laettner and reserve Brian Davis also came through with clutch shots for Duke.

Coach K had said privately his Blue Devils could whip UNLV if they played a perfect game. So they did.

That's just what North Carolina State had done in 1974 to beat a superb UCLA team that featured Bill Walton, one of the greatest college players in the sport's history, and Keith Wilkes, an irrepressible All-American forward.

Make no mistake, the 1973–74 North Carolina State squad was regarded as a powerhouse in many ways equal to the UCLA machine. The Wolfpack had carved out a 27–0 record in the 1972–73 season but were not allowed to play in the postseason because of an NCAA infraction.

The Wolfpack featured David Thompson, a sky-walking, All-American forward, and Tom Burleson, a 7-foot center who could easily dominate any game just like Walton.

But UCLA was UCLA, which is to say merely the greatest dynasty in college basketball history. It might also have been John Wooden's most frustrating team, despite a loaded lineup. It seemed this UCLA team could just turn it on or off by throwing a switch—something no coach would encourage.

The Bruins' record winning streak of 88 games was halted by a one-point loss to Notre Dame in the season's 14th game. UCLA, which lost an 11-point lead to Notre Dame in the final three minutes, made up for it by trouncing the Irish in a return engagement in Los Angeles later in the season.

Somehow, this great UCLA team also managed to lose to lowly Oregon and Oregon State on successive nights in Eugene and Corvallis. Suddenly, the Bruins were battling for their lives in the Pacific-8 Conference, which they eventually won by crushing crosstown rival Southern Cal in the last game of the regular season.

North Carolina State endured more of a struggle to win the Atlantic Coast Conference playoff title, beating Maryland, 103–100, in overtime, another postseason classic. The Wolfpack had an easier time in the NCAA playoffs as they charged toward an eventual meeting with UCLA, which also breezed to the regional title.

Because of the tournament's structure that year, UCLA and North Carolina State, easily the two best teams in the country, were going to settle things in the national semifinals.

Not to be forgotten was their earlier meeting in the regular season, in which UCLA had beaten the Wolfpack by 18 points.

"A real whippin'," UCLA's Tommy Curtis said. "I want State to dwell on that 18-point margin."

The trash-talking had begun.

"We know they aren't 18 points better than us," North Carolina State forward Tim Stoddard said, "but what's more important is that they know it."

For a while, it looked like UCLA was going to have things its way, just as it had earlier in the season against the Wolfpack. Two times during the second half, the Bruins held leads of 11 points.

Not so fast, UCLA.

The Wolfpack applied pressure, and got some key baskets from Thompson, tremendous play from a raging Burleson, and a spark from diminutive Monte Towe, a 5-foot-7 point guard who one writer called a "lovable lightning bug."

North Carolina State's press had helped to turn around the game for the Wolfpack. Suddenly, UCLA's lead was cut to 57–56.

At the end of 40 minutes of regulation, the game was tied, 65–65. At the end of the first overtime, it was 77–77.

"We went to the press simply because we were down," Towe said. "We had to take the fight to 'em."

In the second overtime, UCLA jumped to a seven-point lead, 74–67. But there was still 3:27 left on the clock, enough time for the Wolfpack to come back.

And so they did. Miracle of miracles, North Carolina State wiped out the deficit with the high-flying Thompson leading the way. Thompson's bank shot, followed by two free throws, clinched it for the Wolfpack. Final: North Carolina State 80, UCLA 77.

Unbelievably, UCLA had lost a seven-point lead in overtime. Wooden said he had never seen any of his teams do that.

The Bruins had lost for the first time in 39 playoff games. And for the first time in eight years, they failed to win the national championship.

Not to worry. The Bruins came back in 1975 to restore their place atop the college basketball world. All was right in the sport again—as far as UCLA was concerned, anyway.

Fast forward to the national final between Duke and Connecticut in 1999.

With two championships and five visits to the Final Four, the cocky, consistent Blue Devils could be called the "Team of the Nineties."

Not so Connecticut, which had never won a national championship and was a 9½-point underdog to Duke.

"The Blue Devils seemed at times to be playing in a league by themselves," *Sports Illustrated* said of Duke, which came into the championship game with a fancy 37–1 record.

The Blue Devils featured national player of the year Elton Brand and a deep, fast bench. But UConn was no slouch itself in the speed department.

"The more tape we watched, the more we learned that we're pretty quick ourselves," UConn assistant Tom Moore told *Sports Illustrated*.

Much of that quickness helped swallow up Brand, who faced a double-team time and again.

"I never knew where the double-team was coming from," Brand said.

The Blue Devils were also unable to keep track of UConn's up-tempo offense and were stifled at crucial times by the Huskies defense. Spearheading UConn's 77–74 upset of Duke was Richard Hamilton with 27 points, seven rebounds, and three assists.

The game was so beautifully orchestrated by both coaches (Krzyzewski of Duke and Jim Calhoun of UConn) that even the losing side could appreciate it.

"Twenty years from now, when I'm going bald," Duke forward Shane Battier said, "I can look back and say I played in one of the greatest championship games ever."

And one of the biggest upsets.

12.

Not Only a Man's Game

Humble Beginnings

If you believe James Naismith invented basketball only for men to play, then you don't recognize the Women's National Basketball Association (WNBA), the gold medals earned by the United States in four straight Olympics, or the superpowers Pat Summitt and Geno Auriemma have built at the collegiate level.

Boy, are you missing out.

No, Dr. Naismith had everyone in mind when he devised the game in 1891 in Springfield, Massachusetts.

But it took a woman, Senda Berenson, to introduce the sport to women a short time later at Smith College, not far from the YMCA training center where Naismith had first concocted the game.

For decades, though, the women's game crashed into obstacles created by chauvinists and college presidents, by legislators and lobbyists. It didn't establish a stronghold at the college level until the 1950s and '60s, and only then on smaller levels.

To suggest March Madness eventually would include women's basketball back then would have been, well, madness.

"I was an all-state player in high school (in Gibsonville, N.C.), but there was no opportunity to play in college," said Kay Yow, who went on to a Hall of Fame career as a coach. "There was no real career in coaching for women at that time. I mean there were no role models. There was nothing there. And it was a way of life.

"I grew up at a time that I think that people accepted the way it was, more or less. We answered questions in those days, we didn't question answers."

Yow graduated from East Carolina in 1960 with an English degree. She began her coaching career at the high school level before moving up to North Carolina State and, eventually, leading the U.S. women to a gold medal at the 1988 Summer Olympics in Seoul.

She was a pioneer in the women's game. So was Cathy Rush, who was winning national championships before the NCAA was staging them, leading tiny Immaculata to the first three titles in the Association for Intercollegiate Athletics for Women (AIAW) tournament.

That first championship came in 1972, a watershed year for women's sports. Title IX, as significant a federal law as nearly any in the second half of the twentieth century, was passed, giving women equal opportunities in all educational areas, including athletics.

It would take the NCAA a decade to organize a national tournament for women's basketball, but, thankfully, the AIAW filled the void.

So did colleges such as Immaculata, a Catholic school for women in Malvern, Pennsylvania, with an enrollment under 400 in 1972, and with no gym of its own. And Queens College, a city university in the New York City borough.

And Delta State from the heart of the Mississippi Delta in Cleveland, Mississippi.

AIAW restrictions on scholarships and recruiting in the early years of its national tournament led to such small schools having such a large presence in the women's game. The NCAA didn't exactly sit idly by and watch the AIAW take charge of the female version of college basketball. As the NCAA's members adjusted to Title IX—and in some cases, fought the idea of equality in sports for both genders—the organization also was planning for the day when it would stage a women's event.

Before that would happen, though, women's college hoops had to take baby steps.

Rush recalled those early days at Immaculata, where practices were held while novices training to be nuns played volleyball or roller-skated in the same area. Her players wore tunics and jumpers with box pleats made of wool, then later skirts—hardly like the streamlined outfits of the future. Rush was making less than $500 per year for coaching.

"The stunning part was we had women who could really play the game," said Rush, who had a 149–15 record (.910 winning percentage) in seven years coaching the Mighty Macs. "It was a clear indication that, given the opportunities the men had, women could be just as successful as the men in the sport."

Among those players were Marianne Crawford (later Stanley), Rene Muth (later Portland), and Theresa Shank (later Grentz). All three would make their biggest impact as coaches in the women's game, with Stanley and Grentz joining Rush in the Women's Basketball Hall of Fame. Rush also is in the National Basketball Hall of Fame in Springfield, Massachusetts.

She joked after being a five-time finalist before her election that she had lost more nominations to Springfield's Hall of Fame than games.

"Being here with coaches and players, all of us as coaches know that we're good coaches when we have good players, and we're great coaches when we have great players," Rush said. "And I had some great players."

Grentz probably was the greatest, having led Immaculata to the first three AIAW championships.

"She was no-nonsense. She could scare you anytime," said Portland, who went on to coach at Penn State. "She was the Bill Walton of women's basketball."

At 6-foot, Grentz had good size for the women's game of the 1970s. She also had hops—Rush once called her the best jumper in the sport—and hoops intelligence. Grentz could recognize defenses and immediately break them down, a quality she refined as one of basketball's most successful coaches at St. Joseph's, Rutgers, and Illinois.

"We often used her to bring up the ball, even against smaller, peskier guards," Rush recalled. "Theresa was the whole package: offense, defense, shooting, rebounding, ball-handling. Everything."

The AIAW staged the initial women's tournament at Illinois State. The 16-team field turned out to be strictly a Philadelphia story.

Immaculata, the first Catholic college for women in the Philadelphia area, was one of the underdogs—a big one at that. Perhaps the biggest challenge for the Mighty Macs was simply getting to Normal, Illinois. Nothing Normal in that trip: The players held fund-raisers, selling such items as toothbrushes to earn enough money for the journey. They came up a bit short, and three players were left at home. The rest flew standby, slept four to a room, ate cheaply—and thought nothing of it.

Seeded No. 15, the Macs were expected to be short work for higher-ranked teams such as Mississippi College, Indiana State, Fullerton State, and West Chester, a neighbor back home that wasn't particularly friendly when it had previously routed Immaculata by 32 points. West Chester was so deep that it had four squads it could suit up, and while Immaculata beat the Golden Rams during an undefeated regular season, the Macs weren't playing against West Chester's best. When they did, West Chester romped in a rematch during AIAW regional play.

What chance could a "lucky loser" have—Immaculata had been invited to play in the national tournament despite the regional loss to West Chester?

Plenty.

"It was possible for a small school like Immaculata to compete on a national level because everybody competed in the same pool of teams," Crawford told ESPN. "There wasn't a separation of divisions by small school versus large school.

"I think Immaculata being an all-women's college provided an incubator for women to pursue any opportunity that they thought was possible. And they were encouraged to believe that anything was possible."

Including bringing the first AIAW crown back to Malvern, Pennsylvania.

The Macs beat South Dakota State by 13 points, then took games over Indiana State and a stunning three-point victory against Mississippi College, which had won an invitational tournament in 1971 for an unofficial national championship.

Should Immaculata defeat West Chester in the title game, an official championship banner would hang back on campus.

Rush had no doubts it would happen. Well, maybe a few doubts.

"When we went to Illinois State, we weren't sure how strong the other teams were," she said. "We knew about West Chester, of course, but we saw two different teams from them, one during the (regular season) schedule and one at Towson (in the regional final). We had confidence in our players, but we also were operating in the dark a bit."

Not for the final game, the rubber match between two rivals separated by just 10 miles.

Rush has joked that both teams knew everyone in the stands. Immaculata had perhaps a half-dozen fans on hand—and none of the nuns who would beat buckets like they were drums at home contests.

The Mighty Macs didn't need any support, as it turned out. They beat West Chester, 54–48. The sellout crowds and vast television audiences were decades away. The media section was nonexistent. Headlines about the Macs' mighty triumph? As Diane DiBonaventuro, a future assistant director of athletics at the school, noted, "In 1972 the only way of following the progress . . . at that first national championship was by waiting for the phone call to arrive from one of the players after the game."

The phone calls were celebratory. So was the greeting back home, to the delight of Rush and her national champions.

"The reception was something that I will never, ever forget in my whole life," Rush said. "When we got off the plane and saw family, friends, all the Immaculata family, we all cried. At that point, it became bigger than it had (been) after the game."

The Macs were on their way. So was the AIAW national tournament.

To Auriemma and Summitt, now the preeminent coaches of the women's game, these women were the groundbreakers who enabled them to eventually build UConn and Tennessee into powerhouses.

"Back when I started, my first recollections are of people like Cathy Rush because I am from the Philadelphia area," Auriemma said. "I remember Theresa Grentz and remember what Immaculata, Wayland Baptist, and Delta State did for the game. Also what Sue Gunter and Kay Yow did down at LSU and NC State before people were even allowed to have a program."

Summitt, who like Auriemma is a Hall of Famer, calls those women "trailblazers." She believes the fact every game in the female version of March Madness is now shown on national TV is a credit to the coaches, players, and administrators way back when who performed before family and friends, in front of folks who sat in virtually empty gyms and offered the kind of support that has grown steadily.

"There's no real comparing the game now to the game played back then," Summitt said. "But we wouldn't have come this far without those women who came before us and fought so hard to get the game recognized, to push beyond whatever obstacles were there. And there were many of those obstacles."

With more roadblocks ahead.

Moving Forward

Led by Grentz, Immaculata won the next two titles, beating Queens College before 3,000 fans in 1973, and then Mississippi College. The Macs also beat Queens, 65–61, in February 1975 at Madison Square Garden, the first women's showcase game at the famed arena, where 12,000 fans showed their support.

Delta State, guided by Margaret Wade, the first woman and first women's coach inducted into the National Basketball Hall of Fame, snapped the Macs' majestic streak by beating them in the 1975 and '76 finals. And by 1977, the big schools were becoming big players in women's hoops: Delta State won again, beating LSU.

Rush recognized what was coming.

"We were in the semifinals, but we were not giving scholarships and the school wasn't about to do so," said Rush, who left the job at Immaculata after the 1977 AIAW tournament, when she was making all of $1,200 a year. "That era had passed. The schools that brought in scholarship athletes—and that meant the major universities all over America—were going to take over."

The NCAA wouldn't take over for another five years, but the AIAW's influence began to wane even as the more familiar sports powers began dominating: UCLA, Maryland, and Tennessee charged to the title game. Old Dominion, with championships in 1979 and 1980 behind the great Anne Donovan and Nancy Lieberman, and Louisiana Tech (1981) managed to keep the less-renowned schools in the spotlight.

But 1981 was a critical year for the women's game and its attempts to grab a share of March Madness. That year, the NCAA member schools voted to establish Division I championships for women in several sports, including basketball. AIAW leaders, sensing their influence would disappear once the NCAA began organizing such events, sued. Their claim that the NCAA didn't have the interest of women's basketball and its practitioners at heart had little sway in court and was dismissed.

The AIAW wasn't about to take its ball and go home, though. It adamantly held a 1982 national tournament. So did the NCAA.

The battle was on.

For a year.

Sonja Hogg's Louisiana Tech squad set the tone for '82, eschewing a defense of its AIAW crown to play in the NCAA tournament. It was one of many harbingers.

It was a natural choice, both Hogg and Summitt contended.

"Sixteen of the top 20 ranked teams went to the NCAA," said Hogg, whose budget for the Lady Techsters already was over six figures, large enough that she could hire Leon Barmore as an assistant; Barmore would maintain the school's prominence on the court when he replaced Hogg in 1985.

"It was quite clear where our game was headed once the NCAA decided to be involved," Hogg continued. "The AIAW was great for us, but the NCAA had more to offer for the future. The men's tournament already was taking off and we saw the possibilities for the women's tournament."

Added Summitt: "It was tough emotionally for me, but professionally it was clear-cut. We felt emotionally tied to the AIAW, but there comes a times when you have to look at the big picture, opportunities for your sport and women's athletics across the board."

Summitt and Hogg were the perfect pair to lift the sport, too.

"Sonja was all about raising the awareness of women's basketball," Summitt said. "She wasn't just a great recruiter, she was a great promoter. She could sell an Eskimo ice."

Her Eskimos, uh, Lady Techsters romped through the 32-team NCAA event in 1982, averaging 31.6 points per victory for five games and placing three players—Kim Mulkey, Janice Lawrence and Pam Kelly—on the all-tournament squad. They handled Cheyney State, the last of the non-scholarship schools to make a run for the title, and Mulkey believes the backups for LaTech might have been able to win the title. Or the AIAW crown; the Lady Techsters had beaten AIAW winner Rutgers during the season.

"That was in the day when our second string could have been playing in the Final Four," said Mulkey, who went on to coach Baylor to a national championship in 2005. "We had 10 players on that team that could have started anywhere in the country. Not many teams from that era could play with the teams today. I think we could."

Accepting a bid to the AIAW's swan song was a natural choice for Rutgers, whose coach was Grentz. The site of the tournament's Final Four didn't make the decision any more difficult: the Palestra in Philadelphia.

Sort of a full circle for the star of the Mighty Macs' first AIAW championship.

"We knew early on we were going AIAW," Scarlet Knights guard Patty Coyle told USA Today. "To us kids, it didn't matter. We were in a tournament. At the time, the NCAA was such an unknown to the women's game. The AIAW meant more to us. The AIAW was what we grew up knowing."

Coyle and her sister Mary, also a starting guard, were from Philadelphia. So was All-American June Olkowski. It seemed like fate to them that they would beat Villanova and Texas in the Final Four.

"There was no way we were going back to Philly and not winning it," Patty Coyle said. "We just didn't know how we'd win it."

Coyle scored 30 points and they won the title game by six.

With that, the AIAW's tournament disappeared. March Madness, women's style, now belonged solely to the NCAA.

Dynasties

In the three decades that March Madness has had a woman's touch, only 13 schools have cut down the nets to celebrate a championship. Two of them, the Tennessee Lady Vols and the Connecticut Huskies, tower far above the others.

As do their coaches, Summitt in Knoxville, Auriemma in Storrs.

"It's fair to call them the two coaching giants of our game," Yow, a fellow Hall of Famer, once said. "Just look at the records and what they've achieved on and off the court."

Summitt and Auriemma can accurately be compared to the John Woodens and Adolph Rupps and Dean Smiths and Mike Krzyzewskis of the men's game. And while the quality and quantity of competition in the women's game still isn't close to on par with the men's, Summitt and Auriemma should be recognized for establishing and sustaining elite—at times unbeatable—programs for decades.

They also have provided a spicy touch to their teams' rivalry because, frankly, they aren't fans of each other.

In 2007, a 12-year series between the two schools was ended by Summitt after Tennessee officials notified the Southeastern Conference of potential recruiting violations committed by UConn, including a tour of ESPN headquarters for Maya Moore—who eventually led the Huskies to two championships. The NCAA determined it was a secondary violation, but the bad blood had been spilled. The only time the schools have faced off since has been, well, never.

"We don't play them for a reason," Summitt said.

"We don't have any problems getting games and we don't have any problems getting players," Auriemma countered. "From the time that series ended, we've done OK."

OK, as in taking seven NCAA titles—including five while the annual series was intact—and a record 90-game winning streak that even surpassed the mark set by Wooden's UCLA squads.

It's Summitt, though, who has the overall edge, as the first coach anywhere to 1,000 victories. Sure, longevity is the main reason—she's been at Tennessee since 1975, and chose to continue coaching in the 2011–12 season despite revealing she was suffering from early onset dementia. She has coached nine more seasons than Auriemma has roared on the UConn sideline. But she also has maintained a top-level program since her hiring, with every recruit since 1976 playing in a Final Four. The Lady Vols first showed up at the NCAA Final Four in 1982; they had lost in two AIAW finals before that.

"She's an amazing coach," said Candace Parker, perhaps Summitt's greatest player, who helped Tennessee win two national championships and was voted the Associated Press' Female Athlete of the Year in 2008. "She brings out the best in you and makes you a better player by the time you leave."

And a better person, her former players say.

"She taught us that being a lady and a wonderful person is way more important than anything that you accomplish on the basketball court," added Tamika Catchings, the national player of the year in 2000 and a four-time All-American. "Pat wanted all of us to be successful women, and have more character and class about ourselves than anything."

Notice how Catchings referred to Summitt by her first name, a bit odd in college sports. It's the way Summitt, uh, Pat wants it.

"I really arrived at that playing internationally and playing for Billie Moore and Sue Gunter, and they went on a first-name basis," Summitt said. "I liked it because off the court, I felt like I could approach them and talk to them and be more than just a coach.

"And I think players need more than that. You're a mom or a counselor. You wear a lot of different hats."

Tennessee became titanic in women's hoops in 1987, at last grabbing a national crown in its fourth final, a 67–44 rout of Louisiana Tech—one of the measuring stick programs in the sport at the time. Summitt's "Corn-fed Chicks" had been considered the outsiders in a Final Four that also included Long Beach State and Texas, which was playing on its home court in Austin.

The Longhorns were also the only women at the time to have gone unbeaten, winning the NCAAs in 1986 with a 34–0 mark. Spotless records would become something of a habit in Knoxville and Storrs.

"We had been to seven Final Fours and played in four title games before we ever cut down the nets," Summitt told the *Tennessean*. "I remember when we went to Texas that year, I felt our team was loose in a good way. They were calm and confident."

Summitt asked her players in the hotel if they were ready to do something special.

"And I just remember Karla Horton at the time saying, 'We're on a mission. We're going to win the championship,'" Summitt said. "It was a strange feeling I had then. I thought, 'You know what, this group is so incredibly focused.'"

That focus has been a hallmark of the Lady Vols in all 22 of their Final Four appearances (both in the AIAW and NCAA tournaments) under Summitt.

After that initial taste of supremacy in '87, the Lady Vols won an all-SEC final against Auburn in 1989 and survived against sensational guard Dawn Staley and Virginia two years later for their third championship in five years. It was just an appetizer.

Summitt's squads would go to all four NCAA finals from 1995–98, winning three. In the first of those four title contests, they encountered a new opponent, a rising program from the Northeast: UConn.

The Superstar Women

Quick quiz: Name the greatest players in NCAA tournament history.

Answer: Do we have enough space to list all of the standouts?

Now try it for the women's game. A bit easier to recognize them, sure, but getting tougher all the time.

Since the NCAA took charge of the women's version of March Madness in 1982, the tournament, particularly the Final Four, has featured players every bit as dominant and memorable as their male counterparts. Here's a look at a dozen megastars of March Madness.

Jennifer Azzi, Stanford

Azzi and her teammates in 1987 spent almost as much time handing out flyers trying to attract fans as they did playing hoops. The Cardinal were a .500 team then, but by 1990 they were a power, the first of Stanford's great squads. Azzi was the catalyst.

"She had great talent around her, but Jennifer really was the leader of the pack," Stanford coach Tara VanDerveer said. "She got it all rolling. She got the train rolling."

Azzi collected plenty of hardware as a senior (Wade Trophy, Naismith Player of the Year, Honda-Broderick National Player of the Year). Most important, she led Stanford to the national championship, an 88–81 win over Auburn in Knoxville, not far from her hometown of Oak Ridge, Tennessee.

Lady Vols coach Pat Summitt wondered how she ever let Azzi escape.

"She just got better and better," Summitt said. "I thought she'd be good. I didn't know she'd be great. But she was great."

Tamika Catchings, Tennessee

The daughter of former NBA player Harvey Catchings, Tamika was a 6-foot-2 force who dealt with a partial hearing loss to help the Lady Vols win the 1998 crown and advance to the final in 2000, where they lost to UConn. The national player of the year in 2000 and a four-time All-American, Catchings led Tennessee to a 134–10 overall record and four Southeastern Conference regular-season titles. The Lady Vols won three SEC tournaments in her career, and she was a Kodak All-American in all four of her college seasons.

(continued)

The Superstar Women *(Continued)*

Catchings' career ended when she tore knee ligaments in January 2001. Her No. 24 jersey later was retired by the school.

"She is a perfect role model for young adults and for what hard work can achieve," Summitt said.

Anne Donovan, Old Dominion

The first big star of the women's NCAA tournament after over-powering performances in the AIAW title chases, Donovan was the nation's top high school player when she headed from Ridge-wood, New Jersey, to ODU. At 6-foot-8, her height advantage was obvious, and Donovan used it to score 2,719 points, grab 1,976 rebounds, and block an almost unimaginable 801 shots in three All-American seasons. The Monarchs went 116–20 and won a national championship during that time, and she sparked the school to the 1983 Final Four as something of a one-woman team en route to earning national player of the year honors.

Donovan was driven to succeed.

"She had to work very hard for what she accomplished," said Ann Meyers, a four-time All-American at UCLA. "She was not strong. She was not quick. . . . There was criticism of her game."

Criticism that faded as Donovan dominated college ball, then went on to success as an international player and coach.

Chamique Holdsclaw, Tennessee

A four-time All-American and the leading scorer in SEC history when she left the Lady Vols in 1999—Tennessee became the first school with three straight women's titles during that time—Holdsclaw was a 1998 and '99 national player of the year. The team went 134–17 during her career, and she won the Sullivan Award as America's top amateur athlete in 1998.

Holdsclaw overcame a difficult childhood in Queens, New York, where her mother was an alcoholic and her father had mental health problems. Those struggles left scars, and she later battled depression that led to a brief retirement from professional basketball.

"I was so embarrassed," she told the AP's Paul Newberry in 2009. "The kids would make fun of me. They would make fun of my mom. They would be saying, 'Why is your mom like that?' It made me almost like an introvert. I was always fun to be around, but a part of me kind of went into my little box."

Considering the issues Holdsclaw dealt with before arriving in Knoxville, her college career is even more remarkable.

Venus Lacy, Louisiana Tech

You don't get a parkway in your hometown—in this case Chattanooga, Tennessee—named after you without some impressive achievements.

Lacy, a 6-foot-4 center, helped the Lady Techsters to the 1988 championship and to the Final Four in '99. Twice she made the all-tournament team showing an impressive array of skills, particularly her defense, rebounding, and clutch scoring.

In 1990, Tech had an undefeated regular season to earn the nation's No. 1 ranking, and Lacy averaged 24.2 points and 12.7 rebounds. She earned player of the year honors that season, then headed overseas to begin her professional career, returning after the WNBA came along.

"You don't come across players like Venus often, and when you do you cherish the opportunity to coach her," Tech coach Leon Barmore said. "Venus always was about improving her game and making the team better. She did it for all (four) seasons."

Rebecca Lobo, Connecticut

Undefeated seasons have become something of the norm in Storrs, and the first perfect record came in 1995, when Lobo was the Huskies' key performer. Named the most outstanding player in the Final Four as UConn went 35–0, the 6-foot-4 Lobo patched up differences with coach Geno Auriemma—they had even stopped talking away from the court for a while—to carry Connecticut to its first NCAA crown. Lobo was the Associated Press' Female Athlete of the Year for '95, as well as college hoops' top player and the Woman of the Year, as selected by the Women's Sports Foundation.

(continued)

The Superstar Women *(Continued)*

"It's all a matter of attitude," she said, citing the importance of a balanced life on campus. "Athletes who take to the classroom naturally or are encouraged to focus on grades should be able to do well in the classroom. I believe the reason you go to college is to get your degree. It's not a minor league or an audition for the pros."

A little more than a year later, Lobo was one of the founding players of the WNBA.

Cheryl Miller, Southern California

To merely identify Cheryl Miller as the older sister of former NBA great Reggie Miller would be paying a huge disservice to her; Miller made it into the Basketball Hall of Fame before her sibling. After being chosen a high school All-American an unprecedented four times, Miller was the MVP of the 1983 and '84 NCAA championship teams at USC. The smooth, versatile 6-foot-2 Miller was so superior to her peers, she won three straight national player of the year awards and shared 1984 outstanding college athlete honors with swimmer Tracy Caulkins.

Miller was more than a scorer, although she poured in 3,018 points as a Lady Trojan, then an NCAA record. She grabbed 1,534 rebounds, and had 462 steals in 128 games—another NCAA mark. She was so dynamic that no position defined her, and after leading Southern Cal past defending champion Louisiana Tech in the 1983 title game as a freshman, Miller was called "one of the few women who can single-handedly turn the tide of the game" by Tech coach Barmore. And Miller got even better after that; her achievements included anchoring the 1984 gold medal-winning U.S. Olympic squad.

Maya Moore, Connecticut

The latest of the greatest, the 6-foot Moore was a four-time All-American who guided UConn to two national championships and won three national player of the year honors. Moore stood out as much in the classroom as on the court, earning Academic All-American honors as frequently as she collected basketball trophies.

Moore began playing basketball when her mother installed a hoop on a door in their apartment; Maya was three years old.

On the night UConn broke the UCLA men's college hoops record of 88 consecutive wins, Moore punctuated her role for the Huskies by scoring 41 points. She also had 10 rebounds, three assists, three blocks, and a steal.

"Every night when you need her to be at her best," Auriemma said, "she's at her best."

Candace Parker, Tennessee

Talk about players who could do it all, Parker was the epitome of versatility. At 6-foot-4, she could run the floor; block shots in the post; defend point guards, forwards, and centers; and make any kind of shot. Including dunks.

In 2008, Parker won a second successive national title and an Olympic gold medal, was named the Associated Press' Female Athlete of the Year, and became the top pick in the WNBA draft, a selection that served as a springboard to rookie of the year *and* league MVP honors.

"Talk about hitting all the high points of one's life," Summitt said. "She enjoyed an incredible run of back-to-back national championships, Olympic gold, and all of her individual accolades. It was an exceptional year for an exceptional athlete and person."

Parker was the centerpiece during one of Tennessee's greatest basketball periods, and also was a primary reason for a surge in the popularity of the women's game through social media.

Dawn Staley, Virginia

One of those rare standouts who didn't win a national championship, Staley was a groundbreaker. A relentless defender and explosive penetrator at 5-foot-6, Staley helped open up the women's game, taking it from a more staid, walk-the-floor style to something resembling a manic fire drill.

"I look at myself as an odds beater," Staley said.

(continued)

The Superstar Women *(Continued)*

The Cavaliers, who have never won the NCAA crown, went to three Final Fours and one title contest thanks to Staley, who set a national record with 454 steals during her stellar four seasons in Charlottesville. She was the national player of the year in 1991 and '92 and a three-time All-American.

"People look at the point guard position and refer everything off of Dawn Staley, because of her leadership," Meyers said. "Players are told all the time they can't do something because of their size, but Dawn is the perfect example of what you can accomplish. Playing with the guys out on the playground and at her size, people are telling her, 'You can't, you can't, you can't.' She could."

Sheryl Swoopes, Texas Tech

Often referred to as the "Female Jordan," the 6-foot Swoopes did her best MJ imitation in the Southwest Conference final in 1993. On her way to MVP honors, Swoopes victimized Texas for a career-high 53 points.

She didn't stop there, carrying the Lady Raiders, previously an afterthought in the sport, past Vanderbilt and Ohio State to win their only national title. She scored a record 47 points in the title game.

Swoopes was named player of the year, took the Sullivan Award for all amateur athletes, and was selected Sportswoman of the Year by the Women's Sports Foundation.

"I can't tell you what Sheryl has meant to this program," said Marsha Sharp, Swoopes' coach at Texas Tech. "She'll be a legend in women's basketball, but not just because of her play. She has a charisma that the crowd loves. You never doubt that she is a team player."

Diana Taurasi, Connecticut

The ultra-intense 6-foot guard joined Miller, Staley, and Holdsclaw in winning consecutive Naismith Player of the Year awards as the catalyst for UConn's three straight national titles in 2002, '03, and '04. She was the outstanding player of the Final Four in the last of those two seasons.

While collecting hardware and championships, Taurasi made herself into a star. She didn't win titles in high school, and in the biggest game of her early college life, she shot 1-for-15 in a national semifinal loss to Notre Dame in 2001. It was her only NCAA tournament loss.

"She just turns it on like no one I've ever seen," Auriemma said. "She's just different. If it wasn't for the way she is, the way she plays, the way she comes to practice and the kind of teammate she is, there's no way the rest of her teammates would have been able to do what they did. . . ."

Taurasi's career overseas hit a snag in 2010 when she tested positive for a mild stimulant, but she was cleared of any wrongdoing.

A Bitter Rivalry

While the Lady Vols were considered women's basketball's preeminent program, Auriemma's Huskies had established themselves as a force, but he had had to coach for a decade before pulling things together. UConn went 30–3 in 1993–94, setting up the team for one of the greatest seasons in NCAA history.

Unbeaten as they traveled to Minneapolis for March Madness '95 with 33 victories in their pockets, the Huskies had added star recruit Nykesha Sales to a squad that included All-American Rebecca Lobo—a dominating presence underneath—Kara Wolters, and Jen Rizzotti. No NCAA basketball team, men's or women's, had won 35 games, and two victories in the Final Four would get UConn to that number.

Formidable Stanford was no challenge for the Huskies in an 87–60 rout. When Tennessee beat Georgia in the other semifinal, it set up a classic matchup for the crown—and a piece of history.

Among UConn's 29 regular-season wins was an 11-point decision over the Lady Vols in Storrs, the first time they had ever faced off, and a meeting of the nation's top two teams that had been televised nationally. Now, they would take the sport's biggest stage for the rematch.

"Tennessee has proven itself over the years," Auriemma said. "It's the kind of challenge we look forward to."

For a half, it looked like too much of a challenge. Lobo fell into foul trouble, and the Lady Vols, led by Nikki McCray, grabbed a six-point lead.

But the Huskies never lost their poise, even though Tennessee had been in this position so many more times. Lobo scored 11 second-half points and UConn blitzed the Lady Vols in the final 20 minutes for a 70–64 victory.

Of all his teams, Auriemma cites the 1995 squad that went 35–0 as his most influential in helping popularize women's basketball.

"I think the 1995 team because of their personality, going undefeated, and where we are located in the country had a big impact," Auriemma said. "The amount of media that congregated here created a lot of new basketball fans, and we followed up with two or three more teams that were of the same vein."

That level of interest would be ratcheted up by the Huskies and Lady Vols for the next 16 years as both schools built their dynasties. Auriemma got a kick out of the acclaim that has come his way—in an ironic way.

"A lot of guys that were coaching when I was playing said I'd never be any good as a player. They were right," Auriemma said. "So I turned out to be the coach of a championship team."

But not again for a few years. Instead, the Lady Vols were more dynamic and dominant than ever in a hat-trick title run from 1996–98. Women's hoops already was a fixture in Knoxville, where Summitt's teams regularly outdrew the men. With the addition of the sensational Chamique Holdsclaw in 1996 to a squad already deep in talent and moxie, Tennessee shrugged off the bull's-eye on its back.

Indeed, Tennessee embraced being everyone's target.

"We knew whoever we played, whether it was at the beginning of the season, during the conference games, and in the tournament, we would get their very best," Summitt said. "That was our challenge, and our teams responded to it the way champions do. I believe those three teams had a lasting effect on our program and, I hope, on our sport."

How good were those Lady Vols? They went a combined 100–14 in those three championship seasons, and that includes 10 defeats in 1996–97 when, nonetheless, they stormed to the national crown.

The '96 tournament was a particular feast for Michelle Marciniak. The pepper-pot point guard with the slick moves that earned her the nickname "Spinderella" had 10 points, five assists, and two steals in an 83–65 championship game victory over SEC rival Georgia, helping her secure the tournament's outstanding player award.

Marciniak had begun her college career at Notre Dame, but quickly recognized it was not the right place for her. So she called Summitt.

"I was talking to Pat and she asked, 'What's wrong? Why do you want to transfer?'" Marciniak said. "I said because I wanted to play for one of the best coaches in the country and I wanted to have the opportunity to play for a national championship team."

Tennessee rarely took transfers back then. Marciniak told Summitt that if she didn't take her, she was going to either Virginia or Rutgers.

"I said, 'Well, come on to Tennessee,'" Summitt said.

Summitt and Marciniak had a special bond. Back when the coach was first recruiting the player in Macungie, Pennsylvania, Summitt was eight months pregnant. She went into labor during the trip, flew back to Knoxville, and gave birth to her son, Tyler.

Summitt and Marciniak also were similar—perhaps too similar—in their headstrong approaches.

"She's been a challenge to coach, I'll tell you that, primarily because we're a lot alike. It's hard to get along with someone that's as stubborn as you are," Summitt said with a laugh. "But I respect the fact that Michelle's a great competitor and she works hard. I never had to go to practice and motivate Michelle. If anything, I had to slow her down. She's very special in many ways."

So was Holdsclaw. Heavy favorites entering the 1996–97 season as Holdsclaw's star soared, the Lady Vols hit a pothole on the road back to the Final Four. Make that a sinkhole.

Midway through the season, Tennessee was wobbling with a 10–6 record.

"Coach Summitt over-scheduled," Summitt admitted after all six of those defeats came against top 10 opponents, including the top five in the rankings at the time they met the Lady Vols.

But that kind of schedule hardened the women. Tennessee had lost Marciniak and fellow guard Latina Davis to graduation, and Kellie Jolly injured her knee before the season began.

"I have to keep reminding myself this is a young team," Summitt said. "We don't have the weapons we had a year ago or that we'll have in another year. This is all we've got and we've got to do the best with it."

The best was yet to come, thanks greatly to Holdsclaw.

Tennessee was 23–10 and seeded third in the Midwest for the NCAA tournament. But, as noted by Jolly, who had returned to the lineup in just three months after recovering from a torn knee ligament, "This is March. It's our favorite month."

By late March, not only were the Lady Vols still around, but they were meeting Connecticut for a spot in the Final Four. Oh yes, one other tiny detail: Auriemma's Huskies were undefeated.

"You respect a team with that kind of record," Holdsclaw said. "But you can't fear them."

Tennessee displayed not one iota of fear in the Iowa City matchup. Using a pressure defense, timely offense from Jolly, and the wizardry of Holdsclaw all over the court, the Lady Vols built an eight-point halftime lead—the first time UConn trailed at the half all season.

"We weren't used to being in those type of situations," said Connecticut standout Sales, who would finish with 26 points and 14 rebounds. "People had to step up and do things to cut their lead and we did, but they just kept throwing things right back at us."

Mostly, the All-American Holdsclaw was throwing in shots and grabbing rebounds, carrying Tennessee with 21 points and 11 boards as the Lady Vols headed right back to the Final Four with a 91–81 victory.

"Our team was able to play loose," Summitt said. "We talked about how we were the underdogs and we wanted to beat the top dogs."

Tennessee joined Notre Dame, Stanford, and Old Dominion in the Final Four. The Fighting Irish were the only opponent in Cincinnati that Tennessee had beaten during the season. The Vols had absorbed losses to Stanford and Old Dominion and fallen out of the Associated Press' top 10 for the first time in 11 years.

Facing Notre Dame in one of the semifinal games, Holdsclaw put on a show worthy of the spotlight.

"She seemed to do whatever she wanted—at will," Notre Dame guard Beth Morgan said.

Holdsclaw scored 31 points, making 13 of Tennessee's 30 total baskets. With Holdsclaw scoring 19 of her points in the second half, the Lady Vols sprinted away to an 80–66 win that clinched the school's seventh title game appearance.

"I played relaxed, I ran the floor. I think it was the best (game) I've had all year," Holdsclaw said. "I was excited. I didn't want to have a letdown on my end and I just gave it all I had."

Asked where Tennessee would be without Holdsclaw, teammate Abby Conklin told the Associated Press: "Spring break."

Instead, the Lady Vols were in their third successive championship contest, this one against Old Dominion, which had hammered them, 83–72, during the regular season but barely squeezed past Stanford in overtime in the national semifinals.

ODU had a strong history of its own, having won the 1985 NCAA championship after a terrific run in AIAW play that included a 1980 final-game win against Tennessee.

"I think when you have an opportunity to be a part of a national championship run, you experience something that's second to none," said coach Wendy Larry, an assistant on ODU's 1980 and 1985 title teams and a player for the Virginia school from 1973–76.

"When I took a head coaching position I wanted to share that type of exhilaration with some of my own players," she said.

Now was that chance, but it meant beating a program against whom everyone in the sport was measured.

"I don't feel pressure to defend a championship," Summitt said. "If Tennessee never wins another national championship, we have our place in the history book."

Add another illustrious chapter.

Summitt was halfway to Wooden's 10 championships following a 68–59 victory built as much on her coaching acumen as the awesome skills of Holdsclaw, the tournament's MVP. Summitt designed a defense constructed on physicality, urging her players to "get in their faces from the opening tip," according to Jolly. It worked, as Tennessee took away ODU's rhythmic offense and limited the creativity of point guard Ticha Penicheiro.

The Lady Monarchs' Portuguese guard was scoreless in the first half and shot only 4-for-13 overall. She set a then-championship game record with eight steals, but it hardly was enough.

Particularly with Holdsclaw on the other side. Her 24 points were a key, but her court presence was the difference—just the way it has to be in March Madness.

And Holdsclaw had two more years remaining in Tennessee Orange. Even though the WNBA had been established, women players did not leave school early to turn pro.

Holdsclaw thoroughly agreed with that approach, one that has served the women's game well on both levels.

"I think what the league needs is mature young ladies who have their degrees and who want to go farther than play basketball as a career," she told the Associated Press. "And I think also by playing college basketball, you develop your name. Then, by your graduation or going pro, it does a greater good for the sport of women's basketball."

The greater good in women's college basketball was centered in Knoxville.

"I feel this championship will always stand out," Summitt said of the 1997 title. "They played the toughest schedule and they didn't fold. And I will tell you, I was tough on them."

Tough? You want to see tough?

Look at what the Lady Vols did to the rest of the women's basketball world the next season.

Thirty-nine games, 39 victories.

No Division I team had ever won that many games in a season. Of all the unblemished squads up to that point, the 1998 national champions probably were the most dominant.

Buoyed by their previous two titles, particularly the 1997 version in which Tennessee had scrapped for most of the season until making a shocking run to the top, the Lady Vols in 1998 shattered the notion of parity in the sport with a 30-point average margin of victory.

Sure, they would be tested, particularly by North Carolina in the Mideast Regional final. But, really, while in most years a dozen schools could win the NCAAs, only one truly was in contention in 1998.

And the sporting world noticed.

"Even average fans, people who didn't even know that much about the sport, began to recognize what Tennessee basketball was all about," Iowa State coach Bill Fennelly said.

Holdsclaw became the centerpiece of the "Three Meeks," joined by Catchings and Semeka Randall. They toyed with the opposition to the point that Summitt turned sarcastic when explaining the '98 team's success.

"I taught Semeka Randall how to shoot, I taught Tamika Catchings how to run the floor, I taught Chamique Holdsclaw how to score with the game on the line," Summitt said with a hearty laugh. "What I'm trying to say is, it takes good players."

This Tennessee team had some *great* players, and only once did its destiny seem in doubt.

In the Mideast Regional final, North Carolina used the same tactics of aggressive defense, ball movement, and sharpshooting that defined the Lady Vols, and the Tar Heels built a 12-point edge with just over seven minutes remaining. A desperate Summitt summoned up the right words, as she nearly always did, and the right strategy.

"It was not exactly what I had anticipated," Summitt said. "When we were down 12, I was asking them if I was coaching the wrong team. They were beating us at our own game. I was wondering if we should change uniforms. But I like what I saw down the stretch."

What she saw was Holdsclaw, who had won a championship in each of the past six years (four in high school) take over, particularly from the foul line, on her way to 29 points. Randall added 20, and a huge disparity in free throws, 33–18 in favor of the Lady Vols, helped boost Tennessee into the Final Four.

Also there, at last, was the highly respected Yow. North Carolina State made it to Kansas City after Yow had compiled 23 seasons and 552 victories, plus that gold medal with the 1988 U.S. Olympic team.

"It does thrill me to be here," she said. "I worked every year to get here. If I hadn't gotten to a Final Four ever, I will have had a very full career. To be here at a Final Four is icing on the cake."

No. 9 Arkansas became the lowest seed to make a women's Final Four, and when the Razorbacks got to Kansas City, coach Gary Blair explained why that was a good thing.

"What we did gave hope to everybody else coaching this game, to never give up on your team," said Blair, who would wait another 13 years before winning a national championship, with Texas A&M. "You get a few breaks and you never know what might happen."

Except when Tennessee was the opponent. Everyone pretty much knew what would happen.

Holdsclaw held court with her younger teammates before facing Arkansas, warning them not to get overwhelmed by the occasion.

"Chamique told us she was excited in her first year coming here and Pat had to pull her aside and tell her she needed to focus," said Catchings, then a freshman.

Perhaps awakened by their scare against North Carolina, the Lady Vols romped past their SEC rival, 86–58, for win No. 38; the 28-point margin was an NCAA semifinals record. The first three-peat in NCAA women's basketball was on the horizon.

"I told the team that we are now right where we wanted to be," Summitt said.

So was Louisiana Tech, which knocked off Yow and NC State, 84–65, to set up a classic matchup: Tennessee would be playing in its eighth title game, the Lady Techsters in their sixth, with two previous wins.

"Looking forward to it," Tech coach Barmore said.

Very quickly, though, Barmore and his team were looking for a place to hide. They had no answers for Tennessee's relentless defense and varied offense. By halftime, the Lady Vols were ahead by 23 points. Get the trophy ready.

"That's the greatest women's basketball team that I, personally, have ever seen," Barmore said after a 93–75 drubbing.

Catchings, destined to succeed Holdsclaw as a premier player, scored 27 points, and Holdsclaw had 25. Jolly added a career-high 20, and before long, everyone was echoing Barmore's praise.

Even Summitt, who rarely gets carried away by her teams' achievements.

"I can tell you it's the quickest, the best defensive team I've coached and the best transition team overall that I've coached," she said. "I also can tell you it's a team unlike any that I've coached in terms of their competitiveness and their will to win.

"A lot of players say they want to win. But this team, their preparation was tremendous."

Thirty-nine times out of 39.

Yet Holdsclaw, channeling her inner soothsayer, said, "You know what? "Next year's team will be the best ever."

It wouldn't. Not even close.

Heroic Huskies

Instead, a new era dawned for the Lady Vols—and for women's basketball in general.

Shockingly, Holdsclaw's senior year ended in the NCAA regionals. And the Lady Vols wouldn't win another championship for a decade.

Instead, talk of any dynasty would move hundreds of miles northeast, to a small town in Connecticut called Storrs, home of Auriemma's Huskies.

Not that Summitt's Lady Vols disappeared. After Purdue won the '99 title, Tennessee surged back to the Final Four in 2000. The first final of the new century would be a benchmark for the two powerhouses, as it catapulted UConn to a glorious period during which the women from Tennessee played second fiddle.

Auriemma had begun to surpass nearly every other coach in recruiting, scouring the nation and even international areas—his shooting guard in 2000, Svetlana Abrosimova, was from Russia—for talent. His persuasiveness brought Shea Ralph, Sue Bird, and Asjha Jones to Connecticut, and they brought the Huskies to the top.

In 1995, UConn had ended a perfect season with a 70–64 win over Tennessee for its first crown. Since then, Auriemma's teams had exited March Madness rather quietly. There was nothing quiet about the 2000 bunch, which was 34–1—guess who beat the Huskies, by one point in Storrs?—heading to Philadelphia for the Final Four.

Nor was there anything muted about the Lady Vols, led by the spirited Catchings.

The semifinals were something of an afterthought. UConn ripped Penn State by 18 points, and Tennessee took Rutgers by 10. On to what Ralph claimed was the matchup the world expected.

"Anyone who follows women's basketball has been waiting for this game," Ralph said of the top two teams in America meeting for the championship. "Everyone penciled Tennessee and Connecticut in their bracket. We're ready for it."

Added Summitt, who is not given to hyperbole, "I don't know that there's ever been a better matchup. It doesn't get any better than this."

At that point in their rivalry, which would go from intense to bitter to being in limbo, the teams had split 10 games. Tennessee's 72–71 regular-season victory at UConn had avenged a seven-point defeat at the hands of the Huskies at home a month earlier.

Auriemma understood the unpredictable nature of the sport and was cherishing UConn's first championship game in five years.

"One little thing can go wrong and you don't make it. Being good is not good enough," he said. "So the fact that we are good enough and fortunate enough to be here, I think we cherish this as much as anything."

Summitt and the Lady Vols would have nothing to cherish about this game.

UConn stormed to a 21–6 lead and never looked back, punctuating its defense with 11 blocks. The high level of energy Ralph brought to every possession and every defensive stand was infectious for the deep and versatile Huskies.

"I don't think I've ever wanted anything like I wanted this tonight," said Ralph, selected the MVP of the Final Four after making 7-of-8 shots, scoring 15 points with seven assists, six steals, and a blocked shot. Not bad for someone who had missed the 1997–98 season with her second right knee injury in as many seasons.

"We came out with a vengeance," she said. "We came out like we wanted something, and we got it. And I think we deserve it."

Did they deserve a nod as the most brilliant of all UConn teams—if not the shiniest gem women's basketball ever had seen? After the players carried Auriemma down the court in a quasi-victory lap, he was asked where the 2000 team ranked.

"Not sure," he said. "But I'd take this group any time."

Auriemma would take several other groups to similar heights, including more than one team worthy of being called the greatest the sport has seen.

In 2001, Notre Dame would replace Tennessee as the Huskies' chief adversary—at least for one year. Each team went 32–2 during the season, 15–1 in the Big East. They split two meetings before facing off in St. Louis, site of the Final Four.

"Us and Tennessee used to be Ali-Frazier," Auriemma said. "This is Ali-Foreman."

That would make the Irish Ali, because they stormed back from a 16-point deficit in the first half and won going away, 90–75.

UConn was without Ralph and Abrosimova, both injured, and simply didn't have the firepower to hang with Notre Dame for 40 minutes.

The Irish beat Purdue in an all-Indiana final, while the Huskies headed home to heal—and build.

The result would rock the basketball world.

By the 2002 NCAA tournament, it was clear all championship aspirations, whether they emanated from the Smoky Mountains (Tennessee), the Pacific Coast (Stanford), the Dust Bowl (Oklahoma), or other points across America, would have to go through Connecticut and the dominant UConn Huskies.

"Connecticut being a basketball state, being a small state, (women's basketball) could really own the state," said Pat Meiser-McKnett, who had directed the search that brought Auriemma to Storrs. "Geno was the kind of person who could provide the leadership."

Auriemma recruited one strong class after another, so while the likes of Bird and Jones were maturing, a Swin Cash or Diana Taurasi or Ann Strother was being added to the mix.

Auriemma created an environment of intense competition just to get on the court, let alone get to the Final Four. It's an approach that has served him well for decades, never more so than from 2002–04.

"The great ones are hoping, and praying in some ways, that it's hard as hell. They want it to be like that. And then they'll go, 'Man, this is why I came here,'" Auriemma said. "And then because it's hard for them to break into the lineup because you have so many good players, the demands of all the things that go with playing in this program, every day they walk around with these incredible expectations. They can't just go, 'I don't feel like it today.'"

For three straight seasons, not only did the Huskies feel like it every day, but also they performed every day.

Auriemma's 2001–02 team surpassed even his unbeaten squad of seven years earlier. Indeed, it was one of his favorites, and not just because the Huskies tended to blow out every opponent on the way to a 33–0 mark entering the NCAAs. And not just because national television had discovered these Huskies and popularized them far away from Hartford and Bridgeport and New Haven;

the national semifinals would draw 29,619 to the Alamodome, the largest crowd ever for a women's college basketball game.

"There's a certain style these kids have. There's a certain flair that they play the game with," Auriemma explained. "That's the kind of stuff I like. I like the way they play."

Driven by the memory of their collapse the previous year against Notre Dame, the Huskies' closest game in the early rounds of the '02 tournament was an 18-point win. Even though the other semifinalists were formidable—Auriemma and Summitt would face off in the semis after Duke took on Oklahoma and the sensational Stacey Dales—UConn was an overwhelming favorite for its third title in seven years.

These Huskies were relentless, whether it was Taurasi pushing the ball upcourt, or the defense pestering and punishing the opposition everywhere. If Cash wasn't leading the charge, Tamika Williams might be. Or Jones was controlling the paint. Or Bird, in her final season at UConn, was making like a player of the year.

"They carry a great deal of mystique," Dales said. "That's one of the driving forces behind how successful they are."

But Tennessee had experienced even more success through the years. And Summitt wasn't bringing a bunch of scrubs to San Antonio. Kara Lawson and Michelle Snow were stars in their own right.

Plus, a victory would push Summitt past Jody Conradt of Texas and make her the winningest coach in women's hoops.

Summitt would have to wait.

The Huskies' dogged defense limited the Lady Vols to 31 percent shooting in a 79–56 demolition. Every one of the Huskies had a solid game, but Bird was spectacular, with 18 points, five assists, and shutdown defense on Lawson.

Not to be outdone, Jones had 18 points and 10 rebounds, while point guard Taurasi scored 17 and hauled in 10 rebounds.

"It was very shocking to see how we played," Tennessee's Loree Moore said. "We didn't get going into our rhythm and they took advantage of that. They just steamrolled."

The Sooners saw what Connecticut had achieved, and having defeated Duke, 86–71, they put up a brave front as they contemplated the final—Oklahoma's first trip that far.

"I don't think the championship trophy has been sent to Storrs," Sooners coach Sherri Coale said. "If it's all right with the rest of you guys, we're going to play for it."

But they wouldn't play well enough to stop that UPS shipment to Connecticut.

Yes, Oklahoma challenged the Huskies like few other opponents had that season. Auriemma called the 82–70 win the most difficult hurdle of all—his team's average victory margin of 35.4 points was an NCAA record—and praised the Sooners' desire and focus. But he knew, just as everyone else in the country knew, just how deserving a champion UConn was.

Again, it was the defense and power game that proved decisive. Connecticut outrebounded Oklahoma, 44–25, the second-largest rebounding margin in a championship game, and held the Sooners to 38.7 percent shooting.

So was the team that made UConn the first school to manage two undefeated seasons the greatest of all?

"When you've got players ahead of you, like Rebecca Lobo and Jennifer Rizzotti, you can't be the greatest," UConn's Williams said about the stars of the 1995 unbeaten team. "Are we up there with one of the best? Yes. Can we challenge one of the best teams? Yes.

"But the game is moving so fast, there is going to be another four or five like us that is going to do some good for women's basketball."

Many of them would represent UConn.

Yet following up such perfection would be a formidable challenge for Auriemma and his Huskies. Gone from the roster were Bird, Cash, Jones, and Williams, all seniors. Ahead, Auriemma knew every opponent would be primed to knock off UConn and sully that sterling record a bit.

His reaction? Bring 'em on.

"Do I think I could put together a team like this ever again?" Auriemma asked after winning his third national crown. "If I said no, then I should get out of coaching. The goal of every coach is every year to try to put together a team like this.

"I'm going to start trying to put together another team that's better than this one."

He had the foundation in Taurasi. Strother had been voted the nation's top high school player. Several other All-Americans had been recruited.

"It's not like we're starting over," Auriemma said. "It's just that from where we are this year to where we're going to be is a big difference. There's going to be times where it's going to feel like I don't know where to go with these guys. But in some ways, I'm kind of looking forward to that."

Bring 'em on, indeed.

Auriemma earned his fourth coach of the year honor in 2002–03 by replacing that all-world group with a bunch of scrappers, led by the dynamic Taurasi and that superb freshman class. Along the way to the Big East title game, UConn broke Louisiana Tech's record of 54 straight wins set in 1980–82, and extended its streak to 70.

No one could stop the Huskies.

Well, almost no one.

Cruising toward another top seed in the NCAAs, Connecticut took on Villanova for the conference championship, hardly a daunting task considering the Wildcats had lost five times that season and weren't necessarily UConn's biggest Big East challenger.

The Huskies grabbed a nine-point lead with under 10 minutes remaining. Business as usual.

Then, March Madness struck early.

Nova went on an 18–2 run, making nearly every shot while clamping down on Taurasi and company. The Huskies looked tired and ill-prepared for the stretch run in that contest—and maybe unready for the stretch run toward another national championship, too.

Villanova, a loser to UConn for 10 straight years, won, 52–48, stunning the Huskies and the rest of the basketball world.

Auriemma almost seemed relieved, and pointed out that the loss had come when there was still time to recover.

"Every team that I have ever had that has won a championship has had to suffer something along the way," he said. "Every team has had to have that feeling in the pit of their stomach that, 'I don't want that to happen again.'

"So tonight—not a bad thing."

There was a bad thing or two, though. Auriemma berated a student reporter from the UConn newspaper after the loss, something he later apologized for at a news conference on campus.

And there was doubt cast about the Huskies' ability to handle the gut-wrenching pressure of March.

Villanova coach Harry Perretta found that laughable.

"If I was 70–1, I wouldn't think there was much of a problem," Perretta said. "You're right, sometimes people overreact. I heard people say, 'What's wrong with them?'

"There is nothing wrong with them. They lost one game in the last 71. I would like to win 70 in a row."

Six in a row was the new goal, and the Huskies responded by ripping through the first three rounds of the NCAA tournament before beating Purdue by nine. Awaiting them in Atlanta was a familiar adversary: Tennessee.

But first, UConn needed to get past Texas, while the Lady Vols were dispensing with the brilliant Alana Beard and Duke in the other 2003 semifinal.

The Longhorns, who hadn't played for the championship since their 1986 perfecto, were rugged and confident. They built a nine-point second-half margin.

Then Taurasi took over. She rallied her teammates in a huddle during a timeout, then began raining down three-pointers, driving to the basket for layups or dishes to her less-experienced fellow Huskies. She went for 26 points, and her long three-pointer provided the winning points in a two-point decision.

"I say it over and over again," Auriemma said. "We have 'D' and they don't. That's probably the biggest reason we won."

And now for the enviable final: UConn, looking for a fourth crown in eight years, and Tennessee, seeking its first since its memorable three-year run had ended in 1999.

If any opponent had deep knowledge of just how dangerous Taurasi could be, it was Summitt's Vols, whom Auriemma began referring to as the "Evil Empire"—the first strong sign of the souring relationship between the coaches. Connecticut won the regular-season meeting in overtime as Taurasi scored 25 points, including the tying basket in regulation and the winner in OT. The previous year, Taurasi had scored 32 at Knoxville.

"She played terrific against us throughout her career. She is tough," Summitt said. "I think we have to understand her greatness and really do what we can do to maybe limit touches here or there or change defenses, or whatever we need to do."

Easier said than done. Actually, it was impossible for the Lady Vols to do.

Not even a sore back could slow down Taurasi, who grabbed hold of the Huskies from the first day of practice and made them into her team: bold, creative, unstoppable.

Taurasi nailed four three-pointers as she scored 28 points. No, UConn wouldn't have won without her scoring, but it was her leadership, her tenacity, and her gamesmanship that carried the first NCAA champion in women's basketball without a senior on the roster.

"She's cut from a different cloth," said Auriemma, who during the season had admitted to dreading many practice sessions because of the unpredictability of his young players and the regular run-ins he'd have with Taurasi. "I've never been around anyone who is just immune to the pressures of the moment and has such joy and passion for the game and shows it on every possession."

Having gone 76–1 over two seasons with a pair of NCAA championships, UConn had established itself as the mecca of women's basketball. At least the northern mecca; Tennessee was the other measuring stick.

And yes, their paths soon would cross again in March Madness.

First, of course, the two dynasties would have to get to New Orleans for the Final Four in 2004.

Madness in March, Again

In a 2003–04 season marked by unpredictability, one in which four teams reached No. 1 in the polls (including the Huskies and Lady Vols), the Final Four makeup was anyone's guess. Naturally, if you guessed UConn and Tennessee, the odds were with you.

Minnesota and LSU were the surprise entrants. The Gophers would take on the two-time defending champions, while LSU would challenge Tennessee in an all-SEC battle.

Auriemma dubbed Minnesota "the best seventh seed in the history of college basketball." Considering the Huskies had lost four times, were a No. 2 seed this time around, and again had fallen in the Big East tourney, who was to say the Lady Gophers couldn't pull off the upset?

Well, not with UConn suddenly finding its groove.

Against Minnesota, Taurasi was the guiding force, but it was Strother and some of the less-heralded Huskies who keyed a nine-point win.

"For the most part, I would think people would like someone else to be in the finals," Taurasi said. "But as long as I'm wearing the Connecticut jersey, I don't care what people think. We're going to be in the finals."

As were the Lady Vols, who survived the Tigers, 52–50, in the other semifinal, one of the most exciting finishes in any women's Final Four.

"They have low blood pressure," Summitt said of her players. "My blood pressure right now is not even worth checking. . . . I told them I was really proud of them, but I don't know how much more of this I could take."

The basketball world would be taking in yet another Huskies-Lady Vols matchup. As Chuck Schoffner of the Associated Press told his readers: "UConn-Tennessee in the final. What else is new?"

Here's something new: in the men's tournament, UConn also had made the championship game, facing Georgia Tech. Never had the same school won both hoops crowns in the same year.

"It would be an absolute dream come true," UConn's Jessica Moore said. "We are pulling hard for the men and I know they are pulling for us. Storrs would be crazy if that happened."

Storrs was half-crazed as the men's team beat Tech one night before the Huskies and Lady Vols would meet. Could Auriemma's women finish off the double dip?

Adding spice to the matchup was the cool relationship between the coaches.

"We really don't have a relationship," Summitt said. "I don't have his cell number. We don't talk. We speak before and after the games. That's it.

"But that's the relationship that Geno worked very hard to create. At one time, I thought we had a pretty good relationship. So I don't know why it went south, but that's the way it is."

Auriemma dismissed such talk.

"That's irrelevant," he said. "Only thing that exists is UConn plays Tennessee, five on five in basketball."

A far too simplistic view, of course. And with the Huskies women going for the unprecedented double alongside the men, as well their own triple—the only other school with three straight NCAA women's titles was Tennessee—could a final get more juicy?

Just like the previous year, the Lady Vols were a formidable foe. Taurasi got all of her teammates involved early and the Huskies grabbed a 17-point edge in the first half. By intermission, Tennessee had whittled the lead to six, and with less than 10 minutes to play, the Lady Vols trailed by two.

But they had no answer for Taurasi—again. Her overall game, from scoring to passing to defense, lifted the Huskies every time they were challenged. She got plenty of help from Moore, Barbara Turner, and Strother, unsung players Taurasi helped turn into champions.

For a final exclamation point on UConn's preeminence in college basketball, Taurasi took the bouncing ball at game's end and punted it deep into the stands.

"UConn domination—bottom line," she yelled.

"Unbelievable," added Auriemma of the dual men's and women's basketball championships. "It's so mind-boggling. An unbelievable accomplishment for a school."

One yet to be matched.

Taurasi's departure also marked the end of one of the sport's most dominant eras. Baylor and Maryland would win the next two championships, the first for each school.

But there always was the feeling Summitt and Auriemma would resurface with yet another majestic team or two. And they did.

First, it was Tennessee.

To say Summitt rededicated herself to making the program a champion again would be untrue; she never lost her drive, nor her winning touch as a recruiter. Nobody was dismissing the Lady Vols as a contender.

But they had gone eight years without a national championship despite only 34 losses in that span and a string of strong players making their way to Knoxville. What they needed was a difference-maker. A superstar.

A Candace Parker.

Parker came to Knoxville in 2004 as the high school player of the year. She redshirted in her freshman season while recovering from knee surgery. Then she took over the sport.

Graceful yet powerful at 6-foot-4, Parker already was being coveted by the WNBA and by Olympic team coaches when the 2006–07 schedule began. Her fame would soar as she carried the Lady Vols back to the top—dunking a few times along the way.

The dunks hardly were what defined Parker's game, but those slams also were helping to increase the popularity of women's hoops, showing up from time to time on ESPN highlights.

"Our team, however, doesn't focus on that because they know that's not me and that's not what I'm about," Parker said.

What was Parker about? Just about everything good a player can do on a court.

"There's nothing that she can't do," Rutgers coach C. Vivian Stringer said. "I think everybody's always impressed with the beautiful athlete, the beautiful body. I mean she can rebound, dunk, shoot the ball, play the point. I mean, how many players in this world can do that? None."

And how many teams could derail Summitt and Tennessee from their seventh and eighth national titles?

None.

Parker already had felt the sting of falling short in March Madness. In 2006, she had watched teary-eyed as North Carolina's women cut down the nets after winning the Cleveland Regional. A year later, she was back in Cleveland, this time for the Final Four. This time, she would not fall short.

"I want my legacy to be that we hung banners during my career," Parker said. "All the greats at Tennessee hung banners. All of us came to Tennessee to win a national championship. We haven't done so since '98."

For a while in the semifinals against, yep, North Carolina, it looked as if her legacy wouldn't be so impressive. She hit only 3-of-12 shots and got into foul trouble. But a second-half surge by Parker (10 points, 10 rebounds, two steals, and a blocked shot) lifted the Lady Vols to a 56–50 win.

Next up: Rutgers and Stringer, one of Summitt's closest friends in the profession. The Scarlet Knights, usually on the fringe of basketball greatness, were in their first NCAA title game. They had beaten top overall seed Duke along the way.

Between them, the Hall of Fame coaches had 1,723 victories in 69 seasons. Stringer's roster had no seniors. And, alas, no Parker.

Summitt still was wary.

"Her kids, they just bring it," Summitt said. "They love their coach."

The kids and their coach couldn't solve the Lady Vols, nor slow down the brilliant Parker.

Tennessee's defense was impenetrable as Rutgers managed only 46 points in a 13-point defeat.

"Maybe we read the headlines or realized it was a national championship game," Stringer said. "We looked like a deer stuck in headlights."

Parker had 17 points, but it was her presence all over the court that made the biggest difference. Rutgers paid so much attention to her—and rightfully so—that other Lady Vols such as Shannon Bobbitt and Nicky Anosike shined.

"We were a team that didn't want to be denied," said Summitt, who was joined on the floor after the win by her mother, Hazel, in a wheelchair. "We weren't going to leave here without a championship."

Certainly Parker wasn't going to.

"I know I followed the program since I was a little kid and know the history behind the program," Parker said. "If you don't win a national championship at the University of Tennessee, then it's deemed a failure."

She had one. Time to go for another. Time for "Rocky Top" to fill another arena.

The venue in 2008 would be the St. Pete Times Forum in Tampa. The opponent would be Stanford. The headliner would be "Ace" Parker.

Having led the Lady Vols back to the Final Four—they were joined by Stanford, LSU, and, naturally, old nemesis UConn—Parker added player of the year honors to her resume. She was a megastar along the lines of Holdsclaw, Taurasi, Lobo, and Cheryl Miller.

Indeed, Parker had become so renowned that she often was referred to by one name. You know, Michael, Shaq, Kobe, Candace.

"I went into the season thinking she's one of the best ever," Summitt said. "Now that we're approaching the end of her career—I've coached Cheryl Miller, Chamique, Lynette Woodard, Nancy (Lieberman), Anne Donovan—Parker is the best."

To back that up, though, Parker needed to carry the Lady Vols to one more trophy before heading to the Beijing Olympics and the pros. All the other accolades would mean little without that second title.

Could she carry her team on one shoulder after twice dislocating her left shoulder in the regionals against Texas A&M? Parker shrugged—with the good shoulder—and vowed she'd play her hardest.

Tennessee needed to play hard for every second of its semifinal before edging SEC foe LSU, 47–46, in one of the most intense games Summitt had ever worked. It was the fifth consecutive year the Tigers fell in the national semis.

Did Summitt and her women ever have to work, too. Alexis Hornbuckle's putback with 0.7 seconds remaining was the difference, her only points of a game in which Parker, virtually operating with one arm, scored 13 points and pulled in 15 rebounds.

Wearing a long-sleeve white shirt under her jersey, Parker clearly was in pain all game. Still, she managed to drive the length of the court in the dying seconds as nearly all of LSU's defenders collapsed on her. Parker passed to Anosike for the clutch winning layup.

Except Anosike missed. Hornbuckle immediately put home the rebound, barely in time.

"I couldn't make a shot all night, but honestly, that was the only one that mattered," Hornbuckle said.

How fitting another rematch with UConn for the title would have been. Stanford had other ideas, winning, 82–73, behind its own Candice: Wiggins.

Wiggins was referred to as "Ice" to Parker's "Ace" in deference to the spellings of their first names. Regardless, they both were ice in the hottest situations, and they both had the skills of any ace.

Wiggins and Parker had played each other for years, dating back to AAU games. Their long-distance rivalry was highlighted by Stanford's four-point overtime victory over Tennessee the previous December.

"I remember the Stanford game like it was yesterday," Parker said. "We talk about how it ruined our Christmas and ending the year on a loss."

After vanquishing Connecticut, Wiggins emphasized the final would not be all about "Ace" against "Ice."

"We both realize we've got great support around us and I think that's what it really comes down to," Wiggins said. "And so it's not me versus her, it's Stanford versus Tennessee."

Perhaps. But Parker, with a brace on her shoulder and all the weight of expectations on her back, was the difference. She had 17 points and nine rebounds, played lock-down defense, and helped keep Wiggins (14 points) from being a major factor. In the final minute of a 16-point win, Parker left the floor holding up four fingers on each hand, symbolizing Tennessee's eight national crowns.

She also became the fourth player to win consecutive outstanding player awards for March Madness, joining Taurasi, Holdsclaw, and Miller.

With so many bright days ahead for Parker, including Olympic gold and WNBA awards, she took a few moments to reflect on her years as a Lady Volunteer.

"I look back at my growth not only as a player, but also just as a person," Parker said, "and I feel like it's been the best four years of my life. I wouldn't change anything about it. I love my teammates and I'm just very, very fortunate to have won two national championships."

Summitt had won all eight of those championships Parker had displayed on her fingers. She soon would win her 1,000th career game. Imagine, 1,000 *victories*!

Again, though, the championship pendulum was about to swing back to UConn.

Back on Top in Connecticut

Auriemma won top coaching honors for 2008, and his persuasiveness had attracted three more huge stars to Storrs: Tina Charles,

Renee Montgomery, and Maya Moore. That trio would be at the core of yet another unbeaten season, and Connecticut's sixth national title.

The Final Four defeat against Stanford struck deep into the Huskies' collective psyches. Auriemma had believed the '08 squad was ready to do something special, and he rarely is wrong about such feelings.

He was wrong that time, so he drove the 2008–09 team just a little harder. He knew Charles, Montgomery, and Moore had the talent, the disciplined approach, and the competitiveness to handle anything he threw at them.

Auriemma wasn't mistaken again. On its way to the Final Four in St. Louis, UConn won each of its 37 games by double digits. It routed every ranked team it faced—10 by the tournament's end.

No matter how much he pushed this group, its leaders ramped up the intensity. It was almost like having three coaches on the court.

Moore deflected the credit back to the bench boss, who won his sixth coach of the year award in '09.

"It's always Coach," Moore said. "He always has us ready to go and puts us in situations in practice that are harder than we would see in games."

What they would see in St. Louis was Stanford again. They couldn't wait.

"We definitely remember," Montgomery said, a wicked smile creasing her face. "You don't forget those."

Montgomery and Moore combined for 50 points as the Huskies sped away from a Cardinal lineup with five players at least 6-foot tall and registered yet another double-digit victory, 83–64.

Most excited by the win? Not any of the players.

"I don't want this team to come up short," Auriemma said almost breathlessly. "I don't want them to stop playing. I wanted them to be in the championship game. You love when your best players, the ones who have given their heart and soul to the program and have accomplished so many things, have a chance to win the last college game of the year."

That last game would be against Big East rival Louisville, whom UConn had vanquished, 75–36—yes, by 39 points—in the conference final a few weeks earlier. This was Louisville's first trip to the championship contest.

Stanford Cardinal or Louisville Cardinals, the opponent didn't matter to UConn.

Charles had 25 points and grabbed 19 rebounds in a 76–54 rout to finish off Connecticut's third unbeaten season. Just as the 1998 Lady Vols and 2002 Huskies had been grilled about being the sport's all-time best, UConn's latest champions were hearing the same questions.

Ladies?

"What Diana (Taurasi) and those teams were able to accomplish in those three years was something special," said Moore, only the second sophomore to win player of the year honors. "I don't think anything I can do will ever take away from anything they accomplished. To get this first one is so sweet. Right now I'll think about this one and celebrate it."

Until, that is, the next one.

The next one came immediately, and once more without a blemish.

It had become almost commonplace, even ho-hum, when the UConn women knocked off another opponent. They spent the 2009–10 regular season and Big East tournament knocking off 33 of them. They pushed their untouchable streak to a women's record 72 following a 60–32—yes, 60–32—romp over West Virginia in the conference final.

"This is one of the best teams *ever*," said Temple coach Tonya Cardoza, a former Auriemma assistant. "Not just the No. 1 team in this country right now, but one of the best teams *ever*."

Certainly not one the Owls could handle. Temple managed all of 12 points in the first half of a second-round loss in the NCAA tournament.

Getting to yet another Final Four seemed routine, and the Huskies handled their chores with aplomb. Their 90–50 demolition of Florida State secured their trip with the biggest margin of victory in a regional final.

"It's the time of the year when you want to play your best," said Moore, the regional's most outstanding player. "We're on a roll right now. We're confident. That's what you guys are seeing. We still have some things we need to improve. We're not perfect."

Uh, yes you are, Maya. And nobody at the Final Four in San Antonio was going to top you.

There were formidable contenders in Stanford, Oklahoma, and Baylor. Formidable, but not fearsome.

The Huskies, averaging 47-point margins of victory through four tournament games, were the fearsome ones.

"They're doing things we've never seen," said Stanford coach Tara VanDerveer, whose team had won 26 in a row after losing to Connecticut earlier in the season.

UConn would have to get past Baylor and its 6-foot-8 center, Brittney Griner—the kind of player rarely seen in the women's game. Auriemma called her "the most unique player in college basketball today."

But the Huskies were a unique squad, a group that didn't flinch when faced with any obstacle. Not even a shot-blocking, rebounding, and scoring dynamo such as Griner.

Leading by only three points early in the second half, the Huskies outscored the Bears, 29–12, the rest of the way. Charles, the Associated Press' Player of the Year, more than neutralized Griner.

Auriemma felt a sense of real achievement with the semifinal win.

"I liked coaching tonight," he said. "We've played a lot of basketball this year and there haven't been a lot of opportunities where we've been challenged and pushed to that extent as we were tonight. We like the challenge and the competitiveness of the game. We feel like we really earned that win, accomplished something."

One more big accomplishment remained, and Stanford was in the way. The Cardinal had disposed of Oklahoma, 73–66, in the other national semifinal to set the stage for another classic rematch with UConn. The Cardinal were chomping for the repeat duel with the Huskies, who had beaten them in the '09 Final Four.

"We've kept them in the back of our minds," Stanford center Jayne Appel said. "They know what we're going to do, we know what they're going to do."

Too predictable, because everyone knew Connecticut was going to win.

It would be quite a test, though, before the Huskies got their seventh national crown.

Remember the 12 points Temple got off UConn in the first half of the teams' second-round meeting? Well, that's how many Connecticut managed in 20 minutes against Stanford, at one point missing 18 consecutive shots.

Auriemma strode off the court at halftime as if in a vacuum, never peering around him, ignoring the cheers from a large Stanford contingent.

Auriemma told the Associated Press he wondered if the Huskies would score again. Moore was thinking something entirely different.

"We knew what we had to do," said Moore, the tournament's most outstanding player. "We knew we weren't going to finish the game the way we started."

Instead, the Huskies stormed back—immediately. Moore led a 17–2 burst to start the second half, scoring 11 points, and the Huskies soon were even. Then in front.

Then in control.

Final score: UConn 53, Stanford 47. Easily the closest outcome in their string of 78 wins.

The Huskies would eventually stretch that winning streak to a record 90 games to break the men's record of 88 set by Wooden's great UCLA teams of the late '60s and '70s.

"I've never been prouder of a group of young people," Auriemma said after the victory over Stanford in 2010. "How they fought back today. It was easy for them to pack it in. People wondered, 'What are you going to do the first time we're in a close game?' We reacted how champions react."

Champions seven times over, one fewer title than Tennessee.

Anyone want to bet that's where it ends?

Didn't think so.

13.

Extra Bounces

March Madness sometimes breaks out in February, when the trek to the NCAAs, if not the Final Four, begins across America.

In the America East and the Mid-American. In the Southland and the Southeastern, the Big West and the West Coast. From the Ohio Valley to the Missouri Valley to the Mountain West, and from the Atlantic 10 to the Pac-10 (now Pac-12).

Depending on the calendar, many of these conference tournaments—as frenzied as anything the NCAA event produces—grab the attention of sports fans in the year's shortest month. College hoops doesn't let go until April, either.

By the opening week of the year's third month, the slam dunks and three-point bombs, fast breaks and 2-3 zones are providing a delicious appetizer.

"The action at the conference tournaments is as exciting and dramatic as what we see in March Madness," said Dick Vitale, the Hall of Fame coach and broadcaster. "It's not fair to call those tournaments a warm-up because so much is riding on them. But they sure get you fired up for what follows."

In all, there are 31 conference tourneys of various sizes, played in various size arenas and showcased on various TV outlets. Indeed, they are so heavily supported by television that some are willing to adjust starting times for their title games.

The America East, for instance, brings all 10 teams to a centralized site for early-round contests, then has played its championship contest at the highest remaining seed on a Saturday morning to get some exposure on ESPN. Otherwise, the only way Boston University and Stony Brook get such national TV attention is when they are being annihilated by Boston College or UConn.

The March games for the America East crown are a lot more fun and a lot more competitive than those regular-season blowouts.

"Our thought is in the early weekend we want the championship atmosphere," said Matt Bourque, the America East's associate commissioner. "We have a reception and banquet for our all-conference choices, and our administrators and coaches can get together to give everyone a tournament atmosphere.

"By making the championship game at the higher remaining seed, we show our teams if you take care of business in the regular season, and then in the early rounds of the tournament, you get to host at your place for a chance at the NCAAs."

Significantly, for the America East and more than a dozen other fringe conferences, the TV cameras want to capture their biggest game.

"That's also a reward for the fans, to play that game in your building, and to have ESPN come to their building," Bourque said. "I think it helps some of our teams build programs."

An excellent example of that is Vermont. For years, the Catamounts were considered a hockey school, and rightfully so with their rich history of success in a sport that fits the region. When Vermont brought in a high-quality coach and very personable guy in Tom Brennan, suddenly the basketball team was getting some attention.

Still, it played before a half-filled building while the hockey team regularly sold out.

Then the Catamounts caught fire in the America East, winning the tournament in both 2004 and '05, hosting both of those final games. And Brennan outcoached Hall of Famer Jim Boeheim in the first round of the NCAAs in a huge upset of Syracuse.

"Now Vermont is our most respected program and plays before sellouts every night," Bourque said. "Those championship games showed what Vermont basketball could be. I think every school and every conference is trying to catch lightning in a bottle."

So is ESPN and any other TV outlets involved with those tournaments.

There's no better example of riding a wave of excitement than the 2011 Big East and NCAA tournaments. No story line excites hoops fans more than a long run of success by a surprise team. And while Connecticut normally is viewed as a college basketball powerhouse (in men's *and* women's play), that March it was an outsider when the conference's 16 teams—yep, 16, the biggest field for any conference tourney—gathered at Madison Square Garden in New York.

Sure, UConn had the requisite star in guard Kemba Walker. It also had three freshmen and a sophomore playing key roles; nine losses on its resume, all in conference, including four of its final five contests; and NCAA sanctions for recruiting violations under coach Jim Calhoun.

The Huskies also faced the unenviable task of playing in the first round of the conference get-together, against DePaul, and even a win over the weak sister of the Big East wouldn't bring much comfort. A gantlet of nationally ranked teams awaited UConn.

"It ends up being a new season for you," Calhoun said. "You've seen it in the Big East tournament and you've seen it in the NCAA tournament. Teams get a little bit going, get on a roll, feel good about themselves, good things happen, and the next thing you know, they are going on. A couple of our guys hope they can get some new life, to be honest with you."

New life. And new hope.

UConn routed DePaul, then upended Georgetown. Playing a third straight night, the Huskies found the energy and fortitude to stun Pittsburgh, 76–74, as Walker swished the winning basket and was mobbed by his teammates.

"Everybody was excited, you know? Coming into this game we're the underdogs, everyone saying we're going to lose," Walker said. "But everyone stayed together, and we came out with this victory. Everyone was excited, so I guess they just jumped on me."

The media were jumping all over UConn by now. Not only was the Big East the Big Show in the Big Apple, but Connecticut's heroics were playing well throughout the country. ESPN made certain of it, replaying Walker's winning shot as often as Vitale yells "PTPer."

Yep, UConn and Walker were "prime-time players," in Vitale-speak and on night No. 4, they faced Syracuse in arguably the most-hyped conference tournament game in history.

Just two years earlier, Syracuse went on a similar roll, and its masterpiece was a six-overtime thriller against the Huskies that left anyone who played, coached, broadcast, attended, or watched the game on television absolutely exhausted.

In that one—a matchup that couldn't happen in the NCAAs until deep in the tournament, if at all—the teams combined to take 211 shots. Eight players fouled out. It was well past midnight when the Orange prevailed, 127–117, in one of college basketball's longest epics.

"I stayed up late to watch it," said Syracuse's Brandon Triche, then a senior at Jamesville-DeWitt High School in upstate New York. "I was late for school the next morning."

Everyone's legs were rubbery late in that game and certainly after it. But in 2011, it was only Connecticut that had to ward off fatigue; Syracuse's previous win over St. John's was its first game in the tournament after getting a double bye. The Huskies were playing an unprecedented fourth straight night.

And winning for a fourth straight night. Only one OT was needed for a 76–71 victory as Walker had 33 points and 12 rebounds in another sensational performance.

"I didn't want to go into another six overtimes, I know that," Walker said. "I was mad we went to the first overtime. As soon as the first overtime came, I thought about six. I wanted the win and didn't want to go to another one and another one."

On to the final. Hey, aren't baseball teams the only ones that play five consecutive days?

Not in 2011. Madness, you say? Well, yes, exactly.

Continuing the insanity, the Huskies edged Louisville, 69–66, for the most improbable conference tourney title in Big East annals. Perhaps anywhere, anytime.

"Now that it's over I can definitely tell you I was tired," Walker said as he cradled the MVP trophy and a strand of the MSG net. "With about two minutes left, I was gassed. I just wanted to win this game so bad my heart took over."

How many hearts skipped a beat through UConn's stunning rush to the Big East crown? Certainly every Huskies fan flirted with palpitations—and this was just the conference tourney.

Hold it. This was not *just* anything. It was the perfect example of what makes the conference events much more than an appetizer for the entree.

"What these kids have accomplished this week has been as moving for me as anything I could possibly think of," Calhoun said. "Whatever was asked of them, they did. Their heart took over, their determination to win, and their skill level. I couldn't be more proud of them."

Also consider: Without the Big East tournament to straighten out its act, would UConn have been a factor in the NCAAs? Would it have carried the madness through March and into April, to the Final Four and, ultimately, its third national title?

Not likely.

As grand and glorious as UConn's surge at the so-called mecca of college basketball was, the granddaddy of conference tournaments is not played near Times Square, but on Tobacco Road.

The ACC tourney began only in 1954, however. Three decades before then, schools from the Southeast put together a regional tournament under the auspices of the Southern Intercollegiate Athletic Association (SIAA), soon to become the Southern Conference. But the event had little definition—one year, the Mercer Bears finished second even though they were not a part of the SIAA.

And while other leagues have been in the postseason tournament business for decades, none has resonated through the years like the ACC's event.

One great reason for that, of course, has been the quality of competition within the league. At various times, just about every school except Clemson has been a power, with North Carolina, Duke, Wake Forest, North Carolina State, Maryland, and Virginia all having enviable moments of glory and triumph. Maryland in 1958 was the only school from outside the Tar Heel state to win the conference tourney in the event's first 17 years.

Another reason was the dilemma and disappointment facing runners-up in the ACC: no NCAA bid was forthcoming for them until 1975. Some of college basketball's best squads never got a shot at winning a national title because they couldn't get through the conference tournament wringer. Their reward often was a trip to the NIT.

"Most of my career you had to win your tournament to get in the NCAA," said Lefty Driesell, whose run at Maryland included far too many runner-up finishes for his tastes. "I've had a lot of teams ranked in the top five or 10 in the country that never got in the NCAA because they didn't win the tournament."

The ACC tournament's influence on the sport never was felt more than in 1974 and '75, and it led to a monumental change in the NCAA tourney's structure that has echoed through the decades—perhaps too much so, according to Driesell.

Maryland was ranked fourth nationally in '74 with stars Len Elmore at center, Tom McMillen at forward, and John Lucas at guard. Top-ranked NC State featured the incomparable sky-walker David Thompson, Tom Burleson, and Monte Towe. The Wolfpack were on a mission after missing the previous NCAAs while on probation.

The winner of the ACC final would head to the NCAAs, and the loser would have no shot at the biggest prize. Considering NC State had finished the regular season with a 24–1 record and Maryland was 21–4 (with two losses to the Wolfpack), that seems almost unfathomable these days.

Back then, it was the law of the land—but not for long.

Driesell's Terrapins stormed to a 13-point lead, hitting 12 of their first 14 shots. Every time NC State missed a shot, the Terps ran the other way.

And each time the Wolfpack had a chance, it would fast-break downcourt. The points piled up, and it was 55–50 for Maryland at halftime.

"We were in trouble," Towe said. "But we'd responded all year."

The Wolfpack did again. It took a three-pronged attack that often ran through the 7-foot-4 Burleson in the pivot for NC State to climb back.

At 97–97, Burleson blocked a shot by Mo Howard, and Lucas' desperation heave missed. Into overtime the schools went, searching for a burst of energy that could carry one of them through—and into the NCAAs.

Through 40 minutes, neither team had committed a turnover. The fans at Greensboro Coliseum were just as exhausted as the players, but they understood what a classic they were witnessing.

Maryland's leader was Lucas, as clutch a player as the Terrapins ever had and a future top overall NBA draft choice. His team led by one point when Lucas missed a foul shot in a one-and-one. NC State went into a delay—no shot clock, remember—before Phil Spence sneaked free under the basket for a layup.

What next for Maryland? With less than 30 seconds remaining, Driesell saw plenty of options.

"There was no panic or anything like that," he said. "We were ready to win the game, and we had the players who could do it."

But after a near-perfect game, Lucas threw away the ball. Towe was fouled and he almost never failed at the free throw line. His two foul shots set the final score at 103–100.

Burleson had the game of his life with 38 points, 13 rebounds, and more intimidation than a real pack of wolves.

"I was like a dishrag that's been all wrung out," he said afterward. "I had nothing left."

Actually, it was Maryland that had virtually nothing left. Its national championship hopes were gone, but Driesell told the Terps he wasn't upset. He was only disappointed they had lost: "My team played its heart out." But the heart of the matter was simply this: a team far better than many that would enter the NCAAs was left out in the cold.

"Now, with the multiple bids out there for the ACC, a lot of people can't relate to it," Towe said.

That includes Driesell.

"They started letting the second-place teams in the tournaments in, and then the third and now they are letting the seventh and the eighth places in," he said. "I think that's ludicrous. It used to be called the 'Tournament of Champions.' It's all money now."

But the change in makeup for the NCAA playoffs began with the uproar in College Park. It soon spread throughout the country. When the NCAA recognized how much interest Maryland's plight had raised—and how an expanded field of 32 teams, with at-large bids for some conference runners-up, would yield significant additional revenues—the first major expansion of the tournament occurred.

"In a way, it opened up a chance for Maryland to win its national championship," McMillen said. "That was probably one of the legacies of that whole crazy tournament. It opened up the NCAAs to a whole lot of ACC teams.

"There are a lot of second chances, which is really good."

Indeed, even a tailender in a conference can rise to life in its postseason tournament and steal away the prize: a trip to the NCAAs.

Sheer madness. And brilliance.

14.

Youth Movement

Hey, kid, you want to make a million-dollar living playing basketball? Just skip college and head right to the NBA.

Or maybe just play a year in college and then jump to the pros.

For decades, that's what high schools prodigies have heard from agents, scouts, supplicants, and hangers-on. Who needs the college game when you can be set for life before you can legally drink alcohol, or maybe even before you have voted?

And the NBA is loaded with such phenoms, dating all the way back to the ABA and Moses Malone skipping college to go from Petersburg, Virginia, to the pros—and eventually a Hall of Fame career.

The list of straight-to-the-pros players has featured a who's-who—and a who-the-heck-is-that—of the hoops world. Darryl Dawkins, Shawn Kemp, and Tracy McGrady have had decent careers; Kevin Garnett, Kobe Bryant, LeBron James, and Dwight Howard have had sensational ones.

Then there were the complete busts, from Bill Willoughby to Taj McDavid, who didn't even get drafted after he opted to bypass college. Do the names Korleone Young, Jonathan Bender, Leon Smith, Ellis Richardson, and Tony Key ring a bell? Probably not, nor should they.

They inhabit the other end of the spectrum, the abyss that players without the proper talent or maturity or makeup descend into after skipping school and seeking their fame and fortune immediately in the pros.

Neither the fame nor the fortune comes.

Willoughby's case provides a lesson in what those players miss by skipping college ball and a chance to lead State U to the national tournament. It also illustrates how such stories can have happy endings.

Willoughby played high school ball in Englewood, New Jersey. Highly recruited and a potential difference-maker at whichever college he chose to attend, Willoughby instead went directly into the NBA in 1975, selected in the first round of the draft by Atlanta.

While he lasted eight years in the pros, he never was a standout. Had he gone to Kentucky, as originally planned, he might have experienced two Final Fours—the Wildcats lost to UCLA in 1975 and beat Duke in '78—and a national crown.

Instead, he took the money and dunked: a five-year, $1.1 million contract with the Hawks.

There weren't enough of those dunks, or any other memorable plays, for Willoughby, who eventually fell into financial ruin and depression.

"I've been through just about everything," Willoughby told the *New York Daily News*. "I'm not going to be held back. I want to be a well-rounded person. I want to show people that I'm not just a basketball player. I want be somewhere where I can make a difference in people's lives."

What did one of the first guys to jump from high school to the NBA do at age 44? He went back to school and graduated from Fairleigh Dickinson University, just a few miles from the Jersey town he grew up in.

The preps-to-pros route has changed since the NBA passed a rule, beginning with the 2006 draft, that no longer allowed the callow phenoms to jump straight into the league. They must spend at least one year in college—the NBA would prefer to make it two years—or they can head overseas, as Bucks standout Brandon Jennings did before moving to Milwaukee, profiting from his time in Europe.

Or they can sit out their first year after high school, then apply for the draft once their college class has reached its second year.

There have been mixed reviews about the so-called one-and-done rule, just as there were feuding opinions about whether college players should be allowed to leave early for the pros in the years following Spencer Haywood's lawsuit that went all the way to the Supreme Court. The court found in his favor in 1971, barring the play-for-pay leagues from banning underclassmen from entering the pro ranks if they could prove a hardship.

That ruling changed the landscape of college basketball forever.

"I tore up basketball as they knew it," Haywood told the *Seattle Post-Intelligencer* years later. "To this day, I'm not welcome back to my university (Detroit). It's only been in the last few years that I've been welcomed back into the NBA family.

"I broke down a college bedrock rule and tore up the NBA. With the players, it still pains me. They don't give me any respect for what I went through for them. Jackie Robinson had support. I didn't."

How big an effect did the Haywood decision have on college basketball and, more specifically, March Madness?

A bit, but hardly what the doomsayers were predicting back when Haywood headed to the NBA. Sure, some excellent players, from Malone to Garnett to Bryant to James, never made it onto NCAA courts. But thousands did, and the success of the tournament as it has grown from 25 teams in 1971 to 68 in 2011 has been steady. The NCAAs surged from a cozy tournament to, well, March Madness.

What has irked coaches, fans, and even some players is the way the pros have determined, in essence, who would play college ball. And after 2006, how long many of them would stick around.

Sure, the rule works well for the NBA, which would actually prefer players under 20 or whose class has not gone through its sophomore season to be ineligible, a suggestion the players' union steadfastly has fought.

Asked about stars such as Texas forward Kevin Durant being a Longhorn for one season, winning some player of the year honors, then heading to his league, NBA commissioner David Stern said, "That's OK with us. It's better than coming right out of high school. We get a chance to see them either in the (developmental) league, in college, or in Europe playing against more elite competition.

"Would we like it to be two years (before being eligible in the draft)? Sure, but what would you give to get that?"

And, when he was president of the NCAA, the late Myles Brand cited "hundreds, maybe even thousands, of young men each year who are now taking their high school studies more seriously rather than thinking, 'I can blow off high school and go right into the NBA.' . . . That's going to put them in good stead for their lives."

On the other side of the argument is one of the coaches most often burned in recent years by the "quick hello, early good-bye" syndrome: Duke coach Mike Krzyzewski.

"They're part of the NCAA marketing machine and college basketball," Krzyzewski said of the one-and-done players. "It's a smart move (by the NBA). They don't have to pay a cent. They get to see a kid for a year longer. And they're marketed. I think it was fool's gold, really. Oh, we get a kid for a year. I don't think college basketball has benefited from that."

Indeed, Coach K worries about how many of those players are doing a disservice to the college game, and to the NCAA tournament.

"I'm not saying it's a bad culture," Krzyzewski said. "I'm saying it's a different culture that leads to the NBA. Now you're forcing them to go into our culture for eight months. I'm not sure that's (good). We've already seen problems from it."

The trend of players leaving school early likely never will change. There's even a theory adhered to by some basketball scouts and pro personnel directors that if someone stays all four seasons, he's probably not going to star in the NBA, anyway.

"The glass half-full side says 'Well, at least we get to see the great ones for one year instead of none,'" notes Jim O'Connell, the Hall of Fame basketball writer for the Associated Press. "My side, where the glass is not only half-empty but also cracked, says colleges should make a stand that they are colleges and not a farm system.

"There are no asterisks on teams' accomplishments—like when a program did something wrong—but there are some titles won where people say right away, 'Well, they had so-and-so for just the one year and then he was gone.'"

O'Connell believes the rule will only change if the NBA owners and players negotiate it into a collective bargaining agreement or if a player with time and funds available decides to try and fight it in the courts.

Or through the legislature. Tennessee congressman Steven Cohen once claimed the NBA's minimum age of 19 to be a "vestige of slavery" and sought an investigation of the rule.

Stern's reply: "What the congressman didn't understand, and we'll be happy to share our view with him, this is not about the

NCAA. This is not an enforcement of some social program. This is a business decision by the NBA, which is we like to see our players in competition after high school.

"I don't know why our (nation's) founders decided that age 25 was good for Congress, but I guess they thought that was about maturity. And for us, it's different. It's a kind of basketball maturity."

Former Duke star and current TV analyst Jay Bilas, who also happens to be a lawyer, has proposed that high school seniors would be eligible for the NBA draft, but if the player enters college, he must stay a certain number of years. That could be one year, as it is now, or two or even three; four is unlikely because other sports, most notably the NFL, don't force athletes to stay in school that long, offering a juicy legal precedent for anyone looking to sue for the right to get into the pros.

As ESPN analyst and former coach Dick Vitale often said, "It's unfair to an athlete who has to go to school for one year when he has no desire to be in the classroom. College is supposed to be for those who want an education, for those who want to be there.

"It's time to end this mockery. If these kids want to make themselves available for the NBA, then so be it. If the NBA sees fit to draft them, so be it. The league should determine which players legitimately have a chance."

It's difficult to find proof that the early-entry rules have damaged the college game or the NCAA tournament. Sure, Magic Johnson didn't stay through his senior year at Michigan State. But Larry Bird remained at Indiana State for the full complement, and they faced off in the 1979 title game. More than three decades later, the Spartans' victory still had the highest TV rating for any championship contest.

You don't want to go that far back? OK, consider that more recent NBA standouts Kevin Durant, Blake Griffin, Derrick Rose, and Carmelo Anthony all provided special, even glorious, March Madness moments. They barely stuck around on campus, but left their mark on the game and the tournament while there.

Sure, fans can claim that more 'Melo in Syracuse would have been intriguing and might have created more March fireworks for central New York. Others applaud having him for that one incomparable tournament run.

"John Wall, the impact he has made on Kentucky has been monumental," Vitale said during the 2009–10 season. "A kid like that, you know he's there for one year. It's almost like a tease."

Meanwhile, seniors have continued to have a steady impact on the tournament and the sport in general. In recent years alone, Jimmer Fredette, Nolan Smith, Jon Scheyer, Tyler Hansbrough, and Juan Dixon played huge roles in the drama that is college hoops.

Some players simply aren't ready for the NBA at 19 or 20. Others enjoy the college experience, particularly the opportunity to go Mad in March, and stick around.

But those who make a quick appearance will continue to be here today, gone tomorrow as long as the pros' arms are open to them.

And the colleges won't turn them away, either.

"Some coaches may say they don't want one-and-dones," Kansas coach Bill Self said. "I'm not totally buying into that. I think if you drop a one-and-done in anybody's lap, they would probably say, 'He definitely made our team better and our program stronger,' as long as he came to school for the right reasons."

NIT-Picking

For some, it's a loser's tournament. For others, it's a win-win situation.

The National Invitation Tournament has been nothing if not controversial and polarizing through the years.

Before there was March Madness and the NCAA playoffs, the NIT had the field to itself—at least for a year.

The National Association of Intercollegiate Athletics (NAIA) was actually the first organization to produce a national basketball tournament. It was established in 1937 by James Naismith, basketball's inventor, to crown a national champion among small colleges.

One year later the NIT came on the scene, a product of the Metropolitan Basketball Writers Association.

The NIT participants in 1938: Colorado, Long Island, NYU, Oklahoma A&M, Bradley, and Temple, the eventual winner. New York–area teams had the greatest success in the early days of the NIT, with Long Island and St. John's combining to win four of the first seven tourneys.

(continued)

NIT-Picking *(Continued)*

One year after the NIT opened in New York's Madison Square Garden, the NCAA came out with a tourney of its own. It was more wide-ranging geographically than the NIT.

The NCAA field was drawn from each of the organization's eight regions, with the inaugural tourney featuring the following schools: Oregon, Utah State, Texas, Oklahoma, Wake Forest, Villanova, Ohio State, and Brown. The first NCAA finals were played in 1939, on the campus of Northwestern University in Evanston, Illinois. The winner: Oregon.

New York was the place to be for a postseason tournament, though.

Some of the nation's best college basketball teams loved coming to the Big Apple because of all the media attention. That, and the ability to recruit great talent from the playgrounds in the nation's largest city.

The NCAA tournament quickly realized the value of playing in the Garden.

During the Second World War, the NIT champion met the NCAA champion in an annual charity game to raise money for the Red Cross. The NCAA tournament champions (Wyoming, Utah, and Oklahoma A&M) won all three games.

That was about the last time any good feeling was generated between the two tournaments—particularly after the point-shaving scandals of the 1950s.

It would be many years before college basketball rebounded. For its part, the NCAA never returned its Final Four to the Garden.

For the NIT, the scandals were a personal setback because a lot of the gambling activity had taken place in and around the Garden. Even though the NIT continued to play in the "world's most famous arena," it was simply never the same.

Before long, the NCAA tournament had far surpassed the NIT in the sport's importance. The NCAA was considered the true national championship; the NIT was a little brother who picked up teams that weren't invited to the "Big Dance," a fast-growing phenomenon. Indeed, by comparison, the NIT was called the "Little Dance."

The NIT was often the butt of media humor: the "Nobody's Interested Tournament," the "Not Invited Tournament," and the "National Insignificant Tournament."

David Thompson, North Carolina State's All-American forward of the 1970s, once termed the NIT "a loser's tournament." And such schools as Georgetown, Georgia Tech, Louisville, and Oklahoma rejected invitations to play in the NIT after failing to make the NCAAs.

In 2006, Maryland coach Gary Williams rejected an NIT invitation. But Williams was forced to reconsider when told the university had previously agreed to use the Terps' home court for one of the NIT venues. Economics won out, but the Terps, in a shocker, lost an opening-round game to Manhattan.

Two years later, Williams changed his NIT thinking: if invited, his squad would gladly play in the NIT, he said.

The reason? Williams saw it as an opportunity to further develop the younger players on his team and give the Terps more national exposure. It became a trend for other schools, as well.

Sometimes, coaches have used the NIT for other reasons, such as Marquette's Al McGuire in 1970. Unhappy with the regional placement of his eighth-ranked team, the Warriors' iconoclastic coach spurned an NCAA bid and joined the NIT field instead. The Warriors went on to win the NIT title that season.

Safe to say, that would never happen again. It is now a violation of NCAA rules to reject an invitation to its tournament, in large part thanks to McGuire's out-of-the-box thinking.

When McGuire passed away in 2001 following a successful career in broadcasting, he left behind a legacy of free thinking and basketball expressions that became part of the sport's vocabulary. Think of McGuire and you almost automatically think of such colorful expressions as "white knuckler" to describe a tight game or "aircraft carrier" for a very large player in the middle.

It was his memorable stand against the NCAA in 1970, though, that might have been his biggest contribution in helping shape the sport.

Meanwhile, the NCAA continued to build its field. Adding teams with machine-gun-like ferocity, the NCAA looked like it was making a concerted effort to bankrupt the NIT. In fact, it was, at least according to the NIT.

The NIT filed an antitrust suit, claiming the NCAA was trying to put it out of business by expanding its field, leaving fewer quality teams from which to choose for the NIT.

(continued)

NIT-Picking *(Continued)*

By 2011, the NCAA featured 68 teams in its postseason field, more than twice the number of NIT participants, with more anticipated for the future. The NIT had 32 teams after cutting back from an unwieldy 64 teams in 2006.

Finally, after four years of legal wrangling, the NCAA in 2005 settled matters by purchasing the rights for 10 years to both the postseason and preseason NIT, which also has become a fixture on the college basketball scene.

The NCAA still isn't the only one sponsoring tournaments on the March dance card.

Along came two more postseason tournaments, the College Basketball Invitational (CBI) and the CollegeInsider.com Tournament (CIT).

Established in 2008, the CBI's event includes 16 teams. The CIT has 24, bringing to 140 the number of teams that will continue to play basketball in March—or about one-third of the nation's college hoops programs.

"The NCAA is not happy with this new tournament," said the *Providence Journal* in March 2008 of the CBI. "They aren't saying so publicly, but then they can't."

For the record, the CBI champion in 2011 was none other than Oregon, which will always be remembered as the first NCAA champion.

Epilogue

Everyone loves March Madness, right?

Maybe not.

Consider the topics that come up for debate—sometimes with vociferous disagreement—when college basketball's biggest month (or so) is discussed:

- Expanding the field;
- The RPI (Rating Percentage Index);
- TV's role in Selection Sunday;
- Eliminating campus sites, making the NCAA tournament a big-venue event going to the highest bidder.

So what are the pros and cons of each, and where is the college hoops championship headed?

Size Matters

There are three schools of thought regarding how many teams belong in the NCAA tournament: the 68 now in it; quite a few less; or quite a few more, approaching—even surpassing—100.

The field has gone from 25 in 1970 to 32 in 1975 to 40 in '79. The next year, it increased to 48, but only for three tournaments. In succession, the NCAA went to 52 schools in 1983, 53 the next year, and 64 in 1985.

That's where it remained until 2001, when a play-in game between the two lowest-rated entries was added for a field of 65.

In 2011, three more play-ins, dubbed the first round, were added. Some suggested calling it the money-grabbing round because all it seemed to do was add more TV programming. The field jumped to 68.

The selection committee defended its decision, naturally, to go to 68 by claiming the crop of worthy teams was so deep in '11.

"The last teams in and comparing them and really vetting the qualities of those teams, there was a lot of discussion because there were so many teams to consider," said Gene Smith, the Ohio State athletic director who headed the committee. "We just had a lot more teams that we were scrubbing from that perspective. Usually, you have two or three teams that you feel bad about leaving out. This year, it was seven or eight."

One they didn't leave out, a school that certainly would have been denied in a 64-team field, was Virginia Commonwealth. The Rams made the selectors look pretty wise when they stormed into the Final Four.

"The bump to 68 went pretty well and I think it could be a number they stay with for a while," said Jim O'Connell, an Associated Press college basketball writer and Basketball Hall of Fame member, after the 2011 tournament won by Connecticut. "Remember it was 64 or 65 from 1985 until this past season, so they don't just change the number for any old reason."

But ESPN's Jay Bilas, a former Duke star, wasn't as impressed with the expansion, even if it was just three additional teams.

When VCU and Alabama-Birmingham were chosen, he said straight into the TV cameras: "These are horrible decisions. They need basketball people on the committee. I wonder if some of these people even know the ball is round?"

His point, however, should be well-taken. While VCU turned out to be a phenomenal choice, the field can get bogged down with mediocrity. Sure, the Big East had 11 of its 16 teams in the field with winning records and impressive resumes, but should a school that finishes 10th or 11th in its conference and without a .500 record in conference games be invited to the NCAAs?

Then again, UConn went 9–9 within the Big East in 2011, caught fire, and won 11 straight to take the conference tournament and then the NCAA championship.

So maybe instead of the field holding steady or being narrowed, more teams should be admitted? A 96-team field was discussed, and likely will be again.

"I'm real comfortable with the size of the field that we're blessed to have," Smith said. "As we went through the debate last year nationally and got feedback from all the different conferences relative to expansion, the feedback was loud and clear. We ended up where we are with 68 teams, the opportunity for 37 at-large teams. I do not anticipate (expansion) will be something that will happen in the near future."

Here's another reason why further expansion is a long shot, according to O'Connell:

"One thought why the number may not go to 96 is that the tournament is in such a perfect three-week window, with the conference tournaments the lead-in and the Masters the sign of spring arriving right after it. As long as CBS holds the rights to the tournament and the Masters, it seems to make a lot of sense to keep it a three-weekend event."

CBS, incidentally, owns those broadcast rights—in a shared deal with Turner Sports—until 2024.

RPI or RIP?

Ah, the Rating Percentage Index. Some would like to see it Rest In Peace.

As the Associated Press describes, "RPI has been used by the NCAA since 1981 to supplement the selection of at-large teams and the seeding of all teams for the NCAA basketball tournament."

The RPI is derived from three components: Division I winning percentage (25 percent), schedule strength (50 percent), and opponent's schedule strength (25 percent). Games against non–Division I opponents are not used in calculating the RPI, and margin of victory is not considered.

Albert Einstein did not design it, even if it seemed like something that sprung from his brain.

It also is only one of the factors used to determine the selection of at-large teams and the seeding of all schools. But television, particularly ESPN, has turned it into something almost mystical with the attention it pays to the RPI throughout the regular season.

That has turned off some people.

"If it was a be-all answer, then people would have a right to scream that it's unfair in a lot of ways, sometimes to the power schools and sometimes to the mid-majors," O'Connell said. "Just like everything else in the sport, it's not perfect, but it's the best they have come up with. And, to be fair, there has been some juggling of the formula over the years when that kind of complaining got loud.

"But I believe all the chairmen over the years who have said the RPI is one of the factors the committee looks at, but it is not a number that alone can keep a team out of or get a team in the field."

Regardless, it is a handy device for complaints when things don't go your way on Selection Sunday.

In recent years, things have almost never gone the way of Virginia Tech when the field has been announced. And Tech coach Seth Greenberg verbalized his outrage; the Hokies were denied a bid for four straight years from 2008–2011, despite pretty solid credentials in most of those seasons.

"We need to get rid of the RPI totally from people's train of thought," he said. "Because one second, the head of the committee says the RPI is inconsequential, and the next second, he says they can use the RPI to eliminate a team."

While Tech fans shared Greenberg's pain, supporters of other schools might have been rejoicing their teams' entry into the tournament. And if there are complaints about the influence computerized stats have on the selection process, well, it's not just the numbers the RPI spouts out that determine the field.

"The human element in the picks gives the tournament some flexibility that adds to its appeal," said Stephen Shapiro, assistant professor of sport management at Old Dominion, who conducted a study of "major conference bias" and spoke to *USA Today* in 2010. "Teams just need to feel the picks are made consistently every year."

In or Out? Watch the Tube

So how exactly do teams find out if they will be a part of March Madness—or simply will walk away mad and wind up in the NIT or another of the lesser postseason events?

They do like the rest of us: watch TV.

They tune in to CBS and go through the same drama, forced as it is for so many teams that already know they are going to the tournament and merely want to find out which region they are placed in, who they are playing, and how high (or low) they are seeded.

It does make for some interesting television viewing, though mainly in a voyeuristic way as we see the reactions from the Virginia Techs and Colorados (of 2011) or the many other schools who get bypassed. Their disappointment, sometimes accompanied by anger, is far more compelling than whether Duke is lined up atop the East or where the bushel-full of Big East, Big 12, and Big Ten teams are headed.

"Shock," Colorado coach Tad Boyle said of his reaction to not making the 2011 event, a fact he learned while sitting in front of a TV screen, surrounded by his disheartened players. "In the back of your mind, you feel like your name is going to pop up. When it doesn't, you're extremely shocked and disappointed."

There are the occasional controversies, of course, usually spiced by complaints from coaches who feel slighted. Such as Kentucky's John Calipari in 2011, whose reaction when informed the Wildcats were a fourth seed was, "They did it to us again."

Calipari had been vocally unhappy with his team's seeding in previous tournaments.

This time, the Wildcats had won their second consecutive SEC tournament, had defeated Florida twice in 10 days—including the conference tourney—and yet were seeded two spots behind the Gators, who were seeded number two.

"I'm a little bit surprised," Calipari said. "It was a tough road for us (and) it was a tough road last year. I don't think it's personal, but *wow*! This team has really worked hard all year and I think our RPI is seven. You're a seven and it gets you a (fourth ranking in the tournament)? But at the end of the day you're in the tournament and you still have to win games."

And at the end of the day, you're in the tournament even if the hosts of the selection show aren't quite sure who you are. Years ago, Gonzaga's name elicited blank looks from the announcers, along with a mispronounced GON-ZOH-GA rather than GON-ZAH-GA. Season after season, that private school in Cincinnati would get into the event and announcers would call the Musketeers

"Eggsavier" rather than "Ex-zavier"—as coach Chris Mack notified the broadcaster Kenny Smith via Twitter.

Mack's top scorer was identified as Tu Holladay instead of Tu Holloway.

"It doesn't make a difference," Holloway said with a chuckle. "As long as they get 'Tu' right. As long as they're not saying 'Three Holliday' or something like that, I'm all right."

Mack seemed to enjoy the repartee.

"As long as they're still saying our name, they can say it how they want to," Mack told the Associated Press.

No matter the controversies and confusion, the announcement of the lineup of teams by the selection committee kicks off an all-American frenzy across the nation. The onslaught in popularity of office pools and brackets for March Madness has led the NCAA to the conclusion that anything involving the tournament is worthy of a TV slot. And the networks are only too happy to oblige—CBS and Turner because of all the money they are spending, ESPN because it fills hours and hours of programming, much of it mind-numbing.

In the end, the manufactured suspense leading up to the NCAA playoffs can't match the actual excitement of the games themselves. But it does create some intrigue.

"I've been on pins and needles for a couple of days now," Georgia forward Trey Thompkins once said of the buildup to March Madness. "I wanted to be in the tournament so bad. It's been nerve-racking for me."

Home in the Dome

March Madness no longer means campus sites. Games are played in large arenas, often in domes built for the National Football League (NFL), where thousands upon thousands of fans can pay thousands upon thousands of dollars to attend the Final Four. If the NCAA tournament ever was quaint, it now has become among the biggest mega-events in sports. And the national semifinals are as huge as anything short of the Super Bowl.

Good idea?

Certainly it is for the NCAA's coffers. That, in turn, means more money for the participating schools, and for the Division I conferences that stretch from the Atlantic to the Pacific, from the Canadian border to the Mexican.

Not so good is seeing empty seats at early-round contests, particularly when conference tourneys have full houses for some of their games.

"We've been in domed stadiums for so long now that there aren't that many people around who remember that weekend in East Rutherford in 1996, the last time for a Final Four in a standard arena," O'Connell said.

And, of course, the New Jersey Meadowlands arena is miles from the nearest D-I campus.

"The domes have gotten much better over the years as far as being a venue is concerned, and Reliant Stadium (where the NFL's Houston Texans play) in 2011 was bigger than ever, but it seemed a little more like a basketball facility. We're not talking Hinkle Fieldhouse, Cameron Indoor Stadium, or Allen Fieldhouse, but it was the best huge place to watch a game," O'Connell said.

Jamming as many fans as possible into the building is part of the plan, if not part of the tournament's mystique. Many players seemingly aren't concerned about that, but other aspects of the large venues may be on their minds.

"The players all say the shooting background doesn't affect them, but I find that hard to believe," O'Connell added. "When you have been shooting all season with a closed wall as a backdrop and then for the biggest games of the season the ball sails into a picture where depth is definitely a factor, it doesn't make a lot of sense."

Not that anything will change in the future.

"They will never play another Final Four in any venue except a dome, and whenever it's possible to work a dome or two into the regionals they will do the same," O'Connell said. "I know every Final Four some writers will stand courtside and point at seats that would stink for a football game. Every conversation ends the same way: 'But people buy them to be here.' Domes are one step past a trend."

Yes, the domes are here to stay. So are the brackets. And more televised games than you ever imagined: every contest, beginning in 2011, is made available on national TV; of course, you have to be able to find truTV to watch some of them.

The RPI? Its role will be debated whether the field remains at 68 or reaches 168.

One thing won't be debatable: March Madness is a phenomenon worthy of its name, even if that title is slightly inaccurate. Then again, how nice that the NCAA tournament stretches into April.

Anyone for some May Madness, too?